James B. Davies and Glenn M. MacDonald

Information in the Labour Market: Job-Worker Matching and Its Implications for Education in Ontario

PUBLISHED FOR THE ONTARIO ECONOMIC COUNCIL BY
UNIVERSITY OF TORONTO PRESS
TORONTO BUFFALO LONDON

© Ontario Economic Council 1984
Printed in Canada

ISBN 0-8020-3403-9

Canadian Cataloguing in Publication Data

Davies, James B., 1951–
  Information in the labour market
  Bibliography: p.
  Includes index.
  ISBN 0-8020-3403-9
  1. Education – Canada. 2. Education – Ontario.
  3. Education and state – Canada. 4. Industry and
  education – Canada. I. MacDonald, Glenn M., 1952–
  II. Ontario Economic Council. III. Title.
  LC91.D38 1984   379.1′54′0971   C84-098259-3

This report reflects the views of the authors and not necessarily those of the Ontario Economic Council or of the Ontario government. The Council establishes policy questions to be investigated and commissions research projects, but it does not influence the conclusions or recommendations of authors. The decision to sponsor publication of this study was based on its competence and relevance to public policy and was made with the advice of anonymous referees expert in the area.

Contents

vi Contents

Acknowledgments

We would like to thank John Ham, Alan Harrison, our colleague Chris Robinson, Sandra Tychsen of the Ontario Economic Council, and anonymous referees for their careful reading of and comments on the manuscript. Martin Dooley also provided valuable comments on data used in Chapter 5. Diligent research assistance was provided by Ian Skaith and Irene Majski. Numerous valuable comments and suggestions were made by participants in first and second review seminars for this study. Thanks are also due our University of Western Ontario colleagues who have put up with us during the years in which we were involved in the project. Finally we would like to acknowledge the expert manuscript preparation by Yvonne Adams, Brenda Campbell, Leslie Farrant, and Marg Gower.

INFORMATION IN THE LABOUR MARKET:
JOB-WORKER MATCHING AND ITS IMPLICATIONS FOR EDUCATION IN ONTARIO

1
Introduction

The economics of information has, over the last decade, been a fertile source of new and insightful economic analysis. Its full range of application and policy implications has not yet been exploited. In this book we utilize a simple informational model to help explain recent trends in education in Ontario and provide some guidance for policy formation in that area.

The need for a thorough understanding of trends in education as a foundation on which to build policy practically goes without saying. The resources involved are substantial; for example, in the 1980–81 school year in Ontario expenditures on education totalled $5.5 billion at the elementary-secondary level and $2.1 billion at the post-secondary level. Together these amounts represented 7.6 per cent of average provincial personal income for 1980 and 1981. True aggregate resources devoted to education were even larger. The figures quoted do not include the value of the time spent in study by the 1 918 000 elementary and secondary, and 236 000 post-secondary students.

Recent trends in education present important challenges for policy formation. The fraction of the post-secondary school age population attending colleges and universities has more than doubled over the past two decades. However, almost all this increase took place during the 1960s; during the 1970s there was only a small rise in the post-secondary participation rate. In addition, in the late 1960s community colleges became increasingly important – a trend not witnessed again in Ontario until the last five or six years. Finally, enormous shifts in the type of education chosen by students have occurred. Arts enrolment rose to almost half the total university enrolment in the late 1960s but has since declined to about one-third. Commerce and business administration, on the other hand, tripled its enrolment share in Ontario over the 1970s.

To some extent the changes we have observed have been caused by policy makers. However, to a large degree they have been the result of autonomous forces. What is the appropriate policy response to such changes? Should the system move to accommodate current trends, or are they likely to be reversed in the near future? What are the efficient policies?

Answers to these questions require reasonable explanations of the existing facts. Such explanations require a coherent theoretical framework.

Our primary theoretical framework is a simple informational model. Its basic premises are simply that some individuals are better suited to certain jobs than others, and activities that help them discover the best job-worker matches are an important part of education. Education is productive in that it improves the allocation of resources. Viewed in this way, the value of some types of education whose worth is sometimes called into question – for example, general arts and science study at the universities – becomes more evident. In addition, the explanations of some of the recent trends in education – such as the movement away from arts towards more vocational study – become clearer. These new insights provide an immediate gain in terms of our understanding of appropriate policy initiatives.

For the problem at hand, as with virtually all real world issues, no single theory provides a complete explanation of the phenomena in question. So, in the interests of providing as comprehensive and useful an explanation as possible, we shall also examine the usefulness of the human capital and signalling theories of education. In the former, education is a productive activity that augments skills. In contrast, the signalling model treats education as unproductive 'credentialism.'

The remainder of this chapter consists of a brief overview of Chapters 2–6. First, we examine the alternative theories of education, beginning with the earlier views, namely, human capital and signalling (Chapter 2), and proceeding to the informational model (Chapter 3). Then we investigate the basic guidelines that should govern public intervention in education (Chapter 4). An examination of recent trends in education and training (Chapter 5) and an analysis of the current policy debate (Chapter 6) follow.

II. OVERVIEW

II.1 *Chapter 2 – Earlier models of education: human capital and signalling*
In Chapter 2 we provide straightforward expositions of the elements of human capital and signalling theory. We do so partly to make the book self-contained, but also because both models are sometimes applied incorrectly in policy analysis. We hope that a simple but careful exposition of these theories will prove useful beyond its application herein.

Both human capital and signalling are theories of investment. Current income is given up while one is in school so that greater income will be obtained later. But there is a basic difference between the theories. In human capital theory education provides useful skills and so is explicitly productive. In contrast, signalling theory takes skills as fixed and sees resources devoted to education as merely changing the distribution of an economic pie of fixed size: schooling is pure credentialism.

This basic difference is the source of disparate policy recommendations. For example, anything that provides an artificial limit on investment in education is detrimental, according to the human capital view; for such impediments merely interfere with a productive act. But according to the signalling view, impediments to credentialism save scarce resources currently being wasted.

Given the very different policy recommendations emanating from these models, it is important to try to judge which is the relevant model in different applications. While there may be some aspects of education that largely represent signalling, we argue that the empirical evidence on the whole does not support the broad applicability of the signalling model. In our view, where education does not represent skill acquisition, it is readily apparent that considerable information investment is taking place. Thus the information model provides an alternative explanation to signalling for the non-human capital element of education.

II.2 *Chapter 3 – The informational model of schooling and job-worker matching*
This chapter presents the central theoretical framework utilized in this book.

Like the human capital and signalling theories, the informational model is one of investment. The basic suppositions are that workers differ in terms of their ability to perform various tasks required to produce goods and that not all goods use these tasks in the same proportion. For example, workers might differ in terms of their endowment of strength and dexterity, and some jobs require more or less of those traits than others.

At the outset of education neither the worker nor the firm typically has good information concerning the workers' capabilities. In the informational model education is treated as an activity that yields information on a worker's traits and hence on the kind of jobs to which he is suited. Education is a process of investing in 'person-specific information.' According to this view, as in the human capital model, education is a productive activity.

An important point here is that the informational component of education does not directly increase the quantity of resources in the economy. Rather, it allows them to be more efficiently utilized. This distinction has important policy implications. For example, if some activities are purely information rather than skill augmenting, it will erroneously appear that they do nothing at all, if it is thought that the only possible (or useful) output of schooling is new skills.

The chapter explores the informational model in some detail. The behaviour of both individual investors and firms is presented, and the market for information is analysed. Consideration of the impact of various alterations in the economic environment follows.

II.3 *Chapter 4 – Education and training policy: basic guidelines*
In Chapter 4 we examine the possible rationales for government intervention in education and training. Basic guidelines for the structure of a given amount of intervention are set out with the help of the human capital and information models.

Three possible rationales for government intervention are of interest. They rest on the perceived need for government action to achieve efficiency, equity, and the amelioration of labour market 'imbalances.'

There may be a legitimate basis for government intervention on efficiency grounds. If there are significant positive externalities from education, general subsidies are called for. Moreover, when there are no private insurance markets for earnings, it is difficult for students to borrow to finance the efficient level of education. Given this situation, a system of student loans is also an appropriate response.

In terms of equity, general subsidies to education usually fail to achieve much; the better favoured generally stay longer in school. Nevertheless, redistribution via education may be feasible if a careful approach is taken and may be more desirable than equivalent cash transfers from the point of view of donors.

With free competition in all markets, labour market imbalances – or more specifically, manpower shortages – would not be a justification for government intervention. It can be argued, however, that imperfections in the markets for education and training that have been introduced by government (e.g., tuition fee rigidity) retard adjustment mechanisms. Removal of these imperfections or offsetting action is of course desirable.

Finally, we point out that in our view there is no economic rationale for direct state *provision* of education and training. Nevertheless a great deal of education and training will of course be provided for the foreseeable future in Canada in public institutions. We ask whether this situation is harmful, and if so, what can be done about it. It is argued that state provision is harmful when there is an absence of competition. The latter can be fostered at the elementary and secondary levels via voucher schemes or tax credits for school fees; and at the post-secondary level (where there is already considerable choice) by allowing price competition – that is, by letting institutions set their fees freely. For the universities this would be a major step towards treating them as the private institutions they are, rather than as organs of the state.

II.4 *Chapter 5 – Education and training in Canada: recent trends and the current situation*

This chapter begins by asking where the human capital and informational models are most relevant in our education system. Most students devote increasing relative effort to skill acquisition over their school careers. Thus many school careers start with intensive information acquisition in elementary and secondary school and proceed to heavy skill acquisition in vocational schools, colleges, or some university programs. However, the majority of students still leave the formal education system *without* heavy skill acquisition. These students – who enter the labour force from high school or with an arts or science BA – undertake most of their human capital accumulation on the job. That this investment pattern is not wasteful relative to that involving heavy skill acquisition while the student is still in school is not widely appreciated – especially in the current labour market policy literature – and is an important message of our study.

We go on to look at trends in enrolment and expenditure at all levels of education and training in Ontario and Canada over the period since 1960. The major enrolment phenomena to be explained are the rapid rise in participation rates in the 1960s and subsequent slow-down in the 1970s, the increasing importance of general arts and science enrolment in the 1960s and subsequent decline for arts, and the increasing importance of college enrolment. On the expenditure side, while real spending per student increased rapidly during the 1960s at all levels of the education system, in the 1970s spending at the post-secondary level increased only mildly for the country as a whole and it decreased substantially in Ontario (almost the entire decline occurring at the universities).

The factors underlying the secular trend towards higher levels of educational attainment are twofold. On the supply side, direct costs of education (tuition, books, equipment, etc.) are continually declining relative to forgone earnings. All three theories of education examined in the first two chapters predict that this reduction in direct costs would increase desired education. On the demand side, the informational model predicts that increased specialization and division of labour increase the relative demand for more educated labour.

Augmenting the fundamental tendency towards increased education attainment have been a host of special demand and supply factors. On the supply side, the geographic extension of post-secondary education in the 1960s alone may have contributed strongly to rising participation rates. Also, the three different forms of support for post-secondary education taken by federal funding since 1960 have had a strong impact on provincial spending priorities. On the demand side, we examine the impact of age cohort size effects on earnings for the baby boom generation, the influence of public sector employment demand on the size and structure of post-secondary enrolment, and the effects of changes in elementary and secondary education. Real spending per elementary and secondary student has risen dramatically over the last two decades. Accompanying changes in curriculum content and flexibility suggest that the typical high school graduate today has investigated a wider range of subjects than his/her predecessor of twenty years ago. This means that more information about personal skills and abilities is now being accumulated before the post-secondary stage. The decreased demand for enrolment in programs like general arts and science, where the emphasis on information accumulation is greatest, as well as the overall slow-down in post-secondary participation rates may owe something to this change.

Finally we discuss what may happen to post-secondary enrolments over the next decade in the light of our analysis of past enrolment trends and the arresting fact that the population of post-secondary age will decline by about twenty per cent over the next ten years before rising again to its current level in the first years of the next century.

II.5 *Chapter 6 – Education and training in Ontario: current issues*
In this chapter we relate the policy guidelines and positive analysis of Chapters 4 and 5 to the current debate surrounding education and training policy in Canada.

A current view is that there is a serious misallocation of public support for education and training in this country. This conclusion is based on apparent evidence in the late 1970s and early 1980s of surpluses of post-secondary graduates in programs like the humanities and social sciences; shortages in engineering, computer science, and other more 'technological' programs; as well as a shortage of workers in some skilled trades. The implied policy would reduce support for general arts and science courses, increase that for more technological courses at the post-secondary level, and increase support for skill training in close co-operation with federal manpower training programs.

Closely related to the argument for a reallocation of resources is the claim that our education and training systems have been insufficiently responsive to changes in enrolment demand and labour market conditions, and that new mechanisms to ensure increased responsiveness must be designed. This view has been embodied in Employment and Immigration Canada's new 'National Training Program' (announced in January 1982), under which manpower training in future will take place, as far as possible, only in occupations in high demand. It has also been expressed in the changes to the form of federal funding for post-secondary education under 'Established Programs Financing' being considered by the federal government.

To some extent the basic policy guidelines we suggest in Chapter 4 are in line with current federal thinking. For example, we argue that if the aggregate support for education and training were to be regarded as fixed, a reallocation of support away from post-secondary institutions towards on-the-job training would be appropriate. This would simply alleviate the current distortion caused by the difference in subsidies to formal schooling and training in industry. The reallocation would not be motivated by a desire to eliminate manpower shortages.

A point we stress is that the current emphasis on 'technological' and higher-skill trade training appears to represent a vocationalism, which largely ignores the role of investment in person-specific information in education. There is a trade-off between skill training and information investment. It is a mistake to believe that every increase in the skill content of education must lead to greater employability and higher earnings. Such increases may come at the expense of information investment and therefore reduce the quality of job-worker matching. Hence an optimal combination of skill and information investment, rather than exclusive reliance on one form of education, must be sought.

II.6 *Chapter 7 – Conclusion*
We conclude by outlining in detail the policy initiatives in education and training that we would recommend for the federal and Ontario governments. The spirit of our suggestions is to bring some of the fresh air of the market mechanism into education and training in Ontario. Although the changes we recommend are not minor, we believe they take significant account of both practicability and political reality. We therefore urge their serious consideration by both policy makers and the public.

2
Earlier models of education: human capital and signalling

I. INTRODUCTION

The model of education explored in this study is not the first, nor is it likely to be the last. The economist's view of education is a very broad one by any standards. As a consequence, education is seen as a multifaceted activity, and some of its features are more important or illuminating in some situations than others. Hence, there is ample scope for numerous models of education. One goal of this chapter is to present the basics of two influential views of education: the 'human capital' and 'signalling' theories.

The human capital and signalling models are very different. They start from assumptions that are quite distinct. It follows that the implications and policy prescriptions arising from these models coincide in some instances and differ radically in others. As an example, both models generate the prediction that additional schooling raises wages. However, if there are capital market imperfections, human capital theory prescribes subsidies to education, while signalling suggests either no action or taxing schooling time. The second goal of this chapter is to try to delineate the situations in which the human capital and signalling models best apply. In doing so, it becomes apparent that there is an important gap in the existing body of theory. A vast collection of circumstances exists in which education is clearly important, but in a fashion different from that envisioned in the human capital and signalling models. The informational model presented in Chapter 3 seeks to fill this void.

Education, in its broadest sense, is simply one activity that involves investment of resources early in life in order that income be greater later on. To provide the reader with some indication of the direction in which the discussion will proceed, it is useful to summarize briefly the basic views of education embodied in the human capital, signalling, and informational models.

Education can be envisioned as either productive or unproductive. If seen as productive, the increase in income associated with investment in education stems from either an increase in skills or a more effective application of a given collection of skills. The human capital model focuses on the direct increase in skills provided by schooling; learning to be an electrician is an example. The informational model highlights the role of schooling in efficiently identifying the most productive application of given skills. To illustrate, an individual's undergraduate record may indicate the presence of the analytic traits required of a portfolio manager or the ability to co-operate and co-ordinate demanded of a shop foreman. The informational model implies that education is productive, because it helps allocate resources to their most valuable use.

The signalling model characterizes schooling as entirely unproductive. Some individuals are innately more skilful than others. If individual workers are privy to this information, but firms are not, engaging in an extended period of schooling is simply a way to 'signal' one's ability to firms. Obtaining a BA degree does not mean that the individual is more productive than previously, nor does it provide any indication of where his skills might best be put to use. Rather, the implication is merely that the individual is clever enough to succeed in acquiring a BA degree.

The differing policy prescriptions implied by the theories follow from whether schooling is viewed as productive. In all three theories the private and social *costs* of education coincide. These costs are simply the resources used while in school (e.g., teachers' time, library services) and the output the individual does not produce while in school. In the human capital and informational models the private and social *returns* to education also coincide: output is greater. The socially and privately optimal levels of education therefore coincide. In contrast, in the signalling model output is fixed. There is no social return. The socially optimal level of signalling is zero! However, the individual's private return is greater income earned at the expense of those who do not choose to signal. Thus, from the social viewpoint, individual behaviour leads to too much education.

In the sections that follow we present simple versions of the human capital and signalling models. We then discuss the characteristics of situations in which each seems most helpful. In doing so some of the range of application of the informational model becomes apparent; however, further consideration of its scope will have to await its development and application in succeeding chapters.

II. HUMAN CAPITAL

The human capital model has come a long way since Becker's (1975) pioneering efforts. It has been extended in many directions, and its less useful encumbrances

Figure 1
Human capital production function

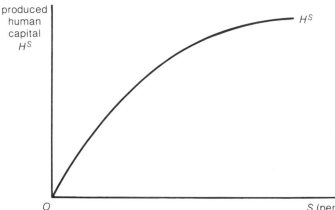

produced
human
capital
H^S

H^S

O S (periods spent in school)

have been eliminated. The simplest (and incidentally perhaps the most elegant)
model is that presented by Rosen (1973) in an essay that has become a modern
classic. Accordingly we focus on Rosen's 'pure schooling' model of human capital
accumulation.

It is useful to devote some attention to the precise notion of human capital.
Human capital is simply the productive resources embodied in a person. The
definition is intended to be all-encompassing; there is but a single kind of human
capital, measured in 'efficiency units.' In other words, human capital consists of a
collection of skills, all jobs use this same set of skills, and they do so in the same
manner.

The reader may find this treatment of skills somewhat restrictive, – all the more
so when it is pointed out that it implies, for example, that the work performed by a
neurosurgeon could be completed by some number of cafeteria cooks, if only the
number were appropriately large. However, in many interesting cases the efficiency units assumption seems much less restrictive, and it is in some of those
instances that the model is more appropriate than in the others. It is also possible
to relax this assumption. A brief description of the 'heterogeneous capital' case is
given at the end of this section.

The pure schooling model of human capital accumulation is an efficiency units
model. Let us call a person's stock of human capital, the number of efficiency
units in his possession, H. In the pure schooling model H is traditionally thought
of as comprising two components. First, a certain amount (H^0) is simply a gift of
nature. One can think of H^0 as what the individual is born with, or the amount
accumulated prior to the age at which schooling ceases to be mandatory. In either
case H^0 is assumed to be exogenous.

The other component of H is obtained through schooling. (This is why the model is referred to as a 'pure schooling' model. Schooling is the only vehicle for obtaining human capital in addition to H^0.) We shall call the number of periods spent in school S. The amount of human capital accumulated by going to school for S periods is labelled H^S. The relationship between H^S and S is referred to as the human capital production function, depicted in Figure 1. Referring to Figure 1, it is sensible to suppose that the longer one stays in school, the larger is H^S. However, this process is subject to diminishing returns; the more schooling one has already had, the less an *extra* period of schooling contributes to the stock of human capital. In sum, a person who has gone to school for S periods has human capital equal to[1]

$$H = H^0 + H^S. \tag{1}$$

H^0 also affects the amount of human capital generated by a given period of schooling. More productive people may learn faster. This is one dimension of ability (another is considered below). Production functions corresponding to greater H^0 lie above and to the left of that depicted in Figure 1.

The predictions of human capital theory follow from the assumption that the number of periods spent in school is optimally chosen by the individual. For present purposes it suffices to suppose that the individual chooses the level of schooling that affords him the greatest level of lifetime wealth. The component of wealth that depends on the number of periods spent in school is the present value of wage earnings. Thus, the best choice of the number of periods in school is that which yields the greatest capitalized wage earnings.

Let us suppose efficiency units of human capital are rented to employers at a fixed rental rate per period, R. Then one-period labour earnings for a person with human capital H amount to RH. Of course these earnings are obtained only for the periods following schooling. The returns to schooling are therefore the value of future wages. The costs are wages forgone during the periods spent in school.[2] Assuming a constant one-period interest rate of r, the present value of labour earnings (called PV) can be shown to be[3]

$$\text{PV} = RH / [r(1 + r)^S]. \tag{2}$$

PV depends on S for two reasons. First, an increase in S raises the stock of human capital to be rented out, thus raising PV. However, raising S also delays the

---

1 Human capital is assumed not to depreciate. This is a minor restriction, easily removed.
2 For simplicity we temporarily ignore the direct costs (tuition, books, ...) of schooling. Their inclusion is dealt with at the end of this section.
3 Expression (2) assumes individuals to live forever. This is merely a convenience. The finite-life version of (2) simply contains a scale factor.

Figure 2
Determination of the length of the schooling period

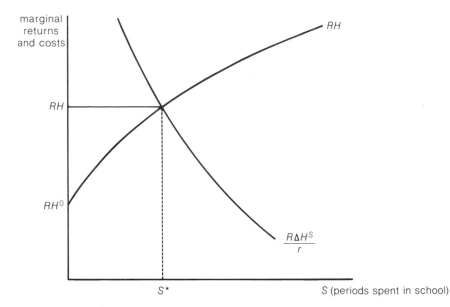

date at which wages are received, thus lowering the present value of the flow of wages. The optimal choice of S is that which just balances these opposing forces.

Suppose we let ΔH^S denote the impact on H of one more period of schooling. Recalling that schooling yields diminishing returns, ΔH^S declines with S. Next, $R\Delta H^S$ is the increase in wages associated with one more period in school (the dollar value of ΔH^S). Then $R\Delta H^S / r$ is the present value (as of the end of the schooling period) of the increase in wages associated with one more period in school. $R\Delta H^S / r$ is therefore the return to one more period in school: the marginal return to schooling time.

What does one more period in school cost? As of the contemplated end of the schooling period, one more period in school means one more period without wages RH. RH is thus the marginal cost of schooling time.

The optimal number of periods to spend in school balances the cost of one more period against the returns:

$$R\Delta H^S / r = RH. \tag{3}$$

See Figure 2. In Figure 2, $R\Delta H^S / r$ is downward sloping, again owing to diminishing marginal returns. Marginal cost RH is upward sloping, as a consequence of the fact that the longer one goes to school, the more human capital one has, and thus the more it costs to spend time out of the labour market. Note that RH is also the level of post-schooling wages; this factor will prove convenient below.

To see why S^* (the optimal duration of schooling, which satisfied (3)) is the best choice, suppose some S smaller than S^* were chosen. Then the present value of the wage gain associated with more schooling $(R\Delta H^S / r)$ exceeds the cost of that extra schooling. Wealth could be raised by spending more time in school so long as S is less than S^*. A similar argument shows that wealth could be raised by lowering S if S exceeds S^*. Thus S equal to S^* is the best the individual can do.

This is a good point for a brief summary. Human capital is an all-encompassing measure of resources embodied in a person. In the pure schooling version of the theory human capital consists of an endowed portion plus that accumulated through schooling. Schooling time yields additional human capital with diminishing returns. Optimal behaviour on the part of individuals involves obtaining the greatest possible capitalized wage receipts. To achieve this goal they balance the wage gains following from extra schooling time against the fact that more schooling time means more forgone income. The appropriate choice is that for which these forces are exactly equal.

The pure schooling model of human capital accumulation has two endogenous variables, schooling (S) and the 'wage rate' (RH). The exogenous variables are the interest rate (r), endowed stocks of human capital (H^0), and any parameters of the human capital production function (the relationship between inputs of schooling time and output of human capital). As an example of the latter, some individuals learn faster than others; this notion may be represented by introducing a 'shift parameter,' A (for learning ability), into the production function. Higher values of A shift the production function upwards.

In contrast to most economic models, the endogenous quantities are not determined simultaneously as functions of the exogenous variables. Rather, the model is recursive. Schooling time (S) is determined as a function of all the exogenous variables through (3). Total human capital at the end of schooling (H) is then the endowed quantity of human capital (H^0) plus the accumulated amount implied by the chosen value of S (H^S). Wages (w) are the rental income (RH) earned by this stock of skills. As such, wages depend directly upon endowed stocks and learning ability, but on the interest rate only through its influence on the choice of S. Schematically,

$$H^0, r, A \rightarrow S,$$

then

$$H^0, S, A \rightarrow RH = w.$$

What are the predictions of this simple version of human capital theory? That is, how do the endogenous variables, S and RH, respond to changes in the

Figure 3
The effect of an increase in H^0 on schooling and wages

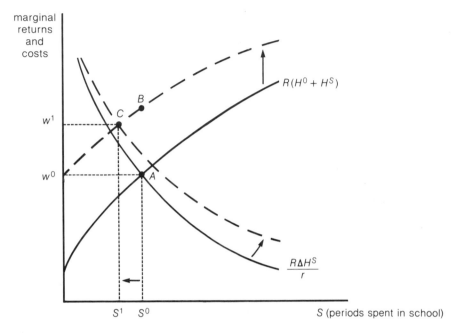

exogenous quantities H^0, r, and A? These questions are particularly easy to answer in this model, because wages are always equal to marginal cost. Thus, we need only decide on how schooling responds to a change in one of the exogenous variables. The effect on wages can then be found by simply asking whether marginal cost is higher or lower at the new level of S. Referring back to Figure 2, wages can be read off the marginal cost curve at the chosen level of schooling.

Consider changes in the endowed stocks H^0. Increases in H^0 raise the marginal costs of schooling. Marginal returns may be increased or decreased, depending upon whether $R\Delta H^S$ rises or falls with H^0. Figure 3 depicts the leading case (S^0 and S^1 represent the old and new levels of S respectively) in which a decline in schooling follows from an increase in H^0. The size of the decline depends on how elastic the marginal returns are; for example, if $R\Delta H^S / r$ is very steep, only a small reduction in S is required to regain equality between marginal returns and cost.

The increase in H^0 affects income in two ways. First, greater H^0 represents a direct addition to the quantity of capital to be rented out, thus raising wages from A to B in Figure 3, if S^0 remained the best choice. This increment to income is

Figure 4
The effect of an increase in r on schooling and wages

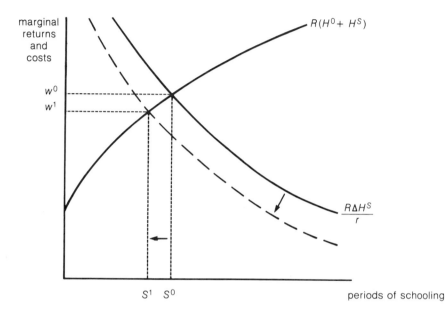

offset to some extent by the reduction in produced stocks of human capital, the move from B to C; on net, however, so long as the increase in H^0 does not cause marginal returns to *decline* drastically, wages must rise from w^0 to w^1. Thus, an increase in endowed stocks of human capital is predicted to raise wages and usually reduce the duration of schooling time.

Next, consider an increase in the interest rate. By reducing the present value of future wages, the marginal return to schooling declines. Marginal cost is unaffected. Schooling is predicted to decline. When the interest rate rises, there is just one effect on wage rates: the reduction in produced human capital causes wages to decline. Altogether, an increase in the rate of interest is predicted to shorten the schooling period and reduce wages. See Figure 4.

Finally, consider an increase in the ability to learn, A. This raises the amount of human capital accumulated for any given amount of time spent in school. Thus, since it raises the forgone wage relevant to any given duration of schooling, marginal cost rises. If the increase in A leaves unchanged or reduces the impact of an extra period of schooling on human capital (marginal returns), time spent in

Figure 5
The effect of an increase in A on schooling and wages

a) ΔH^S falls as A rises

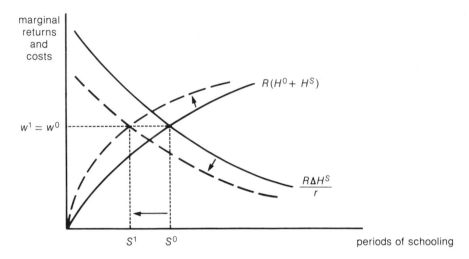

periods of schooling

b) ΔH^S rises with A

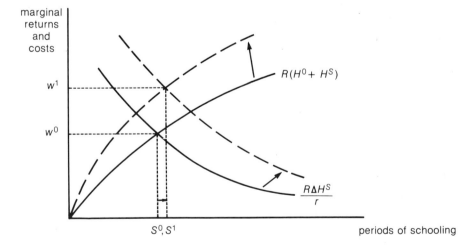

periods of schooling

school declines. The impact on wages is ambiguous. The human capital technology is more productive, but inputs of time are reduced, so output of human capital may either rise or fall. This case is illustrated in Figure 5(a).

The more plausible case is presented in Figure 5(b). An increase in learning efficiency raises the marginal return to schooling. As both marginal returns and costs rise, the effect on the duration of schooling is ambiguous. (The figure is drawn for S^0 less than S^1.) However, the more efficient technology inevitably manifests itself in higher wages.

Finally, three additional topics deserve brief consideration. First, consider the empirical testing of human capital theory. A standard approach involves estimation of wage equations: a regression of the natural logarithm of the wage, which we shall call log w, on the number of years of schooling and various quantities intended to proxy H^0 and A. For example,

$$\log w = aH^0 + bS + cA + e. \tag{4}$$

e is a random error term, and a, b, and c are parameters to be estimated. In the light of the theory of human capital how should the estimate of the parameters in (4) be interpreted?

Consider the parameter b. b is the percentage effect on wages of a change in S, *holding H^0 and A fixed*. How can S change if H^0 and A remain fixed? Only by a change in the interest rate. Thus b represents the percentage effect on wages of a change in the rate of interest, as transmitted through an adjustment in the optimal duration of schooling. It is straightforward to demonstrate that the theory predicts $b = r$.[4] If A or H^0 are not correctly held constant (as occurs if they are poorly 'proxied') $b = r$ is not predicted; for in that case we simply do not know what is generating the movements in S. If H^0 is the driving force, we have seen that schooling and wages are expected to move in *opposite* directions. But if A is the source of the adjustments in S, wages and schooling are predicted to be positively correlated, but $b = r$ is not predicted.

In a similar fashion, the parameter a reflects the percentage effect on wages of a change in H^0, *holding S and A fixed*. If H^0 increases, S is expected to fall. An offsetting reduction in r is therefore required to hold S fixed. It follows that a measures the percentage impact of changes in H^0 on wages, when the rate of interest is adjusted to keep schooling constant. The coefficient c has a similar interpretation. Again, misspecification of A or H^0 severely confuses the exercise.

The point here is that estimates of the parameters of equations like (4) must be treated with considerable caution in the light of the specific nature of the

---

4 The wage is $w = R(H^0 + H^S)$. Let Δw be the effect of S on w. Then
$\Delta w = R\Delta H^S = Rr(H^0 + H^S)$ – from (3) – $= rw$. Therefore $(1/w) \Delta w = r$ or $\Delta \log w = r$.

conceptual experiments they purport to represent. This precaution is even more important, given the practical difficulties associated with holding H^0 and A constant.

Much discussion of schooling is based on stylized facts that emerge from estimation of equations such as (4). The reader should bear in mind that these estimates have content only to the extent that the variables of interest are dealt with properly in the light of the theory.

The second extension of human capital theory involves relaxation of the 'efficiency units' assumption. That is, skills can be viewed as heterogeneous. The analysis presented above can be applied to the accumulation of any particular kind of human capital. If an individual's training is confined to one skill, his/her problem is complicated only slightly by this extension. To illustrate, suppose there are two kinds of human capital, numbered 1 and 2. Then each individual has an endowment of each type of skill (H_1^0 and H_2^0), as well as some degree of learning efficiency for each skill (A_1 and A_2). The wealth maximizing problem then simply involves: (1) figuring out the optimal duration of schooling (S_1 and S_2) for each type of human capital, assuming it is the only type chosen; (2) computing the level of wealth (PV_1 and PV_2) implied by each of these possibilities; and (3) choosing to accumulate the type of skill for which wealth is greatest.

The predictions of the theory are more complicated once heterogeneous skills are allowed for. The difficulties arise simply because a change in H_1^0, for example, may cause either a change in the quantity or type of schooling undertaken. However, the basic qualitative nature of the results is much like that of the results of the efficiency units model. Accordingly, for most purposes the simpler approach suffices. In particular, in later chapters discussion occasionally proceeds in a heterogeneous capital context. The intuition developed in the efficiency units context is generally more than sufficient for a reasonable appreciation of the arguments.

The final extension involves the addition of direct costs of schooling. These direct costs comprise tuition costs as well as expenditures on books and other materials. Since these items may be viewed as increasing the returns to spending one more period in school (i.e., they are in the human capital production function, along with S, H^0, and A), D enters the marginal return to schooling time. However, these direct costs must also be paid during each period of schooling. Thus D must also be included in the marginal cost of schooling. Equation (3), which determines the optimal duration of schooling, is modified to

$$R\Delta H^S / r = RH + D. \tag{5}$$

In terms of new predictions, an increase in direct costs raises both the marginal costs and the returns to schooling, with the former usually rising more than the latter. Accordingly, an increase in D reduces the duration of schooling. Since this implies that less human capital is accumulated, wages also fall.

We may now conclude the summary started above. The optimal level of schooling is determined by equality of marginal returns and costs. The wage rate follows in turn from the choice of schooling. The main predictions of this simple theory are that (1) increases in endowed skills will usually reduce the length of the schooling period and raise the wage rate; (2) increases in the rate of interest reduce both schooling and the wage rate; (3) increases in learning efficiency most likely raise wages, but their impact on schooling time is ambiguous; and (4) increases in the direct cost of schooling reduce both the length of the schooling period as well as wages.

III. SIGNALLING

The study of education as signalling was initiated by Arrow (1973) and Spence (1973). It has since been refined and extended by Spence (1974), Stiglitz (1975), and Riley (1976, 1979b), to name just a few. A simplified version of Riley's (1976) signalling model compares easily with both the pure schooling model of human capital accumulation and the informational model.[5] We therefore focus on that model.

The essential features of the signalling model are quite straightforward. As in the human capital model, individuals possess skills, measured in efficiency units. In the simplest model, however, schooling has no effect on these skills; education is explicitly non-productive. The worker's skills are solely those with which he is endowed: H^0.

Workers are assumed to differ in terms of the amount of these skills they possess. Further, since skills are measured in efficiency units, a worker with more efficiency units is absolutely more productive at all jobs. When one worker is more productive than another in all circumstances, the situation is such that 'ability' becomes an unambiguous concept.

This basic set-up of skills is followed by two assumptions.
1. Each worker knows his ability (H^0). Firms do not have this information nor can they easily obtain it. Production is organized in a fashion that renders rapid observation of the work performed by a given worker next to impossible. This is called the 'asymmetric information' assumption.
2. Workers cannot agree to 'money-back' contracts. That is, it is supposed that the firm will eventually discover the worker's ability. The worker cannot make

---

5 The simplification is as follows. Riley (1976) considers a model wherein schooling yields *both* human capital and signals. We consider only the pure signalling case.

an agreement specifying that he will receive a given wage rate until such time as his ability is observed and then refund any amount that exceeds the observed value of his services. This is referred to as the 'incomplete markets' assumption.

The force behind these two assumptions is clear. Since some workers are more able than others, there are natural tendencies for some to be paid more. However, under the asymmetric information assumption, ability is not observed. It follows that workers, if asked their ability, have an incentive to lie. All workers will claim to have a large value of H^0. If workers could make money-back contracts, the incentive to lie would be removed. But assuming such contracts away, the problem of wage determination in the presence of asymmetric information remains.

How are wages determined in the signalling model? Wages have to be based on something, and if it is to be helpful at all, whatever wages depend on must be observable by both workers and firms. Let us call this entity the signal, Z. In addition to being observable, Z must be related to H^0 in a well-defined fashion. Then, by observing Z, H^0 can be inferred by the firm, and the wage determination problem is solved.

At first blush this structure appears risible. Ability is not observable, but the signal is; thus ability may be inferred immediately. The interest in signalling derives from the specification of the relationship between the signal and ability. As will become evident, inferences about ability are possible only because the signal is chosen optimally. The signalling model derives its predictive content from optimizing behaviour, just as the human capital model does.

The signalling model is a model of a marketplace. The behaviour of firms is a crucial aspect of the structure. This is a consequence of the asymmetric information assumption; if information is to be distributed asymmetrically, there must be at least two economic actors between which information is distributed. This stands in contrast to the human capital model, wherein firms have no interesting role.

We first consider the behaviour of workers, then turn to firms. Workers know their ability. As in the human capital model, their labour market plans consist of schooling followed by work. However, in this case the output of schooling is not skills. Rather, a credential (the signal Z) is obtained.

What is the relationship between schooling time (which we call S), ability (H^0), and the level of the signal (Z)?[6] It is assumed that there is a 'signal production

---

6 A learning efficiency parameter (A in the human capital model) can be included. The predictions arising from its inclusion are discussed below.

Figure 6
Signal production function*

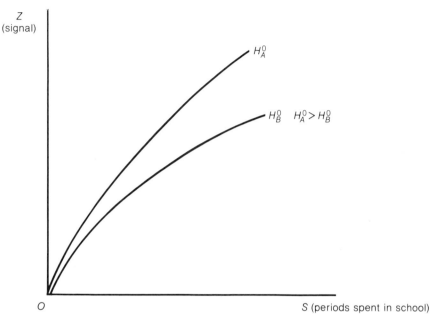

*The upper (lower) curve corresponds to the production function when H^0
takes on the value H_A^0 (H_B^0).

function' that specifies the level of signal obtained by a person of ability H^0 who
stays in school for S periods. The crucial assumptions concerning the production
function are as follows:
1. For any given ability, longer schooling generates a larger signal.
2. For any given duration of schooling, higher-ability workers obtain a greater
   signal.
3. While extra schooling yields a greater signal, the increase is larger for higher-
   ability workers.
A production function embodying these three assumptions is depicted in Figure 6.

Since it is crucial that the distinction among S, Z, and H^0 be quite clear, this is a
suitable point to provide an example of the production relationship. Think of the
signal as a degree. A low value of Z would then correspond to a grade twelve
diploma, slightly higher Z would be a grade thirteen diploma, and so on.

Figure 7
Time required to achieve a given signal

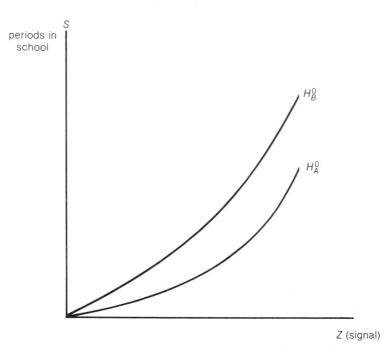

Assumptions 1–3 may be rephrased as (1) given ability, the longer a person goes to school, the more advanced is his highest degree; (2) more able individuals can accumulate a given degree more quickly; and (3) for the more able workers extra schooling time generates a greater increase in degrees.

It turns out that the easiest way to handle the problem is to invert the production function and assumptions 1–3. We then consider how long it takes a person with given ability to accumulate any particular signal. This procedure simply reverses the roles of Z and S in Figure 6, redrawn appropriately in Figure 7. S (on the vertical axis) is the time required for a worker with skill H^0 to obtain a signal Z (on the horizontal axis).

Now suppose the individual is confronted with a wage schedule ($w(Z)$) which depends positively on the level of the signal.[7] Further, as in the human capital

---

7 For the moment the issue of where such a wage schedule might come from can be ignored.

Figure 8
Optimal choice of the signal

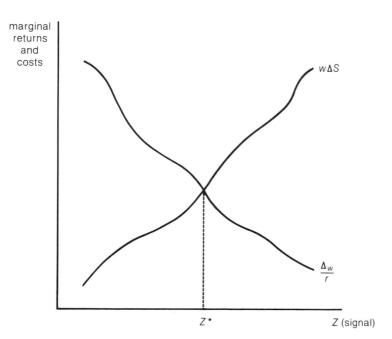

model, assume the individual seeks to maximize the present value of his labour earnings, PV. PV is derived in exactly the same way as in (2):

$$\text{PV} = w(Z)/[r(1 + r)^{S}]. \tag{6}$$

PV depends on the signal (Z) for two reasons. First, a larger value of the signal generates greater wages, hence a larger level of discounted labour earnings. However, for given ability a larger signal can be obtained only through longer schooling. This requires the postponement of work and so reduces the present value of wages received.

How does the individual maximize the present value of labour earnings? He does so by choosing the level of the signal, Z. We could cast the decision in terms of schooling time S; while this would be convenient for comparison with the human capital model, it renders cumbersome the discussion of firms. Consequently, we follow the more conventional analysis.

Figure 9
More able individuals choose larger signals

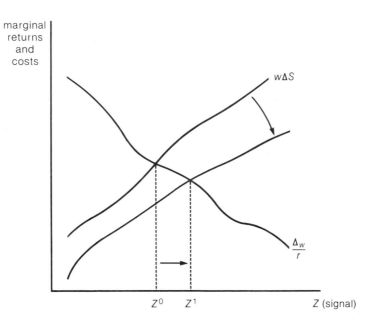

Let us call the impact of increased Z on wages Δw, and the extra schooling time required to obtain a larger signal ΔS. Then the level of the signal that maximizes the present value of life earnings is that for which

$$\Delta w / r = w\Delta S. \tag{7}$$

The intuition here is much like that underlying the choice of schooling time in the human capital model. Increasing the signal raises the wage by Δw. Since this increase is permanent, its present value is $\Delta w/r$, which is therefore the marginal return to signalling. But any increase in Z requires that the schooling period be lengthened by ΔS. Therefore, receipt of wages must be delayed by ΔS. This costs $w\Delta s$, which is the marginal cost of signalling. The optimal choice of Z equates marginal returns and costs, and is illustrated in Figure 8. Since we have yet to say anything about how the wage depends on the level of the signal, other than that it does so positively, marginal returns and costs in Figure 8 do not have the 'nice' shapes implied by the human capital framework.

A brief summary is in order. Workers know their ability. Firms do not have this information and cannot easily get it through observation of work. Thus wages cannot be based directly on ability. However, they can be based on observables such as credentials (the signal). Individuals can accumulate signals by going to school. The choice of signal balances the cost of forestalling receipt of wages against the concomitant perpetual wage gain.

The crucial and subtle part of the signalling argument is as follows. At each level of the signal, a given addition is assumed to require a smaller increase in the length of the schooling period for more able individuals. Equivalently, an increase in H^0 reduces ΔS, the time needed to raise the signal by one unit. Because more able individuals face the same marginal return schedule, and a lower marginal cost, it follows that they will optimally choose a greater signal.[8] See Figure 9 (Z^0 and Z^1 are the choices corresponding to lower and higher levels of ability, respectively).

Next, the signal production function is assumed to be known by everyone, including firms. Also, all workers face the same relationship between the wage they receive and the level of the signal. It follows that for any worker the firm knows the marginal return to signalling, $\Delta w/r$. Because the firm does not know H^0, however, it cannot say what the marginal cost is. (That is ΔS depends on H^0. So $w\Delta S$ also depends on H^0.) However, if the firm observes the choice of signal *and* assumes the worker to be *behaving optimally*, it can infer the marginal cost. That is, marginal cost equals marginal return at the chosen Z. Since each marginal cost curve is associated with a given level of ability, the firm can determine H^0.

To see this inference more clearly, return to Figure 9, where the upper marginal cost curve corresponds to the lower level of ability. The firm knows $w\Delta S$. Suppose it observes a worker choosing Z^0. This is an optimal choice only if the upper curve represents marginal cost. But this marginal cost corresponds to the lower level of ability. Therefore the individual must be of lower ability. If Z^1 is chosen, the worker must be of higher ability.

In brief, the firm knows the marginal return faced by each worker, and can observe his choice of signal. Since the signal is chosen to equate marginal return and marginal cost, the firm has learned the level of marginal cost. Because there is a unique ability associated with each marginal cost curve, knowledge of marginal cost translates into knowledge of ability. In this manner, given Z, the firm makes an inference concerning the worker's ability, H^0. Let us call this inference $\hat{H}(Z)$. According to our earlier discussion, $\hat{H}(Z)$ rises with Z.

---

8 The question of whether more able individuals also take more schooling is addressed below.

Notice that it does not pay the worker to attempt to fool the firm by choosing a high value of Z. Although this deception would succeed, and the firm would pay a greater wage, the present value of labour earnings would be *reduced*, because the value of Z that renders discounted labour earnings as large as possible equates marginal returns and costs.

Now so far wages have had nothing to do with productivity. That is, any wage schedule that yielded greater wages to workers with larger signals would have revealed ability equally well. How then are wages determined?

To determine wages two important assumptions are made. First, since productivity is supposed to be observed eventually, it is assumed that firms are not surprised when they learn the worker's true ability. Their expectations about workers' ability turn out to be correct or 'rational': $\hat{H}(Z) = H^0$. This of course implies that the firm's output is what was expected when hiring took place.

Second, as in the previous section, let RH^0 represent the dollar value of the productivity of a worker of ability H^0. It is assumed that competition ensures the wage offered to a worker with signal Z, $w(Z)$, equals the value of the productivity of a worker with the ability level inferred from that choice of Z: $w(Z) = R\hat{H}(Z)$. Since $\hat{H}(Z)$ is assumed to be an accurate inference, wages equal the value of the worker's productivity.

Thus in the end the signalling mechanism generates a wage schedule having the property that workers are paid according to their productivity. None the less, it is argued that schooling performs no useful purpose. Since productivity is not altered by schooling, neither is total output raised. Thus the size of the economic pie is not increased by schooling, but real resources are expended. Waste occurs because the *distribution* of the product depends on schooling, and individuals devote resources to augmenting their share. Unless social welfare is raised by individuals being paid according to their contribution to output, the whole process is necessarily a social loss.

This loss is the source of the signalling argument against subsidizing education. Specifically, it uses up resources purely in the process of redistributing them. Further, education is often thought of and advocated as an equalizing institution. The signalling argument suggests precisely the opposite. Were there no signalling, all workers (under the assumption that productivity is not observable) would be paid equally. Signalling generates greater wages for the more able, and lower wages for the less well endowed.

We can now add to the summary started above. Given the relationship between ability and the time required to obtain a given level of the signal, more able individuals optimally choose a larger level of the signal. Doing so allows firms to infer the workers' ability. Assuming that firms do not make systematic

Figure 10
An increase in the interest rate

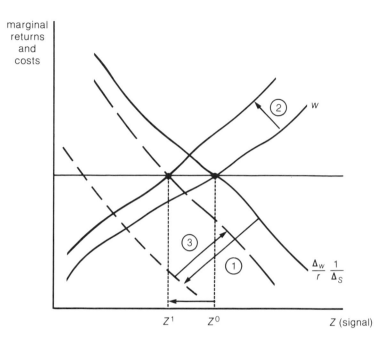

marginal
returns
and
costs

② w

③

①

$\frac{\Delta_w}{r} \frac{1}{\Delta_S}$

Z^1 Z^0 Z (signal)

mistakes, and that they are competitors in the labour market, the equilibrium
wage structure is such that workers are paid according to their actual contribution to output.

What are the observable consequences of the theory? From the viewpoint of
the individual worker, the theory comprises three endogenous variables (wage,
schooling, and signal) and two exogenous variables (interest rate and ability).

What is the impact of an increase in the rate of interest? Since both workers
and firms play an important role in the signalling model, the situation is somewhat more complex than in the human capital model. One prediction is immediately clear. Since individuals are always paid the value of their productivity, and
individual productive capacity is exogenous, an increase in the interest rate
cannot affect the wage received by an individual of given ability.[9]

9 Of course, this theory ignores the general equilibrium effect of a change in interest rates on
   capital accumulation and hence the marginal product of human capital.

It turns out that the relationship between wages and the signal must change when the interest rate does. The argument is as follows. When the interest rate rises, the marginal return to signalling falls.[10] Referring to Figure 10, holding the wage structure constant, the marginal return shifts down to the dashed curve when the interest rate rises (see the arrow marked ①). But since productivity is fixed by assumption, and competition ensures each worker is paid according to his productivity, the wage must remain as before. Thus $w(Z)$ must rise for each level of the signal (see the arrow marked ②). The impact of Z on w, Δw, must therefore rise as well (see the arrow marked ③), because a lower value of Z now yields the same wage as before.[11] But so long as $w(Z)$ rises, Z must fall if the individual's wage is to remain constant. In sum, an increase in the rate of interest lowers the level of the signal, steepens the relationship between wages and the signal, and leaves wages unchanged.

In addition to the above, since the signal falls, the duration of time spent in school is shortened. Thus an increase in the rate of interest reduces schooling time; less potential output is wasted.

Now consider an increase in ability. We have already seen that more able individuals earn more and choose a larger level of the signal (see Figure 9). Whether they go to school for a longer or shorter period is not clear. The reasoning is simple. Although more able individuals wish to accumulate a greater signal, they may do so in a shorter period if the increase in ability raises the impact of additional schooling time on the signal sufficiently. However, the latter effect has to be quite large for schooling time actually to fall. Thus increases in ability are expected to be associated with higher wages, signals, and most likely schooling time.

Finally, in the human capital section we considered the impact of an increase in a 'learning efficiency parameter,' A, on schooling and wages. Larger values of this parameter allowed greater production of human capital in a shorter period, but A itself was not a productive attribute of the worker; that is, it was not part of human capital. We can ask the same question in the signalling context.

Consider a learning efficiency parameter, A, which is not part of ability (H^0) but allows a greater signal to be accumulated faster. First consider the case where

10 Here we have divided the condition determining Z by ΔS: $(\Delta w / r) / \Delta S = w$. Effectively this just changes the units of measurement of marginal costs and returns.

11 It can be shown that the least able individuals do not signal at all. That is, all that signalling does for them is reveal what they would prefer to hide. For everyone else signalling reveals that although they may not be the most able, they are certainly not the least able. The consequence is that all wage schedules go through the point $Z = 0$, $w = RH^0$, where H^0 is the lowest value of H^0 in the population. See Riley (1976).

Figure 11
An increase in learning efficiency

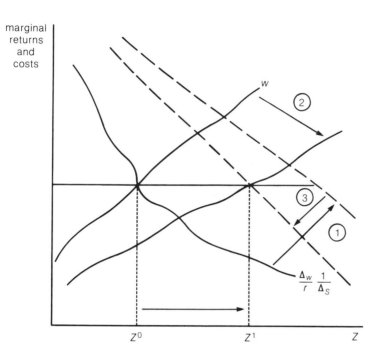

learning efficiency is freely observable by anyone. Holding ability constant, an increase in learning efficiency simply means that a given signal can be obtained more quickly. Again, by assumption the wage earned by the worker is not altered; so the wage structure must change. Referring to Figure 11, greater A means that the time required to increase the signal by one unit has fallen; an increase in learning efficiency lowers ΔS, thus raising the marginal return to signalling to the dashed line (see the arrow marked ①). But to hold the wage fixed the wage schedule must flatten (see the arrow marked ②). Finally, since the wage schedule is *flatter*, the effect of Z on w (Δw) falls (see the arrow marked ③).

Since marginal returns rise and marginal costs fall, the optimal signal rises accordingly. But the impact on schooling time is formally ambiguous. Although a more substantial signal is desired, improved learning efficiency may allow it to be accumulated in a shorter period of time. However, unless the increase in learning efficiency raises the impact of schooling on the signal markedly, schooling time will increase. Thus an increase in observable learning efficiency is predicted to have no effect on wages, to raise the level of the signal, and generally to augment schooling time.

If the learning efficiency parameter is *not* observable, difficulties immediately arise. Suppose an individual is observed to have a given signal and duration of schooling. Given learning efficiency, ability can be inferred just as above. But if learning is not observable, the problem faced by the firm is vastly more difficult. If an individual chooses a high level of the signal, is it because he is a very able worker (high H^0, just as before) or an able learner (high A)? Suffice it to say that in this situation the predictive content of signalling is closely related to the manner in which H^0 and A are related to one another. If able individuals also tend to be efficient learners, the theory remains largely intact. However, if the opposite holds, the theory encounters severe difficulties. After all, the crux of signalling theory is that the firm can infer productive characteristics from optimal signalling choices. If this identification is hindered, an important stumbling block is created.

Finally, one extension is straightforward. As in our treatment of human capital theory, direct costs of schooling have been ignored. They are easily added.

Expenditures on tuition, books, and so on do not alter productivity. They are simply expenditures that allow a given signal to be obtained more quickly. Since productivity is independent of wages, changes in direct costs have no impact on wages. However, since the cost of additions to the signal rises (in the leading case) with direct costs, schooling is predicted to fall when direct costs rise.

Table 1 provides a summary of the predictions of human capital and signalling concerning wages and schooling. Contrary to a common assertion, the two theories are not observationally indistinguishable. While the data required to distinguish between them (at least on the basis of predictions about schooling and wages) are difficult to come by, the fact remains that the theories can be distinguished.[12]

IV. HUMAN CAPITAL, SIGNALLING, OR INFORMATION?

Since we have briefly considered the human capital and signalling models as well as their consequences, it is appropriate to return to the question of their scope. The approach we take is as follows. Let us assume that individuals are observed to

12 Indeed, if one is willing to expand the range of phenomena to be considered, the theories are easily distinguished. For example, signalling is superfluous for the self-employed. Thus signalling theory predicts that the self-employed will exhibit different schooling behaviour from other workers. Human capital theory predicts no difference.

TABLE 1

Summary of predictions

Experiment	Effect on wages		Effect on schooling	
	Human capital	Signalling	Human capital	Signalling
1. Increase in ability (H^0)	+	+	−*	+*
2. Increase in interest rate (r)	−	0	−	−
3. Increase in learning efficiency	+	0	+*	+*
4. Increase in direct costs of schooling	−	0	−	0

* Leading case. In experiment 1, the "non-leading" cases also provide contradictory predictions.

make investments, and that we must choose among the human capital, informational, or signalling models to help us understand the investment process. Under what circumstances would any particular theory be the best choice a priori?[13]

The models differ significantly in terms of the information structure. Schooling requires expenditure of a certain amount of resources; the individual subsequently performs a certain amount of work. If all aspects of this process are known to all before the investment takes place, human capital theory would appear to be most useful. Even if the efficiency units assumption fails, the individual can decide which type of skills to accumulate, and the analysis proceeds much as above.

In the opposite case, where there is *general* ignorance about what an individual would learn from a given investment, and output is costly to monitor, the major problem is one of information gathering. In this case allocation and hence income are based on the information (about existing resources) gathered in school. It is that investment in information that is central; the informational approach dominates.

13 From a methodological viewpoint, a more appropriate approach is to examine the three theories, extract their observable predictions, and on the basis of the data decide which is most appropriate. The view taken in the text follows from such investigations. That is, no theory is unambiguously dominant for all situations. Thus it pays to try to sort out those cases for which each appears to perform best, where part of the sorting-out procedure involves some degree of a priorism.

In the intermediate case, where the worker knows what skills he has but his effort is difficult to monitor, the principal determinant of income is the nature of the inferences the firm makes on the basis of schooling decisions; signalling is more important.

Thus an a priori choice between models comes down to deciding whether the given situation is one of full information for worker and firm, poor information for both, or full information for workers but not for firms. The informational model is cast in the second of these instances. In the next chapter we explore the informational model and examine its predictions.[14]

14 The reader will note that in the chapters following we make relatively little use of the signalling model, focusing instead on human capital and informational explanations and arguments. We do so principally because the empirical basis for human capital theory is strong relative to the evidence on signalling (compare Rosen, 1977 and Riley, 1979 a). Furthermore, many of the phenomena typically ascribed to signalling behaviour can be easily accounted for by the informational model. Thus, for present purposes the human capital and informational models provide sufficient theoretical underpinning.

3
The informational model of schooling and job-worker matching

In the previous chapter we examined the human capital and signalling theories. The former required a world of complete information, the latter an environment where 'informational asymmetries' were central. However, they leave an important gap, namely, those situations where information on some object of interest is generally lacking. The informational model focuses on such situations.

The central ideas of the informational model are very straightforward. When a firm is deciding whether to hire a worker and the worker contemplates accepting a job offer, there is uncertainty about how productive that job-worker match will be. Whenever this uncertainty has any impact on the allocation of resources or the distribution of output, there may be incentives for firms and workers to take action. The appropriate action to take naturally depends on the cause and consequences of the uncertainty.

Two important cases can be distinguished, depending on the underlying nature of the uncertainty. First, suppose the productivity of a given job-worker match depends on factors such as the weather, future government policy, or macro-economic events. Some information concerning these entities exists, but there is little scope for obtaining more. Here risk is essentially exogenous. The economic problem becomes the allocation of given risk between worker and firm. The risk sharing activities are primarily determined by differences between workers and firms in terms of willingness to bear risk. The large 'implicit contracts' literature addresses this problem.[1]

The second case is that in which uncertainty is 'localized.' Localized uncertainty stems from factors specific to the firm and/or its workers. In such an

---

1 A fine survey is provided by Azariadis (1979).

instance the extent of information gathering, which alters the nature of uncertainty, is the core of the economic problem.

The informational model of job-worker matching is a model of how such localized uncertainties result in the allocation of resources to information accumulation. Specifically, we are interested in the case in which the uncertainty stems from imperfect information about the skills of particular individuals. We call this kind of uncertainty *person-specific*.

The rationale for placing the uncertainty on the worker's side is straightforward. Firms use inputs to produce outputs. If there were no uncertainty about inputs, the only localized uncertainty faced by the firm would be related to its technology. Except in the case of a very new good, that all firms (even new ones in an established industry) know and understand their technology seems a plausible assumption. However, on the worker's side significant uncertainties concerning the extent to which their skills match the requirements of the firm's technology typically exist. The manner in which these uncertainties are dealt with is the subject of the informational model.

In order for the accumulation of person-specific information to be of interest, a number of conditions are necessary. First, there must be something of substance about which to accumulate information. That is, there must be some return to that activity. If workers differ only in that some are more able than others in all activities, then new information on the ability of a given worker may reduce risk but will not alter the allocation of workers to jobs, which also occurs if workers' skills differ in a more general way but firms all offer the same job. Information on skills alters the allocation of workers to jobs only if both workers and firms are diverse in a meaningful sense.

On the cost side the allocation of resources to accumulation of information is of interest only if the amount of resources that need to be allocated is not trivial. There are many examples in which the accumulation of person-specific information is clostly. Suppose production is organized in a production-line fashion; then individual contributions are costly to observe on a large scale and difficult to assess. Another example occurs when the period of time between initiation and completion of a task is substantial. If the quality of the worker's work cannot be determined until the task is completed, the information so obtained is very expensive. In all such situations, which are apparently the rule rather than the exception, information is not trivial to accumulate.

In sum, the informational model is concerned with the utilization of scarce resources for the purpose of accumulating information on the skills possessed by workers; *both* workers and firms learn in the process. Such activities have allocative effects (hence they affect the level of output) when workers and firms are heterogeneous. Also, accumulation of information typically involves significant amounts of resources.

In order to model efficiently a heterogeneous economy operating under conditions of incomplete information, we make a number of fairly strong assumptions. All them can be relaxed without significantly altering the structure of the problem at hand. These assumptions are the subject of the next section. The analysis of the informational model begins in Section III with a specification of skills and jobs. Sections IV and V present the returns to and costs of information accumulation. Given costs and returns, discussion of the optimal choice of information accumulation and the theoretical predictions following from that choice are taken up in Sections VI and VII. Section VIII summarizes the model and its implications.

This chapter contains the theory utilized throughout the study. The text presents the model verbally and utilizes some diagrams where helpful. The more technically oriented reader may wish to consult the Appendix, in which the model is presented and explored in a more precise fashion.

II. SIMPLIFYING ASSUMPTIONS

In the informational model individuals accumulate information. To focus the analysis on this process it is useful to make a number of fairly strong assumptions. These assumptions fall under the heading 'simplifying,' because they may be relaxed without altering the information problem in any important way. The more crucial assumptions will be addressed as they are introduced.

First, it is assumed that the activities in which individuals are asked to engage (job requirements) in any particular firm are given. These activities may vary across firms but not within a firm.

Along the same lines, the skills possessed by workers are taken to be fixed. There is no human capital accumulation. Under these two assumptions the productivity of any job-worker match is fixed. We can then direct our attention to the problem of finding efficient job-worker pairings without having the characteristics of the matches depend on the process through which we find them.

The next assumption is that all information is common knowledge, available equally to both firms and workers. This may appear somewhat unrealistic. Workers may reasonably be expected to possess at least some information about their skills that the firm does not possess. However, our model is intended to apply to those situations wherein both workers and firms are ignorant to some extent, as opposed to one-sided ignorance of the kind addressed in the signalling problem. The assumption merely simplifies by making a situation where both workers and firms are uninformed in some arbitrary way into one in which they are equally uninformed. The analytical simplifications are considerable.[2]

In addition to the above, we assume that both firms and workers are risk neutral. This allows us to focus on the purely productive impact of information gathering, without introducing complications following from the separate effect of information gathering on optimal risk-sharing considerations.

Last, we assume that there is only one information producing activity, much like the human capital production function. While we shall refer to it as 'schooling,' it need not be interpreted as such; information gathering could take place in the firm. Indeed, it is possible to construct more complex models involving sequential accumulation of information. Therein early periods of rapid accumulation take place in specialized institutions (such as schools) and later periods involve less intensive accumulation occurring on the job. We take the pure schooling approach purely for simplicity's sake.[3]

To summarize, we abstract from both assignment of workers to tasks within the firm and human capital accumulation. Further, we assume both workers and firms to be risk neutral and to have equal access to all information. Finally, there is but one source of new information. We call this activity schooling.

III. SKILLS, JOBS, AND WAGE OFFERS[4]

In this section we specify two relationships. First, any particular job-worker match yields some amount of output. Since the worker's skills are not known at the time of hiring, neither is this eventual output known. None the less, the problem to be addressed depends importantly on what the possibilities are. The first step is therefore to specify the amount of output that would be produced if a worker with given skills were employed at a particular firm.

This information is used to construct the second relationship. At the time of hiring some information (which may be comprised of both general and person-specific information) will be available concerning the skills of each individual. Naturally, the wage offers made to individuals depend on this information. They

---

2 If asymmetric (but imperfect) information exists, it is possible to embed the present model in a signalling framework. The optimal choice of information quality (below) then becomes a signal, in addition to the role assigned to it here.

3 Strictly speaking, we are therefore assuming that production is organized in a fashion that renders it very costly to measure the output of individual workers.

4 The structure presented in this section can be derived from more basic considerations. See MacDonald (1980).

TABLE 2

Output of potential matches*

		Type of firm	
		α	β
Type of individual	A	$\alpha_0 + \alpha_1$	β_0
	B	α_0	$\beta_0 + \beta_1$

*$\alpha_0, \alpha_1, \beta_0,$ and β_1 are all positive constants.

also depend on the productivity of given job-worker matches (the first relationship). Our second task is therefore to spell out the dependence of wage offers on both information and the underlying productivities of the various potential job-worker matches.

III.1 *The output of possible job-worker matches*

Consider the value of output resulting from a given job-worker match. It depends on the individual's skills and the requirements of the job. To keep things simple we assume that there are just two sets of skills and two types of jobs. It is convenient to categorize individuals according to the kinds of skills they possess, and to label firms according to the jobs they offer. Proceeding in that fashion, we assume there are two types of individuals, called A and B. The two kinds of firms are referred to as α and β. We assume there is a set of natural job-worker matches: A workers are more productive than B workers in α firms; the converse holds for β firms,[5]

The intuitive notion we have in mind is that each job requires the completion of a collection of tasks. These tasks place different demands upon the worker; some call for a strong back, others the willingness to co-operate, and still others the ability to concentrate, and so on. Workers are endowed with these characteristics. A workers possess them in amounts that generate greater output in α firms. B workers and β firms are similarly matched.

Our formalization of these ideas is presented in Table 2. If an α firm employs an A worker, output valued at $\alpha_0 + \alpha_1$ is produced. But if the same firm employs a B worker, output valued at only α_0 is obtained. α_1 is therefore the additional output accruing to an α firm if an A worker is hired instead of a B worker: the

---

5 This 2 × 2 structure is not necessary for the results to follow. What is at the heart of the model is that increased information quality (below) does not reduce expected income. The 2 × 2 structure merely allows us to be very specific about how this occurs.

additional return associated with a good match. The β firms operate in just the opposite fashion. If a B worker is hired, output valued at $\beta_0 + \beta_1$ is produced while only β_0 is obtained if an A worker is hired.[6]

III.2 *Wage offers*
Given this specification of the productivity of the various job-worker matches, we can turn to the relationship between wage offers, information, and the productivity of job-worker matches.

The central problem is that at the time of hiring no one knows exactly what skills the worker possesses; given the contents of Table 2, it boils down to uncertainty concerning whether the worker is an A or a B.

The problem is mitigated to the extent that for each worker there is some person-specific information (the nature of which can profitably be left unspecified until the next section), which can be used to infer something about the worker's skills. Call this information I. Utilizing the information I, the firm can express its views concerning the worker's skills in terms of probabilities. We shall use the notation $P(A|I)$ to denote the probability that a worker is from group A, given some knowledge about him, namely I. To take a simple example, suppose it is known that all blue-eyed workers are A workers, and all brown-eyed workers are Bs. Then if the information I corresponds to knowledge of the worker's eye colour, both $P(A|\text{blue})$ and $P(B|\text{brown})$ take on the value one, while both $P(A|\text{brown})$ and $P(B|\text{blue})$ equal zero. This result makes use of the fact that since A and B are the only possible types of workers, we must have

$$P(A|I) + P(B|I) = 1. \tag{8}$$

If, on the basis of some information I, the firm is 95 per cent certain the worker is an A worker, it is equally appropriate to say the firm is 5 per cent certain the worker is a B worker.

Now suppose an α firm is considering how much to offer a prospective employee on whom there is information I. What must the firm offer? The answer is simply that the firm must make an offer equal to the expected contribution to

---

6 An important aspect of this specification of skills is that it is characterized by comparative advantage. We shall see that in such a situation information affects the allocation of workers to jobs.

  Clearly absolute advantage might also be of interest; some individuals may be more able than others at all jobs. It can be shown that if skills are respecified so that within each of the groups A and B there are less and more able individuals, the analysis to follow is not altered in any fundamental way so long as two conditions are satisfied: (1) the most able workers in group A are more productive at some job than the least able in group B (and vice versa); and (2) there is some uncertainty about who the more able workers are within each group.

output. If a smaller offer is made, it would obviously be advantageous to some other α firm to make a slightly higher offer, and the first firm would not succeed in hiring the worker. On the other hand, if an offer in excess of the expected contribution to output is made, the firm expects to be a net loser on the transaction. Equilibrium in the labour market implies that the firm offers a sum equal to the expected contribution to output.

What is the expected contribution to output in terms of the underlying probabilities and productivities? If the worker is an A, he produces $\alpha_0 + \alpha_1$. The probability with which this event occurs is $P(A|I)$. If he is a B, only α_0 is obtained, the probability of which is $P(B|I)$. So expected output is simply the weighted average of the two possible outputs, where the weights are the probabilities:

$$(\alpha_0 + \alpha_1)P(A|I) + (\alpha_0)P(B|I). \tag{9}$$

To illustrate, assume that if the worker is a B, no output is produced ($\alpha_0 = 0$), and that if he is an A, output valued at 2 is obtained ($\alpha_1 = 2$). Further, suppose that the information is such that the probability the worker is an A is 3/4, and hence the probability the worker is a B is $1 - 3/4 = 1/4$. Then expected output is $(2) \cdot (3/4) + (0) \cdot (1/4) = 3/2$.

The expected contribution to output, the firm's offer, can be put in a more useful form. Since α_0 appears in both terms, (9) can be rewritten

$$\alpha_0[P(A|I) + P(B|I)] + \alpha_1 P(A|I),$$

which, by virtue of (8), equals

$$\alpha_0 + \alpha_1 P(A|I). \tag{10}$$

We shall call expression (10) O^α, the offer made by an α firm to worker with information I. O^α is composed of two portions. α_0 is the least output the firm can obtain from any worker, and is obtained with certainty. That is, it does not depend on the correctness of the job-worker match. The additional α_1 is obtained only if the worker is an A, which occurs with probability $P(A|I)$. Thus the term $\alpha_1 P(A|I)$ represents the expected gain due to correct matching of worker and job.

The offers made by β firms can be arrived at in a similar fashion:

$$O^\beta = \beta_0 + \beta_1 P(B|I). \tag{11}$$

Here, β_0 is the minimum output attainable from any worker, and $\beta_1 P(B|I)$ is the expected gain due to correct matching.

The analysis that follows below can proceed in a less taxonomic fashion if an additional restriction is imposed; we assume that if an individual's information is such that he is viewed as equally likely to be an A or a $B(P(A|I) = P(B|I) = 1/2)$, both α and β firms make him the same offer. In terms of the expressions for O^{α} and O^{β},

$$\alpha_0 + \alpha_1 \cdot 1/2 = \beta_0 + \beta_1 \cdot 1/2. \tag{12}$$

We shall call this *no information offer* $\bar{O}$. The reason this restriction is helpful is as follows. The more likely it is that the worker is an A, the greater is the offer from the α firm and the smaller is that from the β firm. Accordingly, there is always some critical probability such that when $P(A|I)$ exceeds this value, the worker's highest offer is from an α firm; otherwise his highest offer is from a β firm. The restriction (5) simply makes this critical probability equal to $1/2$.[7] Furthermore, we know the offer from α firms increases as the probability that the worker is an A rises, and the offer from β firms falls under the same circumstances. It follows that any information yielding a value of $P(A|I)$ in excess of $1/2$ means O^{α} exceeds $\bar{O}$ which, in turn, exceeds O^{β}. Similarly, if $P(A|I)$ falls short of $1/2$, O^{β} is larger than $\bar{O}$, which is larger than O^{α}. The implications of this relationship will be explained in Section IV.3.

Finally, since workers are fundamentally heterogeneous, even in a world of full information there is no mechanism operating to equalize incomes. Thus the skills of the two groups will not necessarily be valued equally, and one of our groups of workers will tend to be a relatively high-income group. We shall suppose group A to be the fortunate group. In terms of the offer functions, an easy way to represent this idea is to assume that if *full* information prevailed ($P(A|I)$ equals 0 or 1 for every worker), workers employed by α firms would earn more than those employed by β firms:

$$\alpha_0 + \alpha_1 > \beta_0 + \beta_1. \tag{13}$$

Taken together with the restriction that workers who are viewed as equally likely to be either A or B workers receive identical offers from both types of firms, this restriction implies that the minimum output obtainable from any worker is largest in the β firms ($\beta_0 > \alpha_0$) and that the gain due to correct allocation is largest in the α firms ($\alpha_1 > \beta_1$).

---

7 All that is required for the results to follow is that $\alpha_0 + \alpha_1 > \beta_0$ and $\beta_0 + \beta_1 > \alpha_0$. The first restriction implies, for example, that there is some information set for which $P(A|I)$ is sufficiently large that the worker has greatest expected product in an α firm. The restriction (5) simply makes this critical value of $P(A|I)$ equal $1/2$. If either of the restrictions $\alpha_0 + \alpha_1 > \beta_0$ and $\beta_0 + \beta_1 > \alpha_0$ fails to hold, one industry cannot attract any workers. Since output is then equal to zero for that industry, it is safe to assume that a price increase will then force the restriction to be satisfied.

A brief recapitulation is in order. We first constructed a simple pattern of productivity across job-worker matches: α firms and A workers, and β firms and B workers are natural matches. Next, we showed how the productivity of the potential matches translated into wage offers in an environment where the true nature of any particular match of worker and job was unknown. These wage offers, given by (10) and (11), together with the restrictions (12) and (13), constitute all the economically meaningful information about firms.

IV. INFORMATION AND THE RETURN TO ITS ACCUMULATION

In this section we develop the return to information accumulation. In order to do so three things are required. First, in the previous section we were purposefully vague about the precise nature of information. We must now devote some space to this topic. Second, we need to specify the manner in which information is incorporated into the probabilities determining the offers made by firms and hence how information affects these wage offers. Finally, a worker's income depends on the offer he accepts. Thus, although information accumulation affects all wage offers, the worker's expected income is influenced only through those offers which might be accepted once information is accumulated. Thus, the final step is to specify which offers will be accepted under various circumstances and hence to derive the worker's expected income. The return to information accumulation is then simply the impact of information on this expected income.

IV.1 *The nature of information*
There are two kinds of information in our model: endowed and produced. Endowed information, as its name suggests, is available to the worker at no cost. Included in the definition of endowed information are all readily observable characteristics that are correlated with the type of skills possessed by the worker. Height, sex, and family background are examples. Furthermore, general information such as the distribution of skills in the population also qualifies. We summarize all endowed information by a parameter π. π is simply the probability, given endowed information on the worker, that he is an A. To illustrate, suppose general population information of the form presented in Table 3 is available. Roughly speaking, group A tends to be shorter than group B. Also, group A makes up half ($3/8 + 1/8$) the population. So, with no further information on an individual, the probability that he is from group A is $1/2$. Now suppose the individual is observed to be less than six feet tall. Then we know he is from a group 60 per cent of which is from group A (($3/8$) $\div$ ($5/8$) = 0.6). Accordingly, given

TABLE 3

Example of general population information*

		Skills		
		A	B	
Height	at most 6′	3/8	1/4	5/8
	over 6′	1/8	1/4	3/8

* Each cell contains the fraction of the population
with that skill-height pair.

the general population information and the knowledge that this particular individual is from the shorter group, the probability that his skills are of the A-type is $\pi = 0.6$.

Produced information requires an investment of resources by the worker. The technical relationship between these inputs of resources and the output of information, and the choice of an optimal input mix, generate the cost structure for information. This is the topic of Section V. Here we need discuss only how the *output* of the information generating activity, which we call schooling, is combined with endowed information.

Our representation of the information generated by schooling is very simple. Schooling culminates with a verdict on the worker's skills: either 'the worker is an A' or 'the worker is a B.' We shall summarize these statements by using the variable X. The statement 'the worker is an A' will be shortened to '$X = a$.' '$X = b$' summarizes the statement 'the worker is a B.' The output of schooling is therefore simply the *label* X.

The label has two important characteristics. First it is imperfect; that is, knowledge that the label is $X = a$ (or b) does not absolutely guarantee that the worker is an A (or B). The point is simply that any testing procedure has an element of randomness associated with it. However, the label does contain some information; that is, if the worker is an A, then the label $X = a$ is more likely to occur than if it were given that the worker is a B. Put differently, the process schools use to assign labels is more effective than flipping a coin and assigning $X = a$ if the coin turns up heads and $X = b$ otherwise.

To make these ideas operational, we need to be more precise. This is easily accomplished by focusing on the probability that the label is correct. For simplicity, suppose the probability of being correctly labelled is the *same* for both worker types. Let us call this probability θ and use the notation $P(X = a|A)$ to denote the probability that the label is correct ($X = a$) when the worker is an A. $P(X = b|B)$

represents the probability that the label is correct ($X = b$) when the worker is a B. Under our assumptions, $P(X = a|A) = \theta = P(X = b|B)$. That is, the fraction of A workers correctly labelled equals the fraction of B workers correctly labelled, with the fraction being θ. The assumption that the label is imperfect can now be accurately and simply expressed as $\theta < 1$. That the label does contain some information can be represented as $\theta > 1/2$ ($\theta = 1/2$ corresponds to assigning labels by flipping a coin).

Now we have two kinds of information. One is summarized by π, the probability that the worker is an A when the judgment is based solely on endowed information, of either the general population variety or the individual-specific but costlessly observable kind. The other piece of information is the label $X = a$ or $X = b$, which is correct with probability θ.

How do we combine the prior information leading to π with the information X? We want to end up with a number expressing the probability that the worker is an A, given *both* endowed and produced information. This number is then the value of $P(A|I)$ required in the firms' offer functions.

This turns out to be an easy task. Consider $P(A|a)$,[8] which represents the probability that the worker is an A, given the label $X = a$. Suppose that 3/4 of the population with given endowed information is from group A: $\pi = 3/4$. Suppose also that the label is correct $\theta = 2/3$ of the time. What fraction of this population will be given the label $X = a$? 2/3 of the 3/4 who are As will be correctly labelled, and 1/3 of the 1/4 who are Bs will be falsely labelled. So the fraction receiving $X = a$ is $2/3 \cdot 3/4 + 1/3 \cdot 1/4 = 7/12$. Now of the collection labelled $X = a$, $2/3 \cdot 3/4$ are correctly labelled. So as a *proportion* of the group receiving $X = a$, $(2/3 \cdot 3/4) \div 7/12 = 6/7$ are indeed from group A. Therefore, given $X = a$ and $\pi = 3/4$, the probability that the worker is an A is 6/7; so $P(A|a) = 6/7$.

More generally, the fraction of the population (for whom π takes on a given value) that receives $X = a$ is the fraction correctly labelled, $\theta\pi$, plus the fraction incorrectly labelled, $(1 - \theta)(1 - \pi)$. We call this number $P(a) = \theta\pi + (1 - \theta)(1 - \pi)$. $P(A|a)$ is the fraction correctly labelled, expressed as a fraction of $P(a)$.

$$P(A|a) = \theta\pi / P(a).$$

The other relevant probabilities are derived in exactly the same way. This information is summarized in Table 4.

---

8 Here the information I is the label $X = a$ and the general population information. To keep the notation simple the latter is kept implicit in $P(A|a)$.

TABLE 4

Probabilities required for offer functions

$P(A\vert a) = \theta\pi/P(a)$	$P(a) = \theta\pi + (1 - \theta)(1 - \pi)$
$P(A\vert b) = (1 - \theta)\pi/P(b)$	$P(b) = (1 - \theta)\pi + \theta(1 - \pi)$
$P(B\vert a) = (1 - \theta)(1 - \pi)/P(a)$	
$P(B\vert b) = \theta(1 - \pi)/P(b)$	

IV.2 *Offer functions*

In Subsection III.2 we showed that the offers made by α and β firms are ((10) and (11) again)

$$O^\alpha = \alpha_0 + \alpha_1 P(A\vert I)$$

and

$$O\beta = \beta_0 + \beta_1 P(B\vert I).$$

Further, to simplify matters it was assumed that workers for whom $P(A\vert I) = P(B\vert I) = 1/2$ are equally valuable to both types of firms ((12) again):

$$\alpha_0 + \alpha_1 \cdot 1/2 = \beta_0 + \beta_1 \cdot 1/2.$$

Last, since there is no force operating to equalize incomes across heterogeneous workers, we arbitrarily picked the A group to be the fortunate group ((13) again):

$$\alpha_0 + \alpha_1 > \beta_0 + \beta_1.$$

In the previous subsection we derived the probabilities relevant for use in the offer functions. For any particular endowed information π, there are four offers with which we need be concerned: the offers made by α firms if $X = a$ or if $X = b$, and those made by β firms if $X = a$ or if $X = b$.

Consider the offers made by α firms. Call the offer $O_a{}^\alpha$ if $X = a$ and $O_b{}^\alpha$ if $X = b$. Specifically,

$$O_a{}^\alpha = \alpha_0 + \alpha_1 P(A\vert a) \tag{14}$$

and

$$O_b{}^\alpha = \alpha_0 + \alpha_1 P(A\vert b). \tag{15}$$

What are the characteristics of $O_a{}^\alpha$ and $O_b{}^\alpha$? First, since we have assumed that A workers are a natural match for α firms, any information indicating that the worker is an A must raise the offer made by the α firm. Since (relative to $X = b$) $X = a$ represents such information, it follows that $O_a{}^\alpha$ is at least as large as $O_b{}^\alpha$.

Second, if schooling is a nearly perfect indicator of skills (θ is very close to 1), then irrespective of the endowed information, the label $X = a$ means that the worker is almost surely an A. Hence the α firm must offer something close to the productivity of an A in an α firm: $\alpha_0 + \alpha_1$ (Table 2). If $X = b$, the required offer is close to the productivity of a B in an α firm: α_0. So for θ close to 1, $O_a{}^\alpha$ and $O_b{}^\alpha$ are roughly $\alpha_0 + \alpha_1$ and α_0 respectively.

Third, if schooling is essentially useless (θ is near 1/2), the label should have next to no effect on the offers; they should be dominated by the probability that the worker is an A, given only the endowed information (π). Indeed, given $\theta = 1/2$, one can easily check that both $P(A|a)$ and $P(A|b) = \pi$, in which case (14) and (15) are $O_a{}^\alpha = O_b{}^\alpha = \alpha_0 + \alpha_1\pi$.

Finally, suppose that on the basis of the endowed information only, it is concluded that the worker is more likely to be an A than a B: $\pi > 1/2$. Recall that a worker on whom there is *no* information is equally valuable to both types of firm; each offers $\bar{O}$. Then a worker for whom $\pi > 1/2$ is worth more to an α firm than to a β firm without further information. Now suppose some schooling is undertaken and X is revealed. $X = a$ is further confirmation that the worker is a good match for the α firm. But $X = b$ is evidence *contrary* to that in existence ($\pi > 1/2$). When the quality of the labelling process (θ) is the same as that of the endowed information (π) contradictory information 'cancels.' That is, if $\pi > 1/2$, $\theta = \pi$, and $X = b$, we are left with $P(A|b) = 1/2$. Thus, for $\theta = \pi$, the offer $O_b{}^\alpha$ is equal to the no information offer $\bar{O}$.

The same phenomenon occurs when $\pi < 1/2$. $X = b$ is evidence corroborating the expectation that the worker is a B, but $X = a$ is contradictory. When $\theta = 1 - \pi$, $O_a{}^\alpha$ equals $\bar{O}$.

The four essential features of the offers made by the α firms are conveniently summarized in Figure 12:
1. $O_a{}^\alpha$ always equals or exceeds $O_b{}^\alpha$;
2. $O_a{}^\alpha$ approaches $\alpha_0 + \alpha_1$ as θ approaches unity; $O_b{}^\alpha$ approaches α_0 as θ approaches unity;
3. both $O_a{}^\alpha$ and $O_b{}^\alpha$ equal $\alpha_0 + \alpha_1\pi$ if θ equals 1/2; and
4. if π exceeds 1/2 (panel (a)) $O_b{}^\alpha$ equals $\bar{O}$ when θ equals π; if π falls short of 1/2 (panel (b)) $O_a{}^\alpha$ equals $\bar{O}$ when θ equals $1 - \pi$.

The offers made by the β firms can be treated completely symmetrically. They are depicted in Figure 13. letting $O_a{}^\beta$ and $O_b{}^\beta$ be the offers made by β firms to workers receiving $X = a$ or $X = b$, respectively, the basic characteristics are as follows:
1. $O_b{}^\beta$ always equals or exceeds $O_a{}^\beta$;
2. $O_b{}^\beta$ approaches $\beta_0 + \beta_1$ as θ approaches unity; $O_a{}^\beta$ approaches β_0 as θ approaches unity;

Figure 12

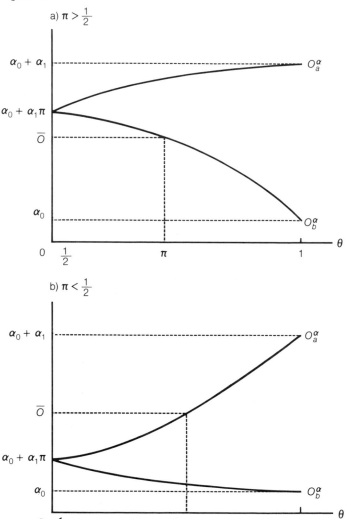

a) $\pi > \frac{1}{2}$

b) $\pi < \frac{1}{2}$

3. both $O_b{}^\beta$ and $O_a{}^\beta$ equal $\beta_0 + \beta_1 (1 - \pi)$ if θ equals 1/2; and
4. if π exceeds 1/2 (panel (a)) $O_b{}^\beta$ equals $\overline{O}$ when θ equals π; if π falls short of 1/2 (panel (b)) $O_a{}^\beta$ equals $\overline{O}$ when θ equals $1 - \pi$.

Given the offer functions $O_a{}^\alpha$, $O_b{}^\alpha$, $O_a{}^\beta$, and $O_b{}^\beta$, depicted in Figures 12 and 13, we can now proceed to analyse the return side of investment in information.

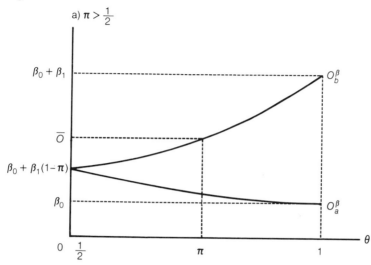

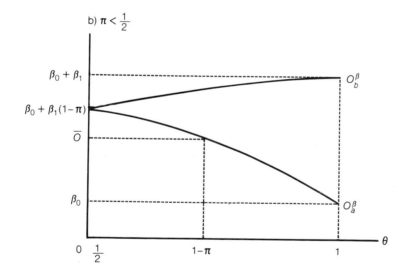

IV.3 *Expected income*

In the previous subsection we showed that the offers a worker might receive depended on who was making the offer (α or β firm), what the endowed information was (π), the label (X), and the accuracy of the labelling process (θ). Below it will be assumed that the worker can choose θ and does so on the basis of a comparison of returns and costs. Since he must choose θ prior to knowing what label he will receive, returns are in terms of *expected* income. We therefore need to construct expected income.

Expected income is easily obtained. With some probability the worker will obtain $X = a$. Given $X = a$, one of the four offers analysed above will be larger than the other three, and it will be chosen. Similarly, $X = b$ will occur with some probability, and one of the offers will be subsequently accepted. *Expected* income is then simply the probability that $X = a$ will occur times the best offer given $X = a$, *plus* the probability that $X = b$ will occur times the best offer given $X = b$. For example, again let $\pi = 3/4$ and $\theta = 2/3$. Then, as above, the probability that $X = a$ will occur is $P(a) = (2/3)(3/4) + (1/3)(1/4) = 7/12$; also $P(b) = 1 - P(a) = 5/12$. Suppose the worker's best offer is 3 if labelled $X = a$, and 2 if labelled $X = b$. Then expected income is $(7/12) \cdot 3 + (5/12) \cdot 2 = 31/12$, which is between 3 and 2.

Symbolically, we call expected income $\mathcal{E}$. Then

$$\mathcal{E} = P(a) \cdot [\text{best offer if } X = a] + P(b) \cdot [\text{best offer if } X = b]. \tag{16}$$

The only remaining problem is to determine what the best offers are if $X = a$ and if $X = b$.

Take the easiest case first. Assume endowed information is such that π equals $1/2$; without further information the worker is viewed as equally likely to be an A or a B. What if $X = a$ occurs? Is the worker worth more to an α or β firm? Since the worker is equally valuable to both firms when he is viewed as equally likely to be an A or a B, and the label $X = a$ makes it more likely that he is an A, he is obviously worth more to an α firm. Clearly then, if $X = a$ his best offer is that from an α firm: $O_a{}^\alpha$. By the same token, if he receives the label $X = b$, his best offer will be from a β firm: $O_b{}^\beta$. Irrespective of the quality of the labelling process, if π equals $1/2$, the label $X = a$ implies he will work for an α firm, and the label $X = b$ implies he will work for a β firm.

The problem is just slightly more difficult when π is not equal to $1/2$. Say π exceeds $1/2$. The worker is viewed as more likely to be an A than a B. Obviously if $X = a$, his best offer is again from an α firm: $O_a{}^\alpha$. But if $X = b$, whether his best offer is from an α or β firm depends on the quality of the labelling process. Referring back to Figures 12 and 13 (panel (a) in both cases), when the quality of the labelling process is less than that of the endowed information (θ is between $1/2$ and π), the information $X = b$ is not strong enough to counteract the endowed information. The highest offer is still from the α firm: $O_b{}^\alpha$ dominates $O_b{}^\beta$. So when the quality of the labelling process is less than that of the endowed information, the latter dominates and the worker's best offer is from an α firm irrespective of the label. When the quality of the labelling process exceeds that of

TABLE 5

Best offers

a) $\pi > 1/2$

	$X = a$	$X = b$
$1/2 \leq \theta < \pi$	$O_a{}^\alpha$	$O_b{}^\alpha$
$\pi \leq \theta < 1$	$O_a{}^\alpha$	$O_b{}^\beta$

b) $\pi < 1/2$

	$X = a$	$X = b$
$1/2 \leq \theta < 1 - \pi$	$O_a{}^\beta$	$\bar{O}_b{}^\beta$
$1 - \pi \leq \theta < 1$	$O_a{}^\alpha$	$O_b{}^\beta$

c) $\pi = 1/2$

	$X = a$	$X = b$
$1/2 \leq \theta < 1$	$O_a{}^\alpha$	$O_b{}^\beta$

the endowed information, the former dominates and the worker's highest offer is from an α firm if $X = a$, and from a β firm if $X = b$.

The case is analogous when $\pi < 1/2$.[9] When the quality of the labelling process is less than that of the endowed information (θ is between $1/2$ and $1 - \pi$), the worker's best offer is from a β firm, irrespective of the data. But if the labelling process is relatively accurate (θ exceeds $1 - \pi$), the label determines which type of firm the worker joins.

This discussion is summarized in Table 5. In panels (a) and (b) the offers received when the labelling process is relatively inaccurate are listed in the top row. The bottom rows and the only row in panel (c) are the same. So long as the labelling process is relatively accurate, $X = a$ means the worker will work for an α firm, and $X = b$ means he will work for a β firm.

Given the information in Table 5, expected income need be constructed for only three cases, corresponding to the top rows of panels (a) and (b), respectively; panel (c) and the bottom rows of panels (a) and (b) come under the third case.

So let us go back to the case where π exceeds $1/2$, and assume the endowed information dominates the label (θ is between $1/2$ and π). Using (16) and the top row of Table 5, panel (a), $\mathcal{E} = P(a)O_a{}^\alpha + P(b)O_b{}^\alpha$. If we substitute in the expressions for $O_a{}^\alpha$ and $O_b{}^\alpha$, (14) and (15), then insert the probabilities from Table 4, a little manipulation yields the initially surprising result

$$\mathcal{E} = \alpha_0 + \alpha_1 \pi. \tag{17}$$

What is surprising about this result is that it says expected income does *not* depend on θ.

9 For $\pi < 1/2$, strong endowed information corresponds to π near 0. Thus in the discussion to follow, θ (between $1/2$ and 1) is compared with $1 - \pi$ (also between $1/2$ and 1).

There is, however, an intuitive explanation. Recall that for the case in question the worker is employed by an α firm, irrespective of the label. Also, whatever the label turns out to be, the worker is paid an amount equal to the value of his expected output given the label. So before the label is known, what does the firm expect the worker eventually to produce? Clearly α_0 will always be produced; hence the first part of (17). The additional α_1 is obtained only if the worker is an A. *Prior* to the labelling process, the probability that the worker is an A is just π. Thus $\alpha_1\pi$ is the expected (prior to labelling) return to correct allocation when the endowed information will outweigh the label.

Equation (17) tells us that if the quality of the labelling process is not sufficient for the label to have some impact on the worker's location, neither will it affect his expected income. The case where π falls short of 1/2 but the worker is employed by a β firm irrespective of the label works the same way; expected income under those circumstances is

$$\mathcal{E} = \beta_0 + \beta_1(1 - \pi), \tag{18}$$

which can be interpreted in the same way as (17). To reiterate, unless the label contains information that affects the matching of worker and firm, expected income (prior to receipt of the label) does not depend on the quality of that information.

The only remaining case corresponds to panel (c) and the bottom row in panels (a) and (b) of Table 5. In this instance the quality of the labelling process is sufficiently high that workers receiving the label $X = a$ are employed by α firms, and those receiving $X = b$ go to work for β firms. The offers so obtained are $O_a{}^\alpha$ and $O_b{}^\beta$ respectively. Accordingly, (16) can be written

$$\mathcal{E} = P(a)O_a{}^\alpha + P(b)O_b{}^\beta. \tag{19}$$

Manipulations similar to that preceding (8) put (19) in the more complex but useful form

$$\mathcal{E} = \bar{O} + \alpha_1\left(\frac{\theta + \pi}{2} - \frac{1}{2}\right) + \beta_1\left(\frac{\theta + (1 - \pi)}{2} - \frac{1}{2}\right). \tag{20}$$

Equation (20) has two important properties. First, raising the quality of the labelling process increases expected income at the rate $(\alpha_1 + \beta_1)/2$. Since the worker is only employed by an α firm should $X = a$, if that label is more accurate his expected productivity is higher in that firm. The same goes for label $X = b$ and the β firm. Consequently, raising θ raises $\mathcal{E}$ and does so at a rate dependent upon the value of correct allocation in the various firm types at which the worker might be employed.

Second, raising the probability (π) that the worker is from group A (based on endowed information) also raises expected income. The rate of increase is $(\alpha_1 - \beta_1)/2$. This rise occurs, simply because we assumed the return to correct matching to be greater in the α firms ($\alpha_1 > \beta_1$).[10]

The equations (17), (18), and (20) are the relevant expressions for expected income. They are depicted in Figure 14, which summarizes the results of this subsection.

IV.4 *Recapitulation*

In this section we assumed that the individual could augment existing information through acquisition of a label. Since we wish to treat the quality of the label as a matter of choice in what follows, we constructed the return to altering the quality of the labelling process.

In order to do this, we first specified the nature of the correlation between label and skills. Next, we explained how the label gets incorporated, along with existing information, to form the firm's belief about the worker's skills, which allowed us to analyse the manner in which the label and its quality alter the offers firms make. Given that relationship, we were able to construct the set of offers the worker would accept, depending on the outcome and quality of the labelling process. Since this quality is necessarily chosen before it is known which label will be received, the worker's expected income becomes the focus of attention. We showed that unless the label is of quality superior to the endowed information, it will have no effect on job-worker matching. Consequently, expected income was independent of the quality of the label. For better-quality labelling processes (those that dominate the endowed information), the label does have an allocative effect. It follows that expected income rises with the quality of the labelling process. Figure 14 summarizes the return to accumulating information.

V. THE COSTS OF INFORMATION ACCUMULATION

In the previous section we addressed the question of how information affects expected income, thus providing the return to investment in information. In this section we analyse the cost of information accumulation.

The label individuals receive in our model is the output of what we refer to as the schooling process. The quality of this labelling activity depends on the

---

10 Notice that neither the *rate* at which increases in θ raise $\mathcal{E}$, $(\alpha_1 + \beta_1/2)$, nor the *rate* at which increases in π raise $\mathcal{E}$, $(\alpha_1 - \beta_1)/2$, depends on either θ or π.

Figure 14
Expected income ($\mathcal{E}$)

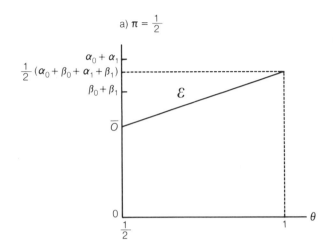

a) $\pi = \frac{1}{2}$

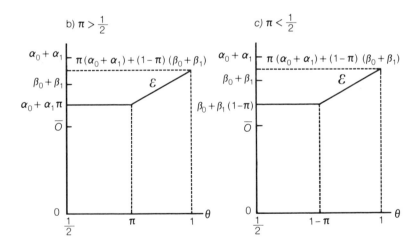

b) $\pi > \frac{1}{2}$

c) $\pi < \frac{1}{2}$

resources devoted to it. Our first step is to specify the nature of this *information quality technology.*

Given the technological relationships between information quality and the various inputs, we can consider the problem of what combination of factors is optimally utilized to produce any given information quality at least cost. The cost associated with this *optimal factor bundle* represents the cost of efficiently acquiring a label of given quality – a cost function in the usual textbook sense.

We shall proceed as follows. The first step is to specify the information quality technology. The optimal factor mix for a given information quality can then be derived. Next we obtain the cost function. Finally the relevant properties of the latter can be discussed.

Given the return side (Section IV) and the cost structure, we can proceed to analyse the optimal choice of information quality (Section VI).

V.1 *The information quality technology*

Our simple information process involves a label, X, and its quality θ (the fraction of the time the label is correct). The information quality technology delineates the manner in which θ may be varied.

Information is the output of schooling. As such, all else constant, it is reasonable to suppose that (1) the longer a person stays in school, the more likely it is that the label he receives at the end will be correct; and (2) this process occurs with diminishing returns. The idea here is simply that for any *given* collection of other factors such as exams, the greater the individual's involvement with each of them, and the more likely it is that they will give accurate results. However, after some point the successive additions of time to the given factors yield smaller increments to accuracy.

Information quality also depends on other factors. For any given input of time the accuracy of the label will be greater the more tests he is required to take, the more material covered by each test, the more the environment is conducive to study, and so on. Of course, for a given time input, use of these other factors is subject to diminishing returns.

A little more formally, let s denote the *fraction* of the individual's life that is spent in school, and let K represent a composite other factor. Our technological assumptions are then that increases in s or K raise θ, but with diminishing returns. The production relationship displays positive but diminishing marginal product for each factor.

Figure 15 depicts the combinations of time input (s) and other factors (K) that yield a given information quality (θ). This *isoquant* is downward sloping, owing to the fact that increments to both s and K augment θ. It is convex to the origin because as the time/other inputs ratio rises, diminishing returns imply that it takes increasingly longer additions of time to make up for a given reduction in other inputs. In the usual terminology, the marginal rate of substitution of time for other inputs (the ratio of the marginal product of time to the marginal product

Figure 15
Information quality isoquant

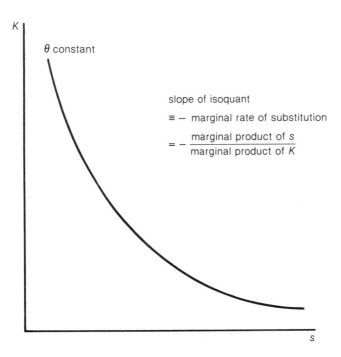

of other inputs) is diminishing. Finally, isoquants corresponding to better quality labels lie everywhere above and to the right of those corresponding to lower quality labels; greater output requires more inputs.[11]

V.2 *Optimal factor utilization*
Whatever information quality is finally chosen, it will be produced at least cost. That is, the value of factor inputs (s and K) will be as small as possible, given the output (θ) to be produced. Accordingly, the cost function on which the choice of information quality is based depends on both factor prices and the level of information quality. In this subsection we make this dependence explicit.

11 One last pair of technological restrictions simplify the analysis to follow. We assume that if K is held fixed and s is raised, the marginal rate of substitution declines. Similarly, holding s fixed, the marginal rate of substitution rises with K. These restrictions ensure there are no inferior factors of production.

First of all, what are the factor prices? We shall let P_K denote the price of the composite factor K. It may then help to think of $P_K \cdot K$ as total tuition.

The price of time is a bit less obvious. What does the individual forgo by staying longer in school? He expects to give up the income he would receive if the label were immediately revealed. This expectation is just $\mathcal{E}$, the subject of Section IV.

Recall that expected income depends on information quality. This fact makes the cost of attaining any given output (information quality) more complex than is normally the case. Specifically, the price of one of the factors of production depends on the level of output under consideration. Since this case is not the standard one, we devote a little extra space to discussion of the optimal factor mix and derivation of the cost function.

Given the prices $\mathcal{E}$ and P_K for the inputs s and K, the cost of any particular input combination is just $\mathcal{E} \cdot s + P_K \cdot K$. The problem then is to ask which combinations of time and other inputs yield a given information quality at least cost.

The solution is quite straightforward. The inputs should be chosen so that the marginal product of a dollar spent on each factor (i.e., the increase in information quality following from expenditure of an extra dollar on that factor) is the same for each one. To see why this equality must hold, suppose a factor combination was chosen that involved the marginal product of one dollar's worth of time exceeding that of one dollar's worth of other inputs. Then by spending one dollar more on time and one dollar less on other inputs, greater information quality could be produced for the same expenditure; in other words, a given information quality could be obtained at lower cost. Thus the factor combination we started with could not have been cost minimizing.

It follows that for each level of information quality and for given factor prices there is a best choice of inputs s and K. Call these choices $\bar{s}$ and $\bar{K}$. The cost of efficiently attaining a given information quality (C) is just the dollar value of s and K:

$$C = \mathcal{E}\bar{s} + P_K\bar{K}. \tag{21}$$

C is the *cost function* for information quality.

v.3 *Properties of the cost function*
The cost function depends on information quality and factor prices. For the following analysis we need to know how cost responds when information quality or a factor price changes. In view of (21), we can most easily obtain this information by examining the impact of some change on factor inputs s and K, and then combine these effects to obtain the change in cost.

First consider an increase in information quality. More output requires more inputs. Thus at constant relative factor prices both $\bar{s}$ and $\bar{K}$ rise; there is a pure *scale effect.* However, from the previous section we know that an increase in information quality raises expected income, $\mathcal{E}$, which is also the price of the time input.[12] Therefore there will be a *substitution effect*. Other factors are substituted for the (now more costly) time input as information quality rises. Both the substitution and the scale effects work towards greater utilization of other factors; so $\bar{K}$ rises as θ does. However, the substitution and scale effects on the use of time oppose each other. The scale effect dominates, unless time and other factors are very good substitutes in production. We shall assume the scale effect outweighs the substitution effect. (This point is argued in more detail in the Appendix.) Accordingly $\bar{s}$ rises when θ does.

When both $\bar{s}$ and $\bar{K}$ rise, it is obvious that total cost rises with information quality. That is, the marginal cost of information quality is positive. It is also easily shown that even if $\bar{s}$ falls when θ rises, greater output of information quality cannot possibly be accompanied by a fall in cost. Therefore marginal cost is invariably positive.

Furthermore, under our assumption of diminishing marginal product, we can show that cost rises at a rate that increases with information quality: the marginal cost of information quality is rising. The intuition is straightforward. A given increase in output raises costs. At low levels of output it does not take a large addition to factor inputs to raise output by a given amount. Accordingly, only a small rise in costs is required. But at higher levels of output a given rise in output requires a larger addition to each factor. Also, one of the factor prices ($\mathcal{E}$) is higher, so a given increase in the time input is more costly than it is at low levels of output. These two effects imply that a given increment to information quality raises costs more at high levels of information quality than it does at low levels: marginal cost is an increasing function of information quality.

Next, consider the impact on cost of an increase in endowed information π. Here a 'low' value of π means an uninformative value, near $\pi = 1/2$.

Recall (Section IV) that endowed information influences expected income. Under our assumptions raising π increases expected income because group A is endowed with skills upon which the market places a higher value. So individuals for whom π is greater face a higher time cost than others. Accordingly, for any given level of information quality their optimal choice of inputs involves less time and more of other inputs; the $\bar{s}/\bar{K}$ ratio is lower.

---

12 The text assumes $\theta > \pi > 1/2$ or $\theta > 1 - \pi > 1/2$, in which case $\mathcal{E}$ rises with θ (recall Figure 14). When $\mathcal{E}$ does not depend on θ, the cost function is constructed in precisely the textbook fashion. However, as will become evident below, individual choice will always yield either no investment (in which case the cost function is irrelevant) or a value of θ satisfying one of the above inequalities.

TABLE 6

Properties of optimal factor choices and cost function

Experiment	Optimal factor choice		Cost (C)
	Time input (s)	Other input (K)	
Rise in information quality (θ)	Rises	Rises	Rises, and at an increasing rate. Marginal cost is positive and increasing.
Rise in π	Falls	Rises	Rises, but at a diminishing rate. Marginal cost rises also.
Rise in P_K	Rises	Falls	Rises, but at a diminishing rate. Marginal cost rises also.

Even though a substitution of other inputs for time is optimal, individuals for whom π is greater face higher total costs. There is simply no way for a rise in one factor price to allow a given level of output to be achieved at lower cost. However, an increment to π increases costs less at high values of π than at low values, because less time is used at high values of π.

Further, a rise in π raises the marginal cost of information quality. The reasoning is clear enough: an increase in output requires an increase in factor inputs and so raises costs; when one of the factors is more costly, the increase in its utilization costs more.

An increase in P_K operates similarly to a rise in π. Any increase in P_K causes a substitution of time for other inputs in the production of a given information quality. Costs are raised, but at a rate that diminishes with P_K. Marginal cost is also raised.

The results of this subsection are contained in Table 6 and depicted in Figure 16.

v.4 *Recapitulation*

In this section we have presented the cost side of the information accumulation problem. We began by assuming an information quality technology wherein time spent in school, in conjunction with other factors, contributed to greater information quality. Noting that the price of time in school is the expected income forgone, and assuming a market for other inputs, we then considered the following question: What is the least cost combination of time and other inputs which yields a given information quality? The dollar value of this efficient choice of

Figure 16

a) Cost as a function of information quality

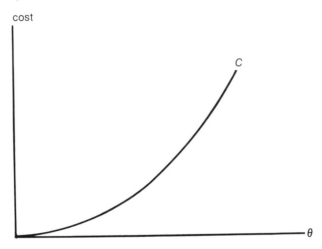

b) A rise in π or P_K

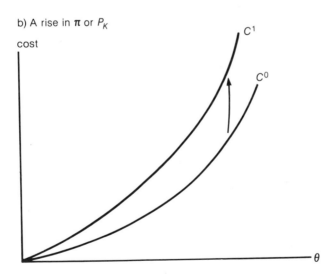

inputs is the cost function for information quality. Cost depends on the level of information quality (θ) and the factor prices ($\mathcal{E}$ and P_K). The endowed information enters the cost side via the price of time. The relevant properties of the cost function were derived and then summarized in Table 6 and Figure 16.

VI. OPTIMAL INVESTMENT IN INFORMATION QUALITY

Sections IV and V presented the return and cost side of information accumulation. In this section we examine optimal choice of information quality. The subsequent section considers the theoretical predictions following from this optimal choice.

VI.1 Optimal information quality

We assume individuals choose information quality so as to maximize returns less costs: $\mathcal{E} - C$.[13] The easiest case is that for which $\pi = 1/2$. In that instance workers receiving $x = a$ work for α firms, and those obtaining $x = b$ work for β firms. As a consequence, expected income always rises with information quality (recall Figure 14, panel (a)); the marginal return to information quality is invariably positive.

When $\pi = 1/2$, what is the optimal information quality to choose? Clearly it is that for which the gain in expected income associated with an increment to information quality equals the additional cost. If we denote the increment to expected income by $\Delta\mathcal{E}$, and the added cost by ΔC, the optimal value of θ is that for which

$$\Delta\mathcal{E} = \Delta C; \tag{22}$$

equivalently, marginal return equals marginal cost.

The solution is portrayed in panel (a) of Figure 17. At $\theta = \theta^*$, the difference between $\mathcal{E}$ and C is a maximum, and the slopes of the two curves are equal.

Now take the case where $\pi > 1/2$. Recall (Figure 14, panel (b)) that expected income does not depend on information quality when information quality is poor relative to the endowed information ($1/2 < \theta < \pi$). Since costs of obtaining information quality are positive, it is obvious that optimal behaviour will never entail a choice of information quality (θ) that is greater than 1/2 but less than π.

---

13 Notice that $\mathcal{E} - C = (1 - s)\mathcal{E} - P_K K$, which is lifetime income less 'tuition.' We use gross income less total investment costs simply because it is similar to familiar analyses of other investment problems.

That is, either $\theta^* > \pi$ or $\theta = 1/2$ (involving no schooling) will be chosen.[14] If $\theta^* > \pi$ is contemplated, θ^* will again be chosen to equate marginal returns and costs, which will generate some net return $\mathcal{E} - C$. This will be the preferred choice of θ if this net return exceeds the expected income attainable when $\theta = 1/2$. In panel (b) of Figure 16, $\mathcal{E} - C$ (when $\theta = \theta^*$) exceeds the vertical intercept of $\mathcal{E}$. Accordingly, $\theta = \theta^*$ (exceeding π) is preferred to $\theta = 1/2$.

Figure 17, panel (c), presents the same analysis for $\pi < 1/2$. Either $\theta = 1/2$ or $\theta = \theta^*$ (satisfying (22)) will be chosen.

To reiterate, information quality is chosen to maximize expected income less costs of investment in information. Depending on the endowed information, the optimal choice is either not to accumulate new information at all, or to accumulate information of sufficient quality to dominate the endowed information.

Naturally, this is not all that can be said. We have seen that for $\pi = 1/2$, it is invariably optimal to choose some information quality greater than $1/2$; $\theta = \theta^* > 1/2$.[15] Further, it is obvious that if π equals unity (perfect endowed information), there is no need to expend any resources on improving information quality; $\theta = 1/2$ is optimal. A logical question is whether there is a critical level of endowed information, call it π_U, such that if $1/2 \leqslant \pi \leqslant \pi_U$, optimal behaviour entails choosing $\theta = \theta^* > \pi$, while if $\pi_U < \pi \leqslant 1$, $\theta = 1/2$ is optimal. In the Appendix it is shown that this is indeed the case. Furthermore, for the $\pi < 1/2$ case, there is a $\pi_L < 1/2$ such that if $0 \leqslant \pi < \pi_L$, $\theta = 1/2$ is optimal, while $\theta = \theta^* > 1 - \pi$ is preferred if $\pi_L < \pi \leqslant 1/2$.[16]

In sum, the existence of strong endowed information ($\pi < \pi_L$, or $\pi > \pi_U$) renders further accumulation of information suboptimal. The reason is simply that if information is going to be accumulated at all, it must be of quality sufficient to override the endowed information. When the endowed information is very strong, the large-scale investment required to obtain equally high quality information is too expensive to be optimal. To reiterate, if π exceeds π_U or falls short of π_L, no investment in information will be undertaken. Should π fall between π_L and π_U, investment will occur.

---

14 When we say 'no schooling,' we do not literally mean that the model predicts that the individual will never attend school. Practically speaking, we refer to schooling beyond some base amount, say grade nine. Further, a more complex analysis allows information to be accumulated sequentially. The decision to go to grade eleven then depends on the outcome of grade ten, and so on.

15 Recall that values of π nearer to $1/2$ (on either side) correspond to the weaker endowed information.

16 We can also show that $\pi_U < 1 - \pi_L$. When the endowed information indicates that the worker is more likely to be in the high-income group ($\pi > 1/2$), the worker's opportunity cost of time is greater. Accordingly, the endowed information sufficient to render investment in information suboptimal need not be so extreme.

Figure 17

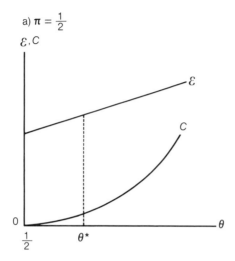

a) $\pi = \frac{1}{2}$

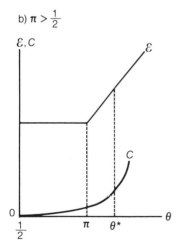

b) $\pi > \frac{1}{2}$

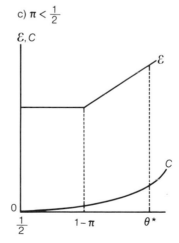

c) $\pi < \frac{1}{2}$

VI.2 *Recapitulation*
In this section we integrated the material on returns and costs of information accumulation. We then characterized the optimal quality of investment and found that unless the endowed information is very strong, optimal behaviour involves supplementing it with produced information. The quality of this information was chosen to equate marginal returns and marginal costs.

VII. THEORETICAL PREDICTIONS

In the preceding section we showed how the optimal information quality is chosen. Prior to that the efficient choice of factors used to produce a *given* information quality was determined. There are therefore three endogenous entities in our model: information quality θ, schooling time s, and other factors K. These variables can be combined to yield expenditures on information accumulation (C) and net expected life income ($\mathcal{E} - C$).[17]

The exogenous variables in our model are the endowed information π, the price of the other factor P_K, and the parameters of the firms' offer functions α_0, α_1, β_0, and β_1. These are the factors whose impact we can examine. It is useful to isolate carefully the influence of these parameters, because many applied issues (some of which are considered in Chapters 4, 5, and 6) can be cast as changes in one (or some) of them.

VIII.1 *Changes in endowed information*[18]
Will individuals who are more likely to be from group A (have a higher value of π) behave differently from others?

Recall that optimal information quality is chosen to equate marginal returns with marginal costs. While we have seen that *marginal* returns ($\Delta \varepsilon$) do not depend on endowed information, marginal costs are greater for those who are more likely to be from group A. Accordingly they choose a lower information quality.

The impact of an increase in π on the factors used to produce information quality is easily obtained. When π rises, expected income rises. Thus for any fixed θ the individual optimally substitutes other factors for time in school. As marginal cost rises and marginal return is unaffected (fn. 10), the optimal θ falls. This scale effect (recall subsection V.3) reduces the utilization of both factors. So as far

---

17 The theoretical predictions concerning π_U and π_L are less useful and are therefore presented only in the Appendix.
18 Here we examine the impact of various changes given that investment is optimal (i.e., $\pi_L \leq \pi \leq \pi_U$).

as schooling time is concerned, both the substitution and the scale effects have the same sign, and optimal s falls when π rises.[19] Since the scale and substitution effects on other factors oppose each other, the impact of an increase in π on K is ambiguous.

The increase in π raises both investment costs (for a given information quality) and expected income. However, because lost income is only a *fraction* of investment costs, it follows that net lifetime income rises with π.

Whether total expenditures on investment rise or fall with π cannot be determined a priori. The reasoning is clear enough. As π rises, the total costs of any given investment rise. But the optimal size of the investment falls, tending to reduce total investment expenditures. The net effect depends on how large a fraction of total costs is time related, and how large the reduction in information quality is.

In summary, individuals who are more likely to be from group A will go to school less and generate less information in the schooling process but achieve greater net life earnings. Effects on the use of purchased inputs, and the total cost of education are ambiguous.[20]

VII.2 *An increase in the price of other factors*[21]
An increase in the price of other factors has no effect on the marginal return to information accumulation. However, the marginal cost is increased. It follows that the optimal information quality declines. Further, there is a substitution effect towards schooling time and away from other factors. Accordingly, an increase in the price of other factors unambiguously reduces the utilization of other factors but has an ambiguous impact on schooling time.

19 The reader will notice that variation in π generates *negative* correlations between income and investment and income and schooling. At first blush this seems unsatisfactory. Of course this is precisely the prediction that human capital theory makes with regard to initial stocks of human capital.

A positive correlation is guaranteed only by variation in factors that affect only the cost side. Variation in P_K (below) yields such a relationship. This highlights the extent to which the common practice of ignoring the direct costs of schooling may be a serious error. It is variation in these costs that the theory (whether human capital or information based) identifies as being the source of the positive income-schooling relation. In a more fully dynamic analysis, the rate of interest plays a similar role.

20 These results have an interesting parallel in human capital theory, where a greater initial endowment would lead to less schooling time under the most reasonable technologies for producing human capital. Thus, according to both the information and human capital theories, the fact that some of the highest earners had very little formal schooling (Horatio Alger) is not anomalous.

21 The analysis here is very similar to that of the previous subsection. It is therefore appropriately brief.

In addition, since information quality declines, so does expected income. Although total investment outlays may either rise or fall, depending on whether the cost saving from reduced investment is outweighed by the rise in price of the other factors, it is easily shown that net lifetime income is reduced by an increase in the price of other factors.

To summarize, a rise in the price of other factors reduces investment, the use of other factors, and net lifetime income. The impact on total investment expenditures and schooling time is ambiguous.

VII.3 Changes in the offer functions

The offer functions contain a considerable number of parameters. Fortunately, the useful conclusions can be obtained by considering only two composite experiments.

First, suppose we consider raising the 'no-information' offer $\bar{O}$, *holding the marginal value of correct allocation* (α_1 and β_1) *fixed*. This change increases the opportunity cost of schooling time without raising the value of correct allocation and so reduces the optimal level of information quality. This reduction diminishes the use of both schooling time and other factors (a scale effect) and also induces a substitution away from time and towards other factors in the production of information quality. Therefore, the utilization of time in the production of information falls, since both scale and substitution effects operate in the same direction. The impact on the use of other factors is indeterminate, however, because the scale and substitution effects conflict, the scale effect reducing their utilization, and the substitution effect increasing it.

The increase in the no-information offer may either raise or lower total investment expenditures (the logic is the same as in the previous two subsections) and clearly raises expected income. But since the rise in income can be shown to outweigh any additional investment expenditures, it follows that net lifetime income rises with $\bar{O}$.

In summary, an increase in the no-information offer lowers information quality and the duration of schooling but raises net lifetime income. The impact on total investment outlays and use of other factors is ambiguous.

Next, consider raising the marginal value of correct allocation (α_1 and β_1), holding the no investment offer fixed (by reducing α_0 and β_0 appropriately). This change increases *both* marginal returns and marginal costs. It can be shown that unless the technology is such that information quality is highly elastic with respect to changes in the time input, optimal investment in information rises with the marginal value of correct allocation. The basic intuition is the opposite to that of the previous experiment. Therein we raised the price of a factor used to produce information with no increase in the return to information accumulation. Here, although a factor price increase is also implied, the main change is in terms of a greater return to investment.

This scale effect works to increase use of both time and other inputs. But the substitution effect reduces the time input and increases use of other inputs. Thus, taken together, the scale and substitution effects of an increase in the value of correct allocation increase the use of other factors and yield an ambiguous effect on schooling time.

Raising the marginal value of correct allocation raises a factor price (schooling time). This raises the costs of a given investment. None the less it has been shown that information quality will generally rise. So total resources devoted to information accumulation clearly rise. Furthermore, expected income is also raised by this change. It can be shown that the gain in expected income exceeds the rise in investment costs, thus raising net expected life income.

Altogether, a rise in the marginal value of correct allocation increases investment in information, the use of other factors, net expected life income and total resources devoted to investment. Only the effect on schooling time is ambiguous.

VII.4 *Recapitulation*
In this section we have considered the effect of change in the economic environment on the quantities determined by the model. Specifically, we analysed changes in endowed information, the price of other factors of production, and the offer functions.

Each change generated a response in terms of the optimal level of investment, because marginal return and/or marginal cost was affected. This provided a scale effect on the inputs to that production process (schooling time and other factors). All parameter changes ended up corresponding to factor price changes as well, and thus induced substitution effects between the factors used to produce information quality. The total change in factor use combines scale and substitution effects.

Finally, the impact on total investment expenditures and net lifetime income could be constructed from the underlying factor price movements, scale effects, and factor adjustments. The predictions in the following chapter are composites of the cases developed in this section, which are summarized in Table 7.

VIII SUMMARY AND CONCLUSION

In this chapter we have presented our theoretical model of the accumulation of person-specific information on productive traits.

The essentials are straightforward. There are two kinds of individuals, and their skills are such that if full information were available, each would 'naturally'

TABLE 7

Summary of theoretical predictions

Change	Information quality	Time input	Other input	Total investment outlays	Net lifetime income
Increase in endowed probability that worker is from group A	−	−	?	?	+
Increase in the price of other factors	−	?	−	?	−
Increase in the no information offer	−	−	?	?	+
Increase in the value of correct allocation	+	?	+	+	+

match with one of two kinds of firms. However, no one is sure of exactly what skills any particular worker possesses, although information on the distribution of skills in the population is readily available.

Given this basic set-up, we developed the offers firms would make to workers on whom any given type of information was available. We then formalized the idea of information by introducing a label that was correlated with the individual's skills. This enabled us to be more specific about the offers individuals might receive, and hence to derive expected income as a function of the quality of the labelling process.

We then turned our attention to efficient production of information. Specifically, we assumed the quality of the label could be augmented by spending more time in school, or by devoting more co-operating factors to the schooling process. Given that both these factors are costly, the issue of how to obtain a label of given quality at least cost was analysed and the properties of the implied cost function for information quality presented.

Once we had carefully developed costs and returns, the analysis of the optimal choice of information quality was straightforward. The optimal quality was simply that for which any further addition to quality would raise costs as much as it would expected returns. We then proceeded to analyse a number of simple comparative statics exercises, which will prove useful in the applications that follow. Changes in the economic environment caused the optimal information quality to change. This scale effect in conjunction with adjustments to the least cost factor mix used to produce any given information quality, yielded predictions concerning schooling time and other inputs. Further predictions on net expected lifetime income and the total quantity of resources used for the production of information were obtained from the underlying changes in information quality and use of inputs.

In the chapters that follow we employ the analysis developed herein to discuss a number of applications to which the informational model of schooling and job-worker matching can be put.

4

Education and training policy: basic guidelines

In the last two chapters we have examined simple versions of three main alternative economic theories of education. In Chapter 5 we ask what light these theories, especially the informational model, can throw on trends in education and training in Ontario (and more generally in Canada as a whole) over the last two decades. In Chapters 6 and 7 we go on to comment on the current debate over government policy towards education and training. In our view, that there is a significant aspect of education – that is, investment in information about inherent skills and abilities – which has been largely ignored is a serious deficiency in that debate.

It is natural for us to be asked whether there is 'enough' emphasis on accumulation of person-specific information in our education and training systems. It is also natural to enquire how it can be ensured that the correct mix of investment in human capital (skills) and in person-specific information occurs. This is a question of the optimal design of public policy with respect to education. In order to answer it, one needs to have a clear conception of how the state should intervene in education and training. The purpose of this chapter is to outline our conception of that role. This acts as background for Chapter 5 as well as the explicitly policy-oriented chapters 6 and 7, since a description of optimal policy requires consideration of the impact of various kinds of government intervention. Understanding such impacts is a crucial step in interpreting recent trends in education and training.

Education in Canada is almost entirely in the public sector. Moreover, tuition at the elementary and secondary levels is free and in the colleges and universities heavily subsidized. Post-secondary students receive, in addition, considerable assistance in the form of scholarships, bursaries, and student loans. Finally, adult workers have some access to subsidized training on the job, as well as to institutional manpower training with not only zero tuition but also generous living allowances.

In the light of the large scale of government's role in education and training in Canada today, it is startling to reflect that in each of the three models of the two previous chapters education proceeds without any public role at all. In fact, we have shown that in both the human capital and informational models (but *not* in the signalling model) the amount and distribution of education is, in a particular sense, 'efficient.' That is to say, no change in the amount of education obtained by any individual could make him/her better off without making someone else worse off; no resources are being wasted.

In the human capital and informational models we know that the pattern of education without government interference is efficient, because private and social costs and benefits of education coincide. Each student continues his/her education until the marginal private return to schooling falls to the marginal private cost. If this is also the point at which social marginal benefit equals social marginal cost, the amount of schooling is optimal not only for the individual, but from the point of view of society as well.

We know that private and social returns to education are the same in the human capital and informational models, because individuals are always paid wages equal to their expected social marginal product.[1] An extra year's education benefits the individual by the increase in wages secured and society by the expected increase in productivity. Since these things are the same, private and social benefits of education coincide.

Private and social costs of education are the same in the human capital and informational models because (1) individuals bear the full costs of education, and (2) education is produced efficiently. Efficient production of education (ensured by the individual's free choice of technique of production, in the face of full-cost pricing of inputs) means that the costs borne by the individual are the true social 'least costs.'

What must one add to the economic theories of education to obtain a role for government? The answer is either considerations other than 'efficiency,' or different assumptions that suggest efficiency is not obtained without government. In this chapter we discuss the role that government should play when we are concerned with 'equity' as well as efficiency, and when there is 'market failure,' that is, a situation in which freely functioning private markets cannot achieve efficient outcomes. The two principal forms of market failure examined arise in

---

1 The equality of private and social returns to education does not hold true in the signalling model. There an individual's marginal product is invariant, but he receives a higher wage the more education he takes.

the presence of signalling, and external effects of education. We also consider whether private markets are capable of either providing students with an amount of information on relative returns to different occupations, and other aspects of the job market, appropriate to make efficient schooling choices, or dealing effectively with certain kinds of 'manpower shortages.'[2]

It is argued in this chapter that there are reasons that government intervention in education and training, through the giving of various subsidies, could be desirable. However, an important point is that there is no economic rationale for organizing the industry in anything other than normal competitive conditions. Specifically, we argue that there is no need for direct state provision of education and training, and that this may be harmful when combined with an absence of competition between state and private sector institutions. We make specific proposals on how current systems can be modified to increase competition. The importance of providing a competitive environment is that it ensures the correct mix and amount of different kinds of education – for example, of investment in human capital or skills, on the one hand, and accumulation of information on inherent skills and abilities on the other.

The chapter proceeds as follows. Section II sets out the alternative rationales for government intervention. Section III investigates further by considering in more detail the *effects* of intervention. Finally, in Section IV we offer what we consider appropriate guidelines for government intervention.

II. ALTERNATIVE RATIONALES FOR GOVERNMENT INTERVENTION

II.1 *Efficiency*
There is a sharp division between the human capital and informational models, on the one hand, and the signalling model on the other. As discussed in Chapter 2, to the extent that education represents merely signalling it is wasteful. Individuals' abilities are neither augmented nor better assessed by going to school. In simple versions of the signalling model, such as the one presented in Chapter 2, school attendance results in no increase in individuals' marginal product over their working careers.

On efficiency grounds, in a world where education represents merely signalling the government should *tax*, rather than support, it; a socially wasteful activity ought to be discouraged. In Chapters 2 and 3 we noted that for the purposes at hand, education is better viewed as human capital and information accumulation

---

2 For illuminating discussions of the rationale for government intervention, see Gunderson (1974a) and (especially) Friedman (1982, Chap. 6).

rather than signalling. In the remainder of this chapter we therefore concentrate on policy prescriptions in a world where signalling is less important.

Turning to the human capital and informational models the no-intervention solution might be inefficient in the presence of positive external effects of education. Such effects have frequently been called on to justify a government role. There are two classes of possible effects. First, there are those that would arise in almost any form of democratic society. For example, education is thought to 'make better citizens.' (See, e.g., Weisbrod, 1964, 28–34.) 'Better citizens' vote more intelligently and support worthy causes. It appears to be generally believed that such externalities are most important in the early stages of schooling. (See, e.g., Friedman, 1982, 88–9.) There is a second class of external effects, which arise only in the welfare state and may be more important at higher levels of schooling, for example, the post-secondary.

In the welfare state personal misfortune results in societal compensation. Costs arising when people become sick or unemployed are borne to a great extent by society at large rather than the individual. This situation introduces a new external effect. There is considerable evidence that, other things being constant, more educated people choose better health and less unemployment. To the extent that these benefits accrue to persons other than the individual, the student may select too little education.[3]

Another externality arises in the welfare state as a result of progressive income taxation. Such taxation reduces the private benefits of education more, proportionally, than private costs (via the reduction in net forgone earnings). In other words, the rest of society shares more in the benefits than it does in the forgone earnings costs. There is thus a positive externality, justifying explicit subsidies to education and training. (See Hare and Ulph, 1979.)

If it is believed that uninternalized positive external effects of education are sizeable, an appropriate policy response would be subsidies that reduce tuition fees below the full-cost level. Determining the appropriate level of such subsidies, it should be noted, is a difficult problem. The value of the externalities in question is extremely hard to quantify. The economist can provide some help, but as argued by Friedman, 'what forms of education have the greatest social advantage

---

3 This argument is clearly of the 'second-best' variety. That is, the externalities in question result from a form of a 'distortion' introduced by government. This distortion consists in the reduction of the private return to schooling below the social return resulting from taking the benefits of reduced likelihood of ill health or unemployment away from the individual.

While some may understandably feel impatience with an argument for more government intervention to undo some harm of existing intervention, practical considerations dictate that social insurance must be viewed as a permanent feature of our society, for good or ill. Useful policy discussions must take this as a datum.

and how much of the community's limited resources should be spent on them must be decided by the judgement of the community expressed through its accepted political channels' (1982, 89).

It can be argued that mere subsidies to tuition fees will not result in all students attending school until social marginal benefits fall to costs. Borrowing problems may prevent this from occurring. The private market for student loans appears to fail. While in the absence of externalities this failure would not automatically imply a need for government-sponsored loans, when there are externalities this market failure produces an especially high social cost. This implies that the benefits of a government-sponsored loan plan may outweigh the costs (including the almost certain need for subsidization of the plan out of general revenue).

At present the Canada Student Loan Plan (CSLP) and supplementary provincial schemes provide fairly sizeable loans on a means-tested basis. (The loans are actually extended by chartered banks and are guaranteed by government. There is an element of subsidy in that interest is paid by government for up to six months after graduation.) It has repeatedly been suggested, however, that these plans do not go far enough. It has alternatively been proposed, for example, that loans should be available to *all* students (not just those from lower income families), or that an income-contingent repayment scheme should be adopted.

In our view the argument for government-guaranteed loans for students other than those from poor families has some merit – after all, we cannot be sure that parents will in all cases provide the support the government expects from them. However, caution is in order. There is a tendency to feel that the market failure implied by the absence of a private market for student loans in itself justifies a government-sponsored plan, and that student loans should therefore be 'available to all.' This position does not stand up to examination. The default risks that preclude a private market also affect a publicly sponsored plan. Raising the borrowing limits under the current loan plans and broadening eligibility dramatically would therefore lead to an increase in the subsidy from general revenue required to support the plan. That is to say, making student loans 'available to all' would impose increased burdens on the taxpayers. These measures are not welfare-improving for all members of society. Whatever else may be said about them, they therefore do not increase efficiency.

It is sometimes felt that something beyond conventional student loans is necessary, because students take less schooling than is socially desirable, since the return to schooling has some risk and students are typically risk averse. This worry has some basis, as shown by Levhari and Weiss (1974), who demonstrate that under plausible conditions risk averse individuals will invest in schooling less than risk neutral ones when the return is uncertain. It is in addition often suggested that students from lower-income families are especially reluctant to borrow large amounts to finance education, that is, that they are particularly badly affected by the risk problem. This concern also has some basis in the economic theory of educational investments, again as shown by Levhari and Weiss, who demonstrate that individuals with a lower endowment of non-human capital are likely to be more strongly affected by risk.

Despite the fact that, in principle, the risk problem may lead to inefficiency, it is far from clear that it is desirable to implement an income-contingent repayment feature in the student loan plan to attempt to deal with it. First, the risk problem may not be as serious as some suppose. The effective variance in returns may be considerably reduced by our progressive tax-transfer system. Also, there is a self-selection mechanism at work that may reduce the problem dramatically. The theory of occupational selection would predict that the least risk averse individuals would enter the most risky occupations. Optimal schooling lengths may therefore be obtained even if the majority of students are risk averse, as long as programs with significantly risky pay-offs take a minority of students.

An income-contingent repayment feature in a student loan plan was suggested initially by Friedman and Kuznets (1945) and Friedman (1955). (See Friedman, 1982, 100–7 for a concise restatement of the proposal.) It has been advocated in Canada by several authors – most recently by Stager (1981). There are many variants, but a representative example is provided by the following scheme, similar to that sketched by Stager. Each graduate would pay a flat percentage of his annual taxable income on his student loan account. This would be applied to the outstanding debt. After a period of, say, thirty years, the remaining debt (if any) would be forgiven.

The main problem with income-contingent loan schemes (aside from the fact that the risk aversion problem may not be very serious) is that they are particularly vulnerable to two standard difficulties in insurance situations: adverse selection and moral hazard. (The income-contingent loan scheme contains an element of insurance, since if the borrower's earnings turn out to be low, he may not have to repay completely.) The adverse selection problem is that individuals expecting low lifetime earnings will have a higher propensity to borrow under the plan; moral hazard lies in the work disincentive effect of the extra income tax that the borrower must pay over his lifetime.[4]

---

4 That these problems may be severe appears to be corroborated by the high default rate experienced by the income-contingent loan scheme operated by Yale University since 1971. For a description and analysis of this scheme, the Yale Tuition Postponement Plan, see Nerlove (1975).

Finally, it appears to be a common view that students may make bad choices because they are ill-informed about alternative educational programs or labour market conditions – in particular, relative earnings in different occupations. It is argued that governments may usefully seek to provide students (and adults as well) with more information to fill the perceived gap. (See, e.g., Economic Council of Canada, 1982, 101–3 or Employment and Immigration Canada, 1981, 83–9.) While such recommendations may seem innocuous, it is not clear that the intervention they countenance is warranted.

There is, in fact, ample empirical evidence that shows that students are typically well informed.[5] And of course there is good reason. Private agents have strong incentives to accumulate information about market opportunities, and much information is available very cheaply – just think how much one could learn from perusing the want ads in a daily newspaper if one had no knowledge of the labour market. To put matters another way, does anyone seriously believe that high school students these days are ignorant of the great promise of a career in computer science, as opposed to one in, say, teaching?

Not only is a great deal of information accumulated privately, in the absence of imperfections it is the *efficient* amount. As with any form of investment, agents will pursue job market information until the marginal benefits fall to marginal costs. If government expends resources to increase information accumulation further, it enters the region where marginal costs exceed benefits. As with any other good, we can have *too much* labour market information.

Of course, just as there may be imperfections preventing individuals from obtaining enough education, there could, in principle, be imperfections preventing people from accumulating enough job market information. Borrowing difficulties may prevent people from doing enough search, and to the extent that investing in job market information increases earnings and reduces the probability of unemployment, the externalities arguments that are pertinent to education are applicable here. We are considerably less sure of the force of these arguments

---

5 In his classic study, *The Market for College Trained Manpower*, Freeman (1971) found that undergraduates make considerable use of information from family, college professors, part-time or summer employment, and the media in assessing alternative careers. (See 194–5.) Their knowledge of forgone earnings, earnings in their intended occupations, and wage growth over the life cycle was quite accurate. (See 196–200.) Crean (1973) found that unemployment rates had a significant positive effect on secondary-student 'retention rates' for most provinces and age groups across Canada. This implies student knowledge of forgone earnings at quite an early stage. Recently, McMahon and Wagner (1981) have found that undergraduate expectations of earnings by occupation, life-cycle wage growth, and a surprising number of other details of the structure of earnings are accurate in the United States.

in the case of investment in job market information, however, since the costs of such investment are much less than those of education or training.

II.2 *Equity*

A major reason we have so much government intervention in education probably lies in considerations of equity, in particular, the desire for 'equality of opportunity.' Yet no student would be forced to discontinue his studies out of financial necessity if the efficiency-based measures suggested in the previous subsection were in force. We have argued for general subsidies to tuition, and generous student loans on efficiency grounds alone.

Although in pursuing efficiency one might obtain, as a by-product, all the 'equality of opportunity' the public desires, there may be arguments for additional equity-based intervention. In particular, some may view the education system as a means for achieving income redistribution. There does seem to be a valid argument for using the education system as a redistributive tool. Suppose we respect the wishes of the donors as well as those of the donees. Donors would no doubt like their transfers to have a *permanent* effect on the welfare of lower-income groups. (In part because this implies less need for future transfers.) They may therefore obtain more satisfaction from a transfer that builds up the resources of (otherwise) poor families than from one that merely subsidizes their consumption. Transfers tied to education are uniquely suited to this role. Human capital and person-specific information are totally illiquid and cannot be squandered.

One should bear in mind that some forms of intervention in schooling that appear redistributive may not be genuinely so. While the expected lifetime incomes of children from poor families are, overall, lower than those from better-off families, there is considerable mobility. Thus, children from poor families who participate in post-secondary education, on average, are destined for middle- and upper-income groups in adulthood. In Section IV we consider whether there is in fact any way we can ensure that support to education motivated by the desire for redistribution is genuinely equalizing.

II.3 *Manpower shortages*

Recently, there have been repeated suggestions that there is a need for governments to do something about manpower shortages. Until the onset in 1981 of severe recession and the slow-down in the energy sector, there were a number of narrow labour markets experiencing extremely tight conditions. They ranged from the markets for particular kinds of university graduates – for example, engineers, geologists, and computer scientists – to those for some kinds of skilled labour – for example, tool and die makers, machinists, machinery mechanics, and welders.[6] Although some of these shortages will likely not reappear unless the fortunes of the energy sector rebound, others (especially the skilled labour shortages) were no doubt only temporarily removed by the recession of the early 1980s. We must therefore ask whether it is true that governments must act to do something about them. We defer our attempt to deal with this question until we have analysed the *effects* of government intervention in the next section.

III. EFFECTS OF GOVERNMENT INTERVENTION

Governments can have three main types of impact on schooling. First, they can affect its *scale*. That is, they can have an effect on the number of years people go to school or, more precisely, on the level of schooling output. Secondly, they can affect the *composition* of schooling output, that is, the relative numbers of students who graduate in different types of programs. Thirdly, they may have an effect on the *technique* of production: what combinations of student's time, s, and other inputs, K, are used in the schools?

The scale effect of any form of subsidy to schooling is unambiguous. As shown in Figure 18, for the informational model subsidies will (in the most plausible case) reduce the marginal cost of information quality, θ, for all levels of θ. If a student chooses an interior solution in the absence of government, he will definitely increase θ and likely raise schooling time, s. On the other hand, students who set $s = 0$ without subsidies may not react at all to a subsidy. Some will find it profitable to go to an interior solution and set $s > 0$, while others will continue with $s = 0$.

As long as there is some reasonable argument that the zero-intervention case gives suboptimal levels of education, the scale effect of government action is in the right direction, even if it may be too large or too small. In contrast, the effect of intervention on the composition of output or the technique of production may be both qualitatively and quantitatively inappropriate.

We can best see the likely effects on the composition of output in the hetero-geneous human capital model briefly sketched in Chapter 2. Recall that in that model there are N different forms of human capital. Figure 19 presents an example where $N = 2$. For convenience we refer to the two forms of human capital and their corresponding occupations as X and Y.

Parts (a) and (b) of Figure 19 show the costs and returns for investment in the X and Y forms of human capital for an individual with endowments H_X^0 and H_Y^0. Without government intervention, if the individual chose to invest in X, he would

6 See Betcherman (1982, Chap. 4).

Figure 18
Scale effects of subsidies to schooling, $\pi > \frac{1}{2}$

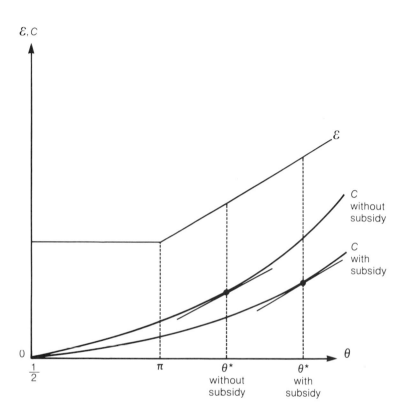

go to school for S_X^* years, while if he chose Y, he would attend for S_Y^* years. The form of schooling chosen would depend on which would provide the largest lifetime earnings.

Part (a) of Figure 19 can be used to help analyse what happens if the government chooses to subsidize one form of education but not another. It shows the downward shift in the marginal cost curve caused by a subsidy. This downward shift would have two effects. First, individuals who study X in the absence of subsidy will go to school longer. Second, some who chose Y initially will switch, because lifetime earnings will now be higher in X. (These changes in program assume an education system that is to some degree responsive to changes in enrolment demand.) The overall result is a possibly large shift of resources away from Y toward X education.

If the pre-subsidy private marginal benefit and cost curves in Figure 19 were also *social* benefit and cost curves, it is clear that the differential subsidy to X would be inefficient. In the equilibrium with subsidy the social marginal benefit of X education would be below cost. The overall value of education output could be increased by reducing the amount of X, and increasing the amount of Y output. The differential subsidy would only *not* cause inefficiency if either the social benefits of X education exceeded private benefits or the social costs of X education were less than the private costs. This might be the case for any of the reasons that we have examined in Section II.

It would require a more ambitious study than the present one to determine whether there are major differences in true rates of subsidy to different programs in the formal education system. Merely looking at relative tuition fees is not sufficient. One must also take into account the aid students receive, their forgone earnings, and the differences in direct costs to the institutions of providing different programs. There is, however, one glaring example of differential subsidy to which we would like to draw attention: that between formal education and on-the-job training (OJT).

The Figure 19 analysis applies to the formal education vs. OJT comparison, as well as to the comparison of different types of institutional education. The major new wrinkle is that employer and employee jointly determine the desired extent of OJT. If we interpret the benefit and cost curves of Figure 19, part (b), as the *sum* of employer and employee costs and benefits, the analysis goes through unchanged. Employer and employee will agree that OJT should be pursued up to the point where the combined marginal costs and benefits coincide.[7]

There is little justification for a zero subsidy to OJT when there are high rates of subsidy to formal education.[8] Not only do we have the efficiency objection just sketched, but we also have reinforcing equity considerations. Those who terminate formal schooling earlier on average have lower lifetime earnings. They also

7 If OJT is purely *general*, the employee is predicted to bear all costs and receive all benefits, because the employer has no incentive to share the costs. He cannot reap any of the benefits, because after the employee has been trained he will leave, unless he is paid a wage equal to his full marginal product. Most OJT is at least partly *specific*, however. (Unlike general training, specific training imparts skills useful in only one firm or a small number of firms.) Employee and employer are predicted to share the benefits and costs of specific training. See the original discussion in Becker (1975, Chap. 2).

8 When we refer to the 'zero subsidy to OJT' we are, of course, referring to the general absence of an *explicit* subsidy. Both OJT and formal education receive an implicit subsidy via the non-taxation of earnings forgone as a result of investment in education or training.

Figure 19
Effects of differential rates of subsidy on the composition of schooling output

a) X schooling (subsidy)

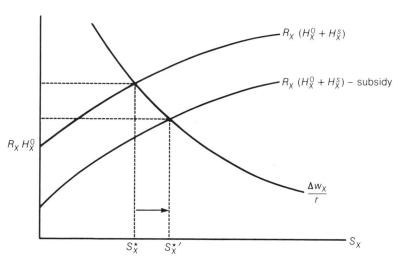

b) Y schooling (no subsidy)

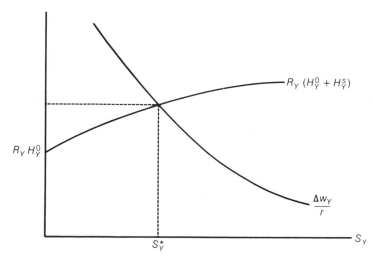

receive less subsidy for education under current arrangements, since while they are working and investing in OJT without explicit subsidy, their contemporaries who go on in formal education are benefiting from very large explicit subsidies.

The substitution away from OJT towards formal education, which our analysis says must have occurred over the last forty or fifty years as effective rates of subsidy to formal education have risen, is not hard to discern. The character of preparation for law, engineering, architecture, accountancy, and journalism, for example, has been greatly changed. In each of these professions almost all training once took place on the job. Now it is customary for entrants to complete an intensive period of (heavily subsidized) formal education before beginning OJT. While some such trend may well have occurred in the absence of government intervention, it has doubtless been accelerated by increased subsidies to formal education.

We would like to emphasize that we are *not* saying that the types of training mentioned in the previous paragraph should not be subsidized. More people train for these occupations than would without subsidies, and this may increase efficiency in the presence of externalities, as discussed in Section II. What we *are* saying is that if we are to take the time path of total government spending on education and training as fixed, it would have been better if less had been spent on formal education and more on OJT.

Finally, what is the effect of state intervention on the *technique* of educational production? The key is to recognize that the type of subsidy generally offered reduces the cost of 'other inputs,' which in the informational model we called K, rather than of the student's own time s. Figure 20 shows how, in the informational model, the privately optimal technique of producing given θ will change if there is a subsidy at the constant ad valorem rate u on the cost of 'other inputs' in education. As long as the student is free to buy as much K as he likes, the subsidy will lead to an increase in the other-inputs-intensity of education. This change in technique is inefficient, since it means that education will no longer be produced using the least-cost method.

In fact, in the public schools the subsidy rate, u, is practically 100 per cent, and in the colleges and universities it is clearly quite high. Thus, if allowed to *choose* K/s freely, students would elect greater goods-intensity than if they paid the full price P_K. Confirmation that this is the case does not seem hard to find. In the universities, where students generally have a formal right to consult teachers outside classes, well-regarded teachers must resort to a number of ad hoc mechanisms (e.g., working at home, careful scheduling of office hours) to restrict the demand for their (free) services. If students paid the true incremental cost of these services, the quantity demanded would be much reduced.

Figure 20
Effect of subsidy on K at rate u on technique of education

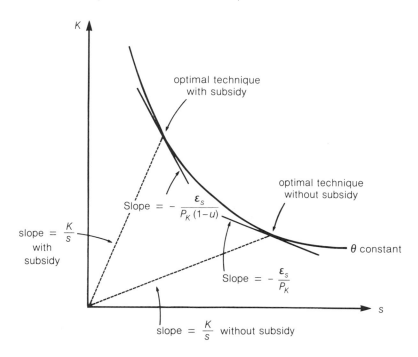

The consequence of the high K/s ratios desired by students in public educational institutions is that K must be rationed. This restriction is undesirable, since it is unlikely that K will be rationed in just such a way that students' K/s ratios are close to the (optimal) ones they would choose without the subsidy. This is especially the case where students are highly heterogeneous. Significant variance in endowments – π in the information model and H^0 in the human capital model – will give substantial differences between students in optimal K/s ratios. How are the institutions to know the correct ratio for each student? They could ask the student. Does he have an incentive to lie? Obviously, yes!

To put the argument more concretely, students differ in the value of their time. Those with more endowed information or human capital have higher expected earnings than others. Since their time is more valuable, efficiency dictates that they should be given less time-intensive education. In more familiar language, for efficiency, 'better' students should be allowed to progress more quickly (e.g., by 'skipping' grades).

The public schools, and more so the colleges and universities, *do* provide a variety of programs and (sometimes) accelerated training for better students. This gives the appearance of a public sector that recognizes the need for differences in composition and technique. There are strong signs, however, that these differences are not sufficient. The existence of private schools appears to indicate that at least at the elementary and secondary levels there is insufficient flexibility and responsiveness to students' needs. After all, in terms of K/s intensity, for example, one would reject *free* public K in favour of privately *purchased* K only if the public K/s ratio were highly inappropriate. (The near non-existence of a private post-secondary sector may indicate that the greater competition at the post-secondary level and geographic mobility of post-secondary students ensures education reasonably well suited to students' needs.) In addition, the relative infrequency of accelerated progress gives a strong indication of inflexibility. In the United States, where this phenomenon is now widespread, it has emerged only as a result of concerted action by universities, educators, and citizens. (See Maeroff, 1983, chap. 3.)

IV. GUIDELINES FOR GOVERNMENT INTERVENTION

What basic guidelines should govern public intervention in schooling? This is a difficult question. It is difficult partly because there are a number of reasons that intervention may be necessary, and simultaneous pursuit of the different policy goals is sometimes conflicting and always difficult to co-ordinate. And the difficulty arises partly from our inability to observe some of the crucial criteria for subsidy – for example, students' ability.

The guidelines for government intervention we can provide necessarily embody compromises between what is ideal and what is practical. None the less, there is considerable room for improvement in education and training policy in Canada. While the current situation is unquestionably a compromise between the ideal and the practical, it is the wrong one.

IV.1 *Intervention to improve efficiency*
As outlined in Section II, it is conceivable that in a world without government intervention there would be generally too little schooling from the standpoint of economic efficiency. The primary reasons, we argued, are that some benefits of education accrue to society at large rather than to the student (these are 'externalities'), and that the private market for student loans appears to fail. The corrective measures we recommended were general subsidies to education and government-sponsored loans to those students who would terminate schooling before social marginal benefits fell to social marginal costs because of the lack of borrowing opportunities. As discussed in Section II, the rationale for government-sponsored

loans is not the failure of the private market for student loans per se, but that failure may prevent the realization of some of the external benefits of education.

While we have argued in Section II that it is prudent to continue to restrict eligibility for loans on a means-tested basis, and to limit amounts borrowed to the requirements of reasonable subsistence, some of the consequences of other measures we recommend in this book might necessitate increased borrowing under the student loan plans. For example, we recommend below that post-secondary institutions should have full control of tuition fees. Especially if provincial operating grants stay constant or fall, in real terms, this might lead to large increases in some tuition fees. Many more students than at present might not be able to continue their education up to the optimal point without the help of loans, and the loan amounts required would be higher. Under these circumstances both the means threshold at which borrowing rights are removed and borrowing limits should be raised.

While it is all very well to know that subsidies to education have an economic rationale, this does not tell us whether current subsidies are too large or too small. How can we tell whether the correct subsidy is being provided? The long-recommended procedure is to estimate the social rates of return to the various levels of education and compare these with the estimated rate of return to investment in physical capital. This approach was widely implemented in the 1960s. Rates of return between 10 per cent and 15 per cent were commonly estimated for the United States, and comparable rates were obtained for Canada. (See, e.g., Economic Council of Canada, 1971, 210.) It has since been argued that the social rate of return to physical capital is in the same range (see Feldstein, 1977), but at the time it was accepted that the estimated returns to education were higher.

In the 1970s there was a considerable decline in the production of rate of return estimates. Freeman's (1975) finding that the social rate of return to a college degree had fallen from an early 1960s level of 11–12 per cent to 8 per cent in 1974 is apparently the last word from the United States.[9] Similarly, Stager's (1982) survey of research on the economics of higher education in Canada reports no estimates more recent than those of Mehmet (1977) for 1969 and 1972. Mehmet's estimates indicate a drop in the average private after-tax rate of return across all university

---

9 Freeman's estimates have been subjected to some scrutiny (see Rumberger, 1980 as well as the rejoinder by Freeman, 1980), but independent estimates for the more recent period are not available. 'Estimates' of the private rate of return based on the schooling coefficient in log wage equations are not relevant for the reasons outlined in our Chapter 2, Rosen (1973), and MacDonald (1981).

undergraduate disciplines from 22 per cent in 1969 to 18 per cent in 1972. (As he notes, of course, 18 per cent is still an attractive return.) More recent estimates are not available.

It has been widely and rather uncritically assumed that the apparent decline in rates of return to education in the early 1970s has not since been reversed (see, e.g., Employment and Immigration Canada, 1981, 154). This assumption has been made despite the fact that we do not really understand why the decline in the early 1970s should have occurred. (Until recently Freeman's (1975) explanation of a gigantic cobweb in the market for college graduates was widely accepted, but Welch (1979) has suggested an alternative explanation in terms of age cohort size effects on earnings.) In the next chapter we discuss the causes of the decline and examine relevant Canadian data, which can help us guess what has happened to rates of return since 1972. It may well be that new estimates of the social rate of return to education in Canada would show an increase after the trough of the early 1970s. This would certainly be consistent with the strong demand for post-secondary enrolment over the last four or five years.

In view of the scale of public expenditure on post-secondary education, and of the considerable ignorance of the pay-offs, it is much to be hoped that a detailed and scholarly examination of the social costs and benefits of post-secondary education (and perhaps other more vocational forms of training) will soon be undertaken.

IV.2 *The second best*

So far in this section we have discussed how governments should respond to the need for intervention created by efficiency problems that would exist in the no-government situation. There is another class of considerations that have to be taken into account. Suppose there were no good reasons for intervention, but government was committed to heavy support for education. Given that we would be in a world where the 'first-best' solution, zero government action, is impossible, what would be the 'second-best' solution?

It is easy to see the answer to the question we have posed if we look once more at Figure 19, where we analysed differential rates of subsidy to different types of training. If a subsidy is placed on X but not on Y education, although marginal benefits and costs of Y education are equal, marginal (social) benefits of X education are below cost. In other words, educating the marginal X trainee produces a net social loss. Given that a subsidy must be paid – the government sets aside a global amount to subsidize education – circumstances can be improved considerably.

Starting from the situation depicted in Figure 19, the government may achieve a 'second-best' solution by reducing the subsidy to X training, and introducing a subsidy on Y. This procedure must result in an improvement. Consider the impact of reducing the X subsidy by a small amount, and simultaneously introducing a small subsidy on Y. X trainees will go to school a little less, Y trainees a little more, and some who would formerly have selected X will switch into the Y program. The large social losses initially caused by the marginal X trainees will be considerably reduced, and will not be offset by equal losses on the Y side. Every time a trainee switches from X to Y, a large social loss from training (in X) will be replaced by a small loss (in Y).

The 'second-best solution' is thus to have some uniformity in subsidies across all forms of training. All types of education will be too greatly encouraged, but none will be encouraged more than any other. Overall damage will be minimized.

The importance of the second-best argument for education policy is clear: it reinforces the presumption that rates of subsidy should be uniform unless solid arguments can be made for a departure on grounds of differential externalities.

IV.3 *Rationing*
So far in this section we have neglected the possibility of non-price rationing of student places. We have recommended guidelines for establishing rates of subsidy. Implicit is the assumption that once pricing policy has been established student demand will be accommodated. In the long run excess (or insufficient) demand by students for any particular type of study will be eliminated, as a matter of policy.

If subsidies have not been carefully determined on the basis of efficiency and equity considerations, it may not necessarily be desirable to allocate educational resources to accommodate demand. For example, we have been told that there are many times as many applicants for performing arts programs at some Ontario community colleges as can be admitted. Tuition fees are uniform across college programs. It may be that the large excess demand for training in the performing arts has something to do with its consumption component. If this is the case, and the uniform tuition fee rule must stand, it is quite appropriate to ration places. It would be a bad idea, from an efficiency standpoint, to shift resources towards this area of excess demand.

In general it is our view that cases where non-price rationing on a more than temporary basis is appropriate are uncommon. Chronic excess demand is a signal that something is wrong. As discussed in Subsection IV.5 below, what may often be at the root of the problem is interference by governments in how educational institutions set the prices for their services.

IV.4 *Equity*
As pointed out in Section II, if redistribution is a policy good, the education system may be an effective tool for accomplishing it. There is, however, considerable practical difficulty. One cannot hope to have much favourable impact on

income distribution by subsidizing even students from low-income families at the post-secondary level, for example. Young people who are still in the formal schooling system at that stage are almost certain to have reasonable lifetime earnings. In order to direct redistribution towards those who will have genuinely low lifetime earnings otherwise, a more sophisticated strategy is required.

A promising way to accomplish redistribution through education and training is to pursue the following two-part strategy. Education is compulsory up to age sixteen. One can therefore have an almost certain impact on the least-favoured by raising the quality of elementary and junior secondary education. (We find in the next chapter that, to the extent one can believe the story told by expenditures, such improvement has been happening across Canada over the last two decades.) The second element in the strategy is to attempt to subsidize on-the-job training. While it is true that those with the lowest expected lifetime earnings likely obtain much less OJT than the more advantaged, it is also clear that past about age sixteen or seventeen OJT constitutes the *only* training they will receive. In Chapter 7 we propose that OJT should be subsidized by paying general age-related wage subsidies of the following form: all workers of a particular age would receive the same flat hourly subsidy, this subsidy would vary inversely with age, and the oldest workers to receive any subsidy would be of about the age of university graduates.

IV.5 *Public vs. private education, and the element of choice*
To a large extent, the entire preceding discussion could apply to a situation where, although there were high rates of subsidy, education was supplied by private firms. Is there any reason we should want education to be produced in the public sector?

It might be argued that the reason the state provides education directly lies in the difficulty of monitoring private schools. However, this argument holds weight only if subsidies exceed the amount that would be voluntarily spent on education. (In this case schools will be established that provide a mixture of education and other services – e.g., various forms of recreation – easily disguised as education.) Given the observed expenditures on private lessons, children's books, etc., it does not appear likely that subsidies exceed the amount that would voluntarily be spent on education.

While it is not our view that direct state provision of education is necessary, the system is firmly entrenched in Canada. The relevant question is therefore not 'should there be state schools, and colleges?' but 'does state provision of education do any harm and, if so, how can this situation be corrected?'

An increasing number of Canadian parents are sending their children to private elementary and secondary schools, despite their considerable cost. This is a tangible indication that state-provided education may, at least for some students, be much inferior to that which could be provided in the marketplace. We have already touched on some reasons why state schools might provide lower quality education. One was that finding the efficient technique of education production for each student is difficult in a non-market setting. (In the market setting parents can select the school that seems to have the right teaching methods for their child.) Another is that there is no natural mechanism that will ensure the provision of the correct mix and amount of different kinds of education – for example, investment in human capital as opposed to accumulation of person-specific information. Rather than having this problem solved simply and efficiently by the 'invisible hand' of the free market, we must attack it through the conscious planning of educators and administrators. This is bound to be a poor substitute, in our view. Finally, in extreme cases discipline or 'standards' may break down severely, because staff are not given the incentives they would have if their schools were selling their output in the marketplace.[10]

For some time a number of economists, of whom Friedman is the best known, have advocated simple schemes for bringing some of the benefits of the market mechanism into the public schools. These include voucher and tax credit schemes. The parent of a school-age child, for example, would receive a voucher for, say, $2000 worth of education. This could be spent at any accredited school. In addition to public schools, in the full-blown version of the scheme private schools would be widely accredited as well. Schools could set their own fees, and parents could supplement the vouchers with their own expenditures. Tax credit schemes would allow the taxpayer a credit up to some maximum for fees paid to accredited independent schools.[11]

The point of the voucher and tax credit schemes is that they would force schools to adopt efficient methods of production and induce them to innovate to offer programs attractive to students. In equilibrium one would expect to find that certain 'bad' public schools would disappear while others become 'good';

10 We have been asked, on occasion, whether there are any suggestions we would make as to how educators can best accommodate information investment explicitly in their planning. In our view, the likelihood of success in efforts to design curricula with the optimal mix of skill and information investment (themselves provided efficiently) in a non-market setting is limited. We therefore hesitate to give advice on how to plan for information investment. (This problem could be solved by the market without the advice of 'experts.') However, if pressed, one could point to standard statistical theory as a guide in devising tests of different skills and abilities. For high confidence in one's results, a large number of repeated, independent observations in each area of interest are indicated. Such an approach lends some theoretical respectability to the current trend towards a large number of self-contained, relatively short 'units' in both school and post-secondary institutions.

11 Manley-Casimir (1982) presents a collection of interesting recent papers on these schemes.

'good' schools would become larger, and the relative importance of private schools would grow. The result is predicted to be a general improvement in the quality of education, with no need for increased state expenditure.

There has been some objection to the voucher and tax credit schemes on the grounds that they would increase inequality in schooling. 'Topping-up' the voucher or spending more than the maximum tax credit would likely be more prevalent among higher-income families. One response is that current systems by no means provide education of equal quality across income groups (see West, 1982). Another might be that despite education not being 'equal,' the method of finance would be progressive. On the one hand, parents would be taxed via the highly progressive personal income tax to raise the required revenues, and on the other, they would receive (roughly) a constant per-child dollar benefit, which is also strongly progressive.

We do not have to rely on theory alone to tell us the likely effects of a voucher system. Whenever alternative institutions receive government funding and there is some freedom of choice, a system with some similarity to the voucher scheme exists. As pointed out by Wilson and Lazerson (1982) such conditions have prevailed quite widely in school systems across Canada. With the exception of British Columbia, the choice has been either between state and denominational schools or among the latter. In British Columbia, under the Independent Schools Support Act of 1977, parents choose between state schools and both denominational and non-denominational independent schools, the latter directly subsidized at a flat per capita rate (initially $500 per student). The consensus appears to be that the quality of Canadian schools has been increased by these arrangements. At the post-secondary level, any qualified student can attend almost any institution in Canada, with heavily subsidized tuition. Although individual institutions do not typically control their fees, the provinces can adjust these fees to keep their colleges' and universities' programs competitive. To a large extent the high quality of post-secondary education in this country and the responsiveness of the college and university sector to changes in student enrolment demand (documented in the next chapter) are due to the high degree of competition implied by these arrangements. Bad post-secondary programs experience great difficulty in surviving.

While post-secondary institutions in Canada exist in quite a competitive environment, we should point out that the nature of the market differs significantly from textbook-perfect competition, with important implications for post-secondary performance. The departure is that prices are highly inflexible. Universities and colleges receive part of their remuneration from tuition fees. These fees are the object of considerable political sensitivity, and are de facto controlled by provincial governments, which typically tax any increase in tuition fees beyond the amount they desire by a dollar for dollar reduction in funding. The other, more important source of revenue consists of the payments received from the provincial government ('formula funding'). These payments are typically related to enrolment, so that they increase the implicit price the institutions receive for training an additional student. Like tuition fees, the relative prices implied by the weighting used in formula funding, although ostensibly related to the costs of different programs, are fairly rigid and unresponsive to short-run changes in costs.[12]

The result of having a rigid structure of prices for university and college services must be a very different expected response to fluctuations in enrolment demand under some circumstances than would be obtained with flexible prices. If demand increases in an area where there are constant marginal costs, and there is no increase in the price of inputs concomitant with the rise in enrolment demand, the increase in demand can readily be accommodated without any change in price. This responsiveness may explain, for example, the observed success of our post-secondary institutions in expanding commerce and business administration enrolments over the last decade (see Chapter 5). On the other hand, where inputs (e.g., teachers and equipment) are highly specialized (as in engineering or computer science, say) marginal cost may be rising in the number of students, and periods of increased enrolment demand may coincide with increases in the relative cost of inputs (especially teachers). Thus, on the usual demand-supply analysis, with a fixed price the number of students enrolled could decline rather than increase.

In fact, although there is sometimes impatience with post-secondary responsiveness to changes in enrolment demand, we typically find that when there is a boom, for example, in the engineering field more engineering students are enrolled. The only way in which such responsiveness can occur, with rising marginal cost, is for the nature of the product to change. In other words, the *quality* of education provided must decline. Presumably this decline in quality must be such that costs are reduced, so that the institution is at least breaking even in providing the form of instruction in question.

Clearly, the type of enrolment responsiveness we get in a post-secondary system with institutions competing for students under fixed prices is considerably inferior to what we would have with flexible prices. With the latter an increase in enrolment demand in a specialized area would lead to a larger supply response (as well as higher tuition fees, of course) if the post-secondary sector operated

12 If fees were under full control by the institutions it would not necessarily be a drawback to have subsidies unresponsive to short-run changes in costs. The value of external benefits to society may not fluctuate with short-run changes in labour market conditions.

approximately like a competitive industry. To achieve this enhanced responsiveness we would argue that post-secondary institutions should be given full control of their tuition fee structures.

Some may object to our view that the post-secondary sector may be expected to behave like a competitive industry. Universities and colleges appear to have many goals aside from profit maximization, and it is thought that phenomena like academic tenure may force behaviour at odds with what we would expect in a competitive market.

It is not unrealistic to think of universities and colleges operating in a competitive industry, especially in Ontario, where there are large numbers of these institutions. For competitive behaviour there should be a possibility of entry (new colleges or universities *may* be inaugurated when a profitable opportunity arises). When entry is possible, existing institutions must behave like profit maximizers. Otherwise they will be forced into a loss position by the more aggressive institutions. As in any competitive industry, firms must maximize profit, because to do otherwise leads to losses and eventually to going out of business.[13]

Academic tenure certainly alters the response of a university to changes in the structure of enrolment demand. This does not mean, however, that tenure is inconsistent with competitive behaviour. Indeed, one possible view is that tenure arose as an optimal incentive structure under competitive conditions.[14] This is not to say that if conditions in the industry change markedly (e.g., turmoil in the structure of demand becomes a long-term phenomenon), tenure as currently observed will continue to be an optimal incentive structure. Its nature may well change in response to altered circumstances and thus lead to a change in the behaviour of universities.

IV.6 *Manpower shortages*
As outlined in Section II, until the onset of recession in 1981 there was considerable concern about shortages of two types of manpower: certain kinds of skilled

---

13 It might seem unlikely that a publicly supported university or college would be forced to close as a result of an irremediable deficit. Political considerations, it is often felt, will keep such institutions afloat. Nevertheless, the Ontario government has been putting considerable pressure on the universities to expunge their deficits. Even if closure of the entire institution is unlikely, closure of individual faculties, or amalgamation with another, more vigorous institution are real possibilities, whose presence ought to give considerable encouragement to profit maximization.

14 Tenure induces extremely hard work on the part of all those embarking on an academic career, at least at our dominant universities. It may be that the result, in terms of the overall quality of a university's faculty is more cheaply obtained than by other means (e.g., annual performance review). This issue clearly warrants some detailed examination.

workers and some types of highly qualified manpower (HQM). Except for the tightness related to the rapid expansion of the resource sector up until 1982 (e.g., of engineers, geologists, and geophysicists), it appeared likely that these shortages would resurface at the end of the recession. What would be an appropriate public policy response?

In a world of competitive labour and education markets there should be no public policy response. As in any other area, the market mechanism may be relied on to eliminate the shortage as quickly as is efficient. Elimination of a shortage (i.e., a return to equilibrium) will generally take longer than in other markets – it takes longer to produce a new engineer than a new cassette deck – but that is not a legitimate excuse for impatience. There is nothing government can do about such technological constraints.

Of course our education and labour markets are not perfectly competitive. They have a number of features that interfere with the adjustment mechanisms that cause shortages. But these features, we shall argue, are principally the by-product of current government intervention.[15] There is a good case for government action to remove these distortions but little case for new intervention to 'solve' shortages.

As we have outlined in the previous subsection, the imposition of a rigid pricing structure on post-secondary institutions interferes with their capacity to respond to increases in enrolment demand in areas with rising marginal cost or specialized inputs. Freeing-up prices as we have advocated would eliminate this problem.

The deleterious impact of government intervention on labour market adjustment mechanisms is felt also in on-the-job training (OJT). Minimum wages interfere with training, because they limit the amount of training that an employer may profitably offer. In the case of general training, for example, if a worker has to be producing rather than training for fifty minutes in the hour in order to generate a marginal product equal in value to the minimum wage, then there is very little room for training. Hashimoto (1982) has recently shown that minimum

---

15 It has been pointed out to us that a 'shortage' may be observed without government intervention in a situation where there is only one purchaser of a certain kind of labour (or a small group of purchasers who collude). (See, for example, Gunderson, 1974a, 721.) Under such monopsonistic conditions workers will be paid less than the value of their marginal product (VMP), because the employer equates the marginal cost of the labour input, rather than the wage, to VMP. There is in a sense a 'shortage' because if labour were available at a constant wage equal to the observed wage rate (i.e., the marginal cost of the labour input was constant rather than rising), more labour than is in fact used would be demanded. We do not regard this argument as especially important, in the Canadian context, because situations of monopsony appear to be non-existent.

wages are responsible in this way for a considerable reduction in OJT in the United States. Clearly, adjustment to a shortage via OJT may be limited if OJT is thus constrained.

Of greater relevance to the skilled labour shortages that have been experienced in Canada is the wage fixing for trainees common in regulated apprenticeship programs. If an apprentice must be paid 60 per cent of a journeyman's wage in his first year, 70 per cent the next, and so on, these constraints may prevent employers who could otherwise provide apprenticeship training from doing so.

We should point out that if our recommended wage subsidies for young workers were eliminated, the interference with OJT caused by minimum wages and apprenticeship regulations would be reduced, and the capacity of OJT to deal with shortages would be increased. An employer forced to pay a minimum wage of, say, $3.00 but in receipt of a $1.00 wage subsidy can afford to offer considerably more training.

Finally, it is important to note that the various influences interfering with adjustment mechanisms that we have identified do not *prevent* the elimination of shortages. What they do, by limiting the training capacity of post-secondary institutions and employers, is mainly to slow down adjustment. Shortages are made more severe, because it takes a longer time to achieve a new steady state.

V. CONCLUSION

In this chapter we have asked what rationale there is for government intervention in education and training. Public action must be predicated on the laissez-faire solution's being unsatisfactory from the standpoint of efficiency or equity. We have argued that there may be a legitimate basis for government intervention, in both these considerations, but that the form and scope of justifiable intervention is limited.

There is an argument for government intervention in education and training on efficiency grounds, we have argued, if there are positive benefits of education and training that accrue to society at large rather than to the student – that is, if there are 'externalities.' As economists are accustomed to point out, externalities justify subsidies. In this case subsidies not only to formal schooling but also to on-the-job-training (OJT) are justified.

Government subsidies that reduce tuition fees are not the only form of intervention justified by externalities. If the private market for student loans is viewed as inoperative, in the absence of government-sponsored student loans some of the external benefits of education would not be realized. Some students would be forced to terminate schooling too early. This suggests the provision of loans in amounts large enough to finance student subsistence at a reasonable standard of living to those students who would not otherwise be able to finance continued education. That is, we have provided an efficiency- based justification for something very similar to the current Canada Student Loan Plan (CSLP).

We have examined and rejected alternative efficiency arguments for government intervention. It is sometimes thought that in the absence of externalities the failure of the private market for student loans implies an efficiency gain from government provision of such loans. We have pointed out that the same high default risk that affects the private market would be present under a government scheme. A government-sponsored student loan plan almost inevitably must be subsidized out of general revenue and therefore cannot be advocated on pure efficiency grounds *in the absence of externalities.*

We have also argued against the contention that an inefficient schooling outcome occurs in the absence of government action, as a result of student risk aversion. The problem is likely exaggerated, and the often recommended remedy – an income-contingent student loan plan – is considerably more vulnerable to default risk than conventional loan plans are.

In addition, if the electorate supports redistribution of income and prefers transfers in kind in the form of education to those in cash, there is a legitimate basis for using education as a redistributive tool. In practice it is difficult to ensure that educational expenditure is genuinely redistributive, because people with lower lifetime earnings generally make less use of the system. We have suggested that redistribution via education can best be accomplished by ensuring high quality elementary and junior secondary schools and by shifting subsidies towards OJT and away from formal education.

An additional reason suggested for government intervention does not hold up under analysis: the existence of manpower shortages. In competitive education and labour markets shortages would be efficiently (although not of course immediately) eliminated. We do point out, however, that governments have introduced certain imperfections in education and labour markets that slow down adjustment mechanisms: rigid price structures for post-secondary institutions, minimum wages, and apprenticeship regulations, for example. Removing these imperfections (a good idea in the post-secondary case) or offsetting them (perhaps with wage subsidies for the young in the cases of minimum wages and apprenticeship regulations) would of course be excellent initiatives.

Our recommendation for general subsidies to education would countenance special subsidies in areas where external benefits are considered especially high (e.g., graduate programs at the universities). Such concern with getting prices right implies a general strategy for the provision of educational opportunities by schools, colleges, and universities. The strategy is to set prices correctly and then accommodate student enrolment demand. For various reasons this policy may sometimes not be practicable. For example, there has always been a policy of uniform tuition fees across programs at Ontario community colleges. If such policies cannot be abrogated, then there may be situations of chronic excess demand (e.g., where the consumption component of training is important), which clearly should not be eliminated by expanding enrolment. However, in general it pays to get the price right and eliminate excess demand or supply.

Finally, quite apart from the issue of whether government should subsidize education is the question of whether it should be in the business of providing education in state schools and community colleges. (Universities are not state institutions, although they receive most of their funding from the state. They do have considerable remaining independence and are therefore in a category distinct from schools and colleges.) While this point is interesting in principle, a more relevant question in the Canadian context is: 'Does it do any harm to have education provided directly by the state, and if so, how can this be reduced?' We have argued that state provision may be harmful, because there is no natural mechanism that ensures efficient methods of production or the correct mix and amount of different types of schooling.

In our view it would be desirable to bring the benefits of the market mechanism increasingly into our schools, colleges, and universities. At the elementary and secondary level this may be done through voucher or tax credit schemes. Confidence in the results is enhanced by Canadians' considerable experience with parental choice between state and independent schools, and by the evident value of competition at the post-secondary level. Indeed, something similar to a national voucher scheme is in force at the post-secondary level, where qualified students can choose to attend practically any Canadian institution, paying more or less uniform (and highly subsidized) fees. The high quality of Canadian post-secondary education owes much to this freedom of choice. The competitive mechanism would work even more effectively, however, with the elimination of certain constraints. The most important step would be to give post-secondary institutions full control over fees. We would then expect the post-secondary sector to fulfil even more closely public expectations on the range and quality of programs and responsiveness to changes in demand conditions.

5
Education and training in Canada:
recent trends and the current situation

I. INTRODUCTION

This chapter asks how the economic theories of education, set out in Chapters 2 and 3, can be used to interpret the structure of our education and training systems. In addition, it describes and analyses enrolment and expenditure trends over the last two decades, focusing in particular on changes at the post-secondary level.

   Section II examines the current structure of education and training. It argues that if we are to appreciate the system's accomplishments, we must acknowledge the role played by information investment in key elements of the system. In Section III we examine enrolment and expenditure trends since 1960 at all levels of education. Particular attention is given to shifts among university programs and between universities and community colleges. Section IV considers possible explanations of these trends. Finally, in Section V we discuss the implications of our analysis for future trends.

II. THE NATURE OF EDUCATION AND TRAINING IN CANADA

Table 8 outlines the levels of educational attainment being achieved by those leaving the formal education system in the spring of 1980. It shows that about 62 per cent of Canadian young people are obtaining at least a high school diploma, and slightly more than half of these go on to obtain some post-secondary qualification.[1] Overall, 13 per cent obtain a community college diploma, and 21 per cent an undergraduate diploma or degree from a university. A very small

---

1 For ease of exposition, we are adopting the fiction that attainment rates will not differ among the different age cohorts of young people represented in Table 8.

TABLE 8

Rates of education attainment by level, Canada and Ontario, 1979-80 (percentages)

Level	Canada			Ontario		
	Male	Female	Total	Male	Female	Total
High school diploma	60.4	63.4	61.9	64.9	63.9	64.5
Community college diploma	11.7	15.1	13.4	9.4	14.3	11.8
Undergraduate diplomas, BAs, and first professional degrees	20.2	21.2	20.7	22.6	24.0	23.3
Graduate diplomas, Masters, and PhDs	4.4	2.5	3.5			

NOTES
1 Rates are calculated by dividing the numbers of graduates by the population aged eighteen, twenty, twenty one, and twenty four on 1 June 1980 for the successive levels.
2 No rate is shown at the graduate level for Ontario, owing to the importance of out-of-province enrolment. Note that this problem also affects the undergraduate rate, although to a lesser extent.
SOURCES
The following Statistics Canada publications: *Education in Canada*, *Elementary-Secondary School Enrolment*, *Enrolment in Community Colleges*, and *Estimates of Population by Sex and Age for Canada and the Provinces*, and authors' calculations

proportion, 3.5 per cent, proceed to achieve a graduate qualifaction at university. The sexes differ in that women have a higher propensity to obtain a community college diploma and a lower rate of achieving graduate degrees.

In order to complete the review of attainment rates, note that the number of young people enrolled in trade and vocational schools is similar to the number attending community colleges. The implication is that a significant fraction of the 38 per cent who do not obtain a high school diploma achieve some trade qualification. Around 30 per cent of young people do not obtain any formal educational qualification before entering the labour force. However, 250000 adults, about 2 per cent of the labour force, enter full-time manpower training each year. If a majority have no form of diploma, a large proportion of the perhaps 30 per cent who 'drop out' of the formal education system may engage in at least a year of full-time training as adults.

Attainment rates are meaningless unless we know what students accomplish in the various forms of education and training. As argued in Chapter 2, most of the functions of the system can be understood in terms of the human capital and information investment models developed above.[2]

In trying to sort out where human capital or information is most important it is helpful to know what theory would predict about the *sequencing* of these two forms of investment in a world where both were present. Suppose there are two forms of schooling. One helps to determine whether one is an A or a B but does not alter skills. The other can be used to augment type-A or type-B skills, or both, but yield no information. A little reflection reveals that the first type of schooling should precede the second. In other words, it makes sense first to explore one's comparative advantage and then to exploit that knowledge by building up one's special skills and abilities. (Note that uncertainty about future remuneration in different occupations would reinforce the tendency to postpone human capital investment.)

We should also note that the education and training systems we want to examine are only the *formal* part of our society's overall education system. Both human capital and information investment may be continued after the termination of formal schooling, *on the job*. Becker (1975) showed, using standard economic analysis, that if total private costs of training are lower on the job, training will take place there, rather than in school. Despite the substitution away from OJT, which the previous chapter argued has been caused by increasing subsidies to formal schooling, the advantages of training in the workplace are so large that a great deal of training still occurs on the job.

Casual empiricism suggests that OJT is mostly a matter of skill acquisition, that is, human capital investment, rather than information accumulation. If much of formal schooling, at least at the earlier stages, represents information investment, many workers may actually acquire most of their human capital on the job. Moreover, this arrangement might be entirely sensible. If information investment takes place most cheaply in school and skill acquisition most cheaply on the job, we should not want a student to learn skills (i.e., accumulate human capital) while still at school.

In trying to gain an overall conception of what our education and training system is doing, we have found it helpful to examine the range of typical schooling

2 We also comment on the importance of the consumption component, mentioned in Section II of the preceding chapter, and the possible importance of signalling, where this seems appropriate. Recall that we have argued, in Chapter 2, that information investment and signalling are essentially competing interpretations of the non-skill-augmenting, non-consumption component of schooling. For reasons outlined in Chapter 2 we believe that information investment, a productive activity, is considerably more important in our education and training system than is signalling (which is completely unproductive).

careers. For the most part they can be summarized in seven distinct stylized careers, as illustrated in Figure 21. This figure shows the proportional split in effort devoted to skill vs. information acquisition as a function of years of schooling. Part (a) of the figure shows the 'academic,' or 'non-vocational' path terminating in a high school diploma. By and large, high school students in the academic stream do not appear to be intensively engaged in acquiring job-relevant skills. We would argue that their education may consist largely of information investment. In contrast, part (b) of the figure shows a schooling career terminating in trade or vocational school. Students following such a career move from the 'academic' information stream in junior high school to heavy skill-acquisition at high school.

At the post-secondary level we have a similar contrast between careers that never reach the stage of intensive human capital investment and those that do. Panel (c) of Figure 21 shows the case of a student who terminates with a three-year degree in arts or science.[3] As shown, in our view such students typically never reach intensive skill acquisition during formal schooling. Panel (d) illustrates the contrasting path followed by a high school graduate who goes on to a community college and studies to become a technician or para-professional. Intensive human capital investment can, of course, also be pursued at university. Panel (e) shows the case of a student who enters a specialized faculty – for example, nursing, home economics, commerce, agriculture – at the start of his/her university career. More delayed skill acquisition occurs for students who complete one or two years of arts or science before entering an honours program or professional school, as shown in panel (f) of Figure 21. Finally, in panel (g) we have the case of a student who pursues graduate studies, similar to the panel (f) path, except that heavy skill acquisition is prolonged by three or four years.

What emerges from this assessment of alternative schooling careers? First, there are two main paths that do not involve any period of concentrated skill acquisition: termination after an academic high school diploma or three-year BA. Most schooling careers follow one of these two paths (principally the former). Second, we see that there is a variety of less-used paths that terminate in a period of concentrated skill acquisition.

By and large it appears that policy makers and the public best understand and appreciate education that terminates in intensive human capital investment. The results of such education are more 'tangible' than those of information investment. In addition, since information investment is not obviously different from

---

3 Our judgment that a three-year BA does not typically involve intensive skill acquisition is coloured by our own experience. We find that while good honours students frequently obtain jobs where they make great use of their skills as economists, this is usually not true of general students graduating with a three-year BA and a major in economics.

Figure 21
Relative importance of information vs. skill acquisition by type of schooling career

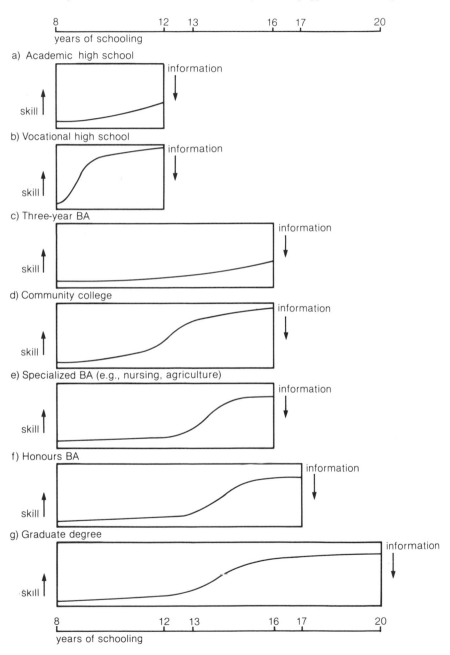

signalling (or pure consumption), there may be a suspicion that students who are not augmenting skills are not productively occupied. Their education may appear simply a form of 'screening,' and the special demand for such graduates may be regarded as 'credentialism.'

We can offer a twofold explanation and defence of the considerable importance in our education system of non-vocational studies. First, to the extent these studies represent investment in person-specific information, rather than signalling or consumption, they are productive and they do build up society's capital stock. Second, formal education that never reaches concentrated skill acquisition is not aberrant, because it is typically followed by intensive human capital accumulation on the job.

There are two types of schooling career that do not fit into the tidy scheme presented above. First, many students alter their plans during post-secondary study, sometimes making dramatic leaps between programs and institutions, often at the expense of additional years of study. That this is so common appears to confirm the importance of information-investment at the post-secondary level. If students knew their true talents and abilities perfectly at the point of high school graduation, costly changes in program at a later stage would be undertaken only in response to a significant change in the relative costs or benefits of different forms of training.[4] Changes in relative costs and benefits do not appear to explain what is observed, since they are usually minimal over the short period that a student spends at the undergraduate level, and there is a great deal of 'cross-hauling' – for example, some students who start in psychology switch to economics, and vice versa.

The other schooling career not represented in Figure 21 is that interrupted by lengthy labour force attachment. The importance of this type of career is sizeable and increasing, as the data on part-time post-secondary studies make clear. It might seem that mature labour force members who return to college or university likely have considerable person-specific information and are returning primarily to augment skills. However, in a period of rapid technological change there may be an important element of self-discovery ('can I cope with computers?'), that is, of information investment.

Of course not all mature labour force members who return to education go back to college or university. A large number enter the training programs run by Employment and Immigration Canada. This form of training is a very different phenomenon from post-secondary education, because (1) it always occurs after a

---

4 One might object that students frequently make changes because they find that they do not enjoy their studies. We would argue that not knowing whether one will enjoy a particular kind of work or study has consequences for one's behaviour very similar to not knowing whether one has the necessary talent. Both forms of ignorance call for some investment in information.

period of labour force attachment, (2) it is much more heavily subsidized, and (3) the trainee has less freedom in course selection.

It is clear that its sponsors view manpower training as principally a matter of skill acquisition. Indeed, this emphasis is increasing. Impatience with the results of manpower training has recently led to a call for more emphasis on equipping people with marketable skills.[5] The whole thrust of the new National Training Program is to identify and teach skills that are in high current demand.

Although the sponsors of manpower training may see their task as one of teaching skills, it is not clear that the trainees share this view. Unlike many workers returning to colleges or universities at their own expense, manpower trainees typically may not know whether there is any particular skill that it would be to their advantage to accumulate. While workers returning to college or university give up earnings and will therefore not go back to school without good reason, manpower trainees are unemployed and generally without good prospects. Their incomes will not be much affected if they enter training. (Most will receive unemployment insurance benefits whether they train or not.) That they wish to train therefore does not indicate they believe there is a high probability of a significant pay-off. Somehow the manpower counsellor and the worker determine which skill should be studied. The worker's attitude may well be, for example, 'I don't know if I am suited to be a heavy equipment operator. The counsellor seems to think I might be. Perhaps I'll give it a try.' In other words, the trainee may regard information investment as an important purpose of his training.

If the architects of the manpower training scheme view their programs principally as teaching skills, but the trainees regard them largely as information investment, it is not hard to imagine that the results of training will differ from those intended. Some portion of the trainees in any program will discover that they are not in fact well-suited to the target occupation. This factor imposes an upper limit on placement rates, which may be very low given the distribution of costs.

III. ENROLMENTS AND EXPENDITURES – RECENT TRENDS

III.1 *Enrolment – the overall picture*
Table 9 sets out the structure of full-time enrolment in formal education and training in Canada, at five-year intervals, over the period 1960–80.[6] Table 10

---

5 See the discussion of current labour market policy literature in the next chapter.
6 Ideally, we should examine full-time equivalent (FTE) enrolments. Unfortunately part-time enrolment figures for community colleges are not readily available. We can gauge the effect of ignoring part-time enrolment by comparing full-time and FTE enrolments at the universities.

TABLE 9

Full-time enrolment, by level, Canada and Ontario, selected years, 1960-80

School year beginning in	Canada						Ontario					
	(1) Elementary and secondary	(2) College	(3) University	(4) Total (1)–(3)	(5) Technical and vocational	(6) Manpower training	(7) Elementary and secondary	(8) College	(9) University	(10) Total (7)–(9)	(11) Technical and vocational	(12) Manpower training
Levels (000s)												
1960	4201.6	49.4	113.7	4364.7	n.a.	n.a.	1422.8	16.6	32.2	1471.6	n.a.	n.a.
65	5159.6	69.4	204.2	5433.2	n.a.	n.a.	1790.9	21.2	59.3	1871.4	n.a.	n.a.
70	5832.3	166.1	309.5	6307.9	219.2	268.6	2073.2	54.4	121.1	2248.7	89.9	70.0
75	5590.3	221.0	371.1	6182.4	253.0	237.0	2056.6	59.6	159.7	2275.9	92.2	66.1
80	5103.8	260.8	382.6	5747.2	n.a.	256.5	1918.1	75.8	160.2	2154.1	n.a.	77.5
Percentage composition												
1960	96.3	1.1	2.6	100.0	n.a.	n.a.	96.7	1.1	2.2	100.0	n.a.	n.a.
65	95.0	1.3	3.8	100.0	n.a.	n.a.	95.7	1.1	3.2	100.0	n.a.	n.a.
70	92.5	2.6	4.9	100.0	3.5*	4.3*	92.2	2.4	5.4	100.0	4.0*	3.1*
75	90.4	3.6	6.0	100.0	4.1*	3.8*	90.4	2.6	7.0	100.0	4.1*	2.9
80	88.8	4.5	6.7	100.0	n.a.	4.5*	89.0	3.5	7.4	100.0	n.a.	3.6*

* Percentage of total excluding technical and vocational, and manpower training
SOURCE: Statistics Canada, *Education in Canada*, various issues

TABLE 10

Average annual growth rates of full-time enrolment, by level, Canada and Ontario, 1960-80

Interval	Elementary-secondary	College	University	Total post-secondary
CANADA				
1960–65	4.2	7.0	12.4	10.9
65–70	2.5	19.1	8.6	11.6
70–75	–0.8	5.9	3.8	4.5
75–80	–1.8	3.4	0.6	1.7
60–80	1.0	8.7	6.3	7.1
ONTARIO				
1960–65	4.7	5.0	13.0	10.5
65–70	3.0	20.7	15.4	16.9
70–75	–0.2	1.8	5.7	4.6
75–80	–1.4	4.9	0.1	1.5
60–80	1.5	7.9	8.4	8.2

NOTE: The average growth rates are geometric.
SOURCE: Calculated from Table 9

throws additional light on these data by presenting the implied average annual growth rates of enrolment for the elementary-secondary and post-secondary levels.

Perhaps the most striking feature of enrolments is the concentration at the elementary-secondary level. In 1980–81, for example, 89 per cent of those enrolled in conventional programs at schools, colleges, and universities were at the elementary-secondary level. The sheer size of elementary and secondary enrolment constitutes a warning to policy analysts. While an economist may feel out of his element in the study of elementary and secondary education, changes at this level have extremely large potential effects on the overall output of the education system, as well as on what goes on at the post-secondary level.

In the first half of the 1960s most of the growth in post-secondary enrolment was at universities rather than colleges. In the latter half of the 1960s, however, this trend was reversed, and both college and university enrolment increased at the fastest rate for any of the four five-year intervals presented in Tables 9 and 10. Since 1970, for the country as a whole, enrolment growth in both colleges and

Whereas in 1965 FTE university enrolment exceeded full-time by 11 per cent in Ontario and 10 per cent for Canada as a whole, by 1980 the difference had risen to 16 per cent for Ontario and 19 per cent for Canada. The rise in the importance of part-time enrolment ocurred gradually over the interval between 1965 and 1980. Thus one should mentally correct the figures provided for the post-secondary sector in Table 9 to give a slightly more buoyant enrolment picture.

universities has decelerated in each five-year period. However, college enrolment has increased faster than university enrolment throughout. Thus, whereas in 1970 35 per cent of post-secondary students were in the colleges, by 1980 this proportion had risen to 41 per cent. This development is extremely interesting, since it suggests that in the 1970s there was a sizeable reallocation of post-secondary resources from universities to colleges. This is precisely the change that several recent documents in the labour market policy literature argue ought to occur in the 1980s (see the discussion of the literature in the next chapter).

Turning to Ontario, again the early 1960s was a period of much slower growth for the colleges than for the universities – average annual growth of 5 per cent vs. 13 per cent. However, the rise of community college enrolment in the late 1960s was even more meteoric in Ontario than in the country as a whole, with the growth rate rising to 21 per cent (compared to 19 per cent for the whole country). Once again, the second half of the 1960s was the period of most rapid growth for both colleges and universities. The pattern in Ontario diverges markedly from that of Canada as a whole in the 1970s. There was not a steady deceleration at both colleges and universities. Over the first half of the 1970s enrolment at Ontario colleges grew much more slowly than for the nation as a whole (10 per cent vs. 33 per cent), while over the second half it grew much faster (27 per cent vs. 18 per cent). Thus college enrolment actually accelerated sharply in Ontario in the later 1970s. In contrast, university enrolment rose at very close to the national rate in Ontario over both the early and the late 1970s. College enrolment actually declined as a fraction of total post-secondary enrolment in Ontario over the early 1970s, from 31 to 27 per cent. In the late 1970s this trend was more than reversed, however, so that over the decade as a whole the proportion at colleges increased from 31 to 32 per cent.

Finally, Table 9 reveals some interesting points about federal manpower training programs (principally the Canada Manpower Training Program, and the Canada Manpower Industrial Training Program). These schemes currently enrol, at both national and Ontario levels, about as many trainees as there are students enrolled in community colleges. While sizeable, they have not grown in enrolment over the 1970s; so that whereas in 1970–71 the total number of manpower trainees for the whole country was 56 per cent of the post-secondary total, by 1980 this ratio was down to 40 per cent. Thus, although in the 1970s there was an enrolment shift away from universities towards colleges, there was also a shift away from manpower training towards post-secondary education. While the former change is in line with the recommendations of much of the recent labour market policy literature, the latter takes the opposite direction to the change generally recommended by much current policy analysis.

III.2 *Expenditure – the overall picture*

Table 11 presents data on total expenditures (i.e., both capital and operating). To a large extent the expenditure picture mirrors the enrolment situation. A striking difference is the lower concentration at the elementary and secondary levels. While in 1980–81, for example, 89 per cent of total full-time enrolment in conventional programs at schools, colleges, and universities was elementary or secondary, only 71 per cent of total expenditure occurred at these levels. It is also interesting to note that while the enrolment share of elementary and secondary schools has been falling since 1970, the expenditure share has been rising. (The consequences for relative per capita spending at the elementary-secondary and post-secondary levels are shown in Table 12.)

Another way in which expenditure trends diverge from those in enrolment, is in the relative spending on colleges and universities. For the country as a whole, for example, over the 1970s college enrolment rose from 35 to 41 per cent of the post-secondary total. The proportional increase in expenditures, from 19 to 29 per cent, however, was much greater. The contrast is even larger for Ontario alone. Although the enrolment shift – an increase in post-secondary share from 31 to 32 per cent for the colleges – was very small, the colleges benefited from an increase from 15 to 26 per cent in their share of total post-secondary expenditures.

The expenditure and enrolment trends of Tables 9–11 give only a crude idea of what must have been happening to the real education inputs offered by the system to students at different levels. There are two reasons: (1) the expenditure data of Table 11 mix capital, operating, and student aid expenditures; and (2) so far we have deflated, using the CPI, which may have followed quite a different path from that of the prices of the inputs used by the educational system.

Table 12 shows operating expenditures per full-time student by level, at five-year intervals over the period 1960–80, deflated by the CPI.[7] It suggests a continuous increase in real per capita spending at all levels since 1960 for Canada as a whole, with the most rapid rate of increase at the elementary-secondary level, an intermediate rate of increase at the colleges, and relatively slow growth at the universities. The result is an indication that while in 1960 real per capita spending at the colleges and universities was, respectively, 3.8 and 6.4 times that at the elementary-secondary level, by 1980 these ratios had declined to 2.1 and 3.4. In

---

7 If full-time equivalent (FTE) data were used, the elementary-secondary picture of course would not change. There would be a downward influence on the trend in per capita spending at the post-secondary level; this would not be especially large, however. Rather than declining by 20.0 per cent from 1970 to 1980, real per capita spending at Ontario universities would have fallen 21.5 per cent, for example. For the country as a whole the 1.9 per cent increase from 1970 to 1980 for the universities would translate into a 1.4 per cent decline.

TABLE 11

Total expenditures in 1971 dollars (deflated by CPI), by level, Canada and Ontario, selected years, 1960–80

	Canada						Ontario					
	(1)	(2)	(3)	(4)	(5)	(6)	(7)	(8)	(9)	(10)	(11)	(12)
School year beginning in	Elementary and secondary	College	University	Total (1)–(3)	Technical and vocational	Manpower training	Elementary and secondary	College	University	Total (7)–(9)	Technical and vocational	Manpower training
Levels (000s)												
1960	1779.4	77.2	365.6	2222.2	63.2	n.a.	645.4	24.0	133.8	803.2	12.9	n.a.
65	2940.0	120.5	898.3	3958.8	187.1	n.a.	1082.8	39.9	337.6	1406.3	50.1	n.a.
70	4949.7	436.1	1816.2	7202.0	468.5	293.7	1898.5	142.3	799.2	2840.0	126.7	84.3
75	5941.5	658.8	1921.0	8521.3	585.8	352.5	2052.5	202.4	748.3	3003.2	147.2	102.2
80	6729.0	802.1	1965.4	9496.4	581.6	383.3	2453.9	244.7	710.5	3409.1	150.1	119.6
Percentage composition												
1960	80.1	3.5	11.5	100.0	2.8*	n.a.	80.4	3.0	16.7	100.0	1.6*	n.a.
65	74.3	3.0	22.7	100.0	4.7*	n.a.	74.1	2.7	23.1	100.0	3.4*	n.a.
70	68.7	6.1	25.2	100.0	6.5*	4.1*	66.8	5.0	28.1	100.0	4.5*	3.0*
75	69.7	7.7	22.5	100.0	6.9*	4.1*	68.3	6.7	24.9	100.0	4.9*	3.4*
80	70.9	8.4	20.7	100.0	6.1*	4.0*	72.0	7.2	20.8	100.0	4.4*	3.5*

* Percentage of total excluding technical and vocational, and manpower training
SOURCE: Statistics Canada, *Education in Canada*, various issues

TABLE 12

Operating expenditures in 1970–71 dollars per full-time student deflated by CPI by level, Canada and Ontario, selected years, 1960–80

Selected years	Canada			Ontario		
	Elementary and Secondary	Post-secondary		Elementary and secondary	Post-secondary	
		College	University		College	University
	Levels (1970–71 dollars)					
1960–61	$ 343	$1295	$2182	$ 375	n.a.	$2649
65–66	483	1381	2621	507	n.a.	3185
70–71	758	1986	4068	810	$2388	4490
75–76	888	2402	4138	894	2776	3836
80–81	1217	2528	4146	1122	2527	3592
	Relative levels (elementary and secondary = 100)					
1960–61	100	378	636	100	n.a.	706
65–66	100	286	543	100	n.a.	628
70–71	100	262	537	100	295	554
75–76	100	270	466	100	311	429
80–81	100	208	341	100	225	320

SOURCE: Calculated from Statistics Canada data appearing in *Education in Canada* and *Financial Statistics of Education*

Ontario a more complex and somewhat disturbing pattern is suggested: while per capita spending rose steadily at the elementary-secondary level, it peaked in 1970 for the universities and in 1975 for the colleges, with a subsequent decline.

Table 12 suggests at least one alarming phenomenon: real per capita spending at Ontario universities appears to have declined from $4500 to $3600 (in 1970–71 dollars) over the 1970s, a drop of about 20 per cent. Can we accept this suggestion as bearing much relation to the truth? That is, did the universities' costs escalate at approximately the rate of inflation given by the CPI? Table 13 answers this question by using separate input price indexes, which we have constructed for each level of education in Canada and Ontario. These indexes put a 70 per cent weight on the average salaries of full-time teachers, and a 30 per cent weight on the CPI.[8] They implicitly assume that the average quality of full-time teachers has

8 In 1979–80 teachers' salaries formed 68–70 per cent of total operating costs at both the elementary-secondary and university levels, for both Ontario alone and Canada as a whole. (See Statistics Canada, *Financial Statistics of Education*, no. 81-208. The calculation cannot be made for colleges from this source.) We are clearly assuming that non-salary expenses

TABLE 13

Operating expenditures in 1970–71 dollars per full-time student deflated by input price indexes,*
by level, Canada and Ontario, selected years, 1970 and 1980

Selected years	Canada			Ontario		
	Elementary and secondary	Post-secondary		Elementary and secondary	Post-secondary	
		College	University		College	University
	Levels (1970–71 dollars)					
1970–71	$ 758	$1986	$4068	$ 810	$2388	$4490
1980–81	934	2360	4319	883	2378	3592
	Relative levels					
1970–71	100	262	537	100	295	554
1980–81	100	253	462	100	269	407

* In each case the input price index puts a 70 per cent weight on average salaries of full-time
teachers, and 30 per cent on the CPI.
SOURCE: Calculated from Statistics Canada data appearing in *Education in Canada* and *Financial
Statistics of Education*

not changed at any level. While this assumption is not precisely correct, it is
sufficiently close for present purposes. Because of data availability problems, the
only two years of the five shown in Table 12 that can be compared are 1970–71
and 1980–81.

Table 13 shows that the picture provided when deflating by the CPI is in many
respects misleading. For both the country as a whole and Ontario alone teachers'
salaries increased very rapidly at the elementary-secondary level over the 1970s
and less rapidly at the post-secondary level. College teachers' salaries rose more
quickly than those of university teachers. The result is that the decline in per
capita spending at the post-secondary level relative to the elementary-secondary
level is reduced. For colleges across Canada as a whole the relative decline almost
disappears, while for universities across Canada as a whole and colleges in
Ontario about two-thirds of the apparent relative decline is eliminated.

---

increased at a rate close to the general rate of inflation. It would be desirable to use a better
price series for these non-salary expenses, but it does not appear that one is available. The
present approach constitutes an improvement over the methods that some others have
employed. For example, the Ontario Council on University Affairs deflates by the CPI when
comparing trends in relative per capita spending in the schools and universities. (See OCUA,
1982, 38.)

In one very important respect, however, Table 13 tells much the same story as Table 12. It happens that over the period 1970–80 the average salaries of full-time Ontario university teachers rose at a rate almost exactly equal to the increase in the CPI. Thus the suggestion that real per capita spending at Ontario universities had fallen from about $4500 in 1970 to $3600 in 1980 (in 1970–71 dollars) appears to have been quite accurate. The 20 per cent decline in real per capita spending stands. As a result there also remains a very sizeable drop in spending relative to the elementary-secondary level. Whereas in 1970 per capita spending at Ontario universities stood at 5.5 times that at the elementary-secondary level, by 1980 the ratio had fallen to 4.1.

As discussed in the next section, since 1965 there has been a considerable enrolment shift at the universities, both for the country as a whole and for Ontario alone, away from arts towards programs that are more costly to provide. This change must mean that real per capita spending *within* university faculties actually declined faster than 20 per cent, on average, for Ontario in the 1970s. In the absence of significant increases in teaching productivity or a decline in the fraction of operating expenditure directed towards research, Ontario universities must have been forced to offer students declining real educational inputs.[9] In other words, the 'quality' of university education has declined in Ontario.

III.3 *Post-secondary enrolment – the detailed picture*
Figures 22 through 25 chart the rise of full-time enrolments in universities and colleges in Canada as a whole and Ontario alone, respectively. As we found above, the most striking feature of the post-secondary enrolment picture is the extraordinary overall growth over the last two decades. Between 1960 and 1982 the number of full-time post-secondary students rose abut 4.5 times in Canada as a whole, and 5.25 times in Ontario alone. Since the post-secondary age population (those aged eighteen to twenty-four) only approximately doubled for both Canada and Ontario, this indicates slightly more than twice the participation rate for Canada and considerably more than twice the rate for Ontario.

A second important feature of post-secondary enrolment growth is that it did not occur at a constant rate. The annual growth rate for total post-secondary enrolment, for the country as a whole, rose gently to 14 per cent in 1967, declined

9 Some tangible indications are provided in OCUA (1982). Between the 1972 and 1980 academic years the amount spent by Ontario universities on library acquisitions dropped steadily from $12.7 million to $8.2 million in 1972 dollars, while between 1976 and 1980 furniture and equipment expenditures decreased from $23.4 million to 17.9 in 1976 dollars. (Input-specific price indexes developed by OCUA are used.) Finally, the full-time academic staff complement fell from 13 267 in 1977 to 13 051 in 1980. (See OCUA, 1982, 42–4.)

Figure 22
Full-time enrolment in Canadian universities, annual growth rates vs. time, 1961–82

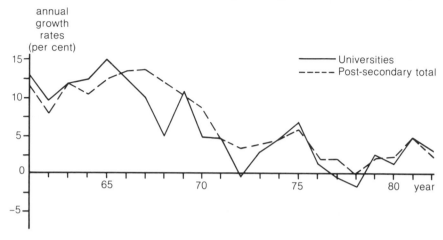

Figure 23
Full-time enrolment in Canadian community colleges, annual growth rates vs. time, 1961–82

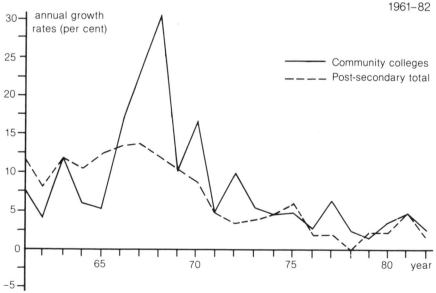

Figure 24
Full-time enrolment in Ontario universities, annual growth rates vs. time, 1961–82

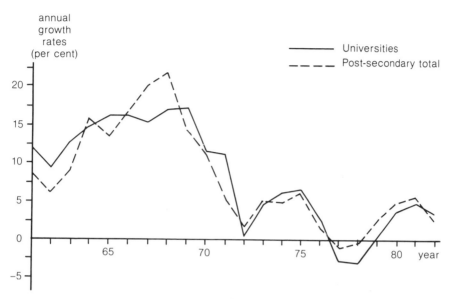

to 3 per cent in 1972, experienced a short-lived increase to 6 per cent in 1975, and then fell to a fairly steady 2 per cent over the period 1976–80. Over the last two years there has been another resurgence. Turning to Ontario the major differences are that the gradual increase in the growth rate over the 1960s, did not peak until 1968 and did so at a higher rate (22 per cent); the decline to 1972 was more precipitous, ending with a growth rate of just 1.6 per cent; during the 1976–80 period there were two years of negative growth: 1977 and 1978; and the recent period of resurgence has been more marked. In other words, fluctuations in post-secondary enrolment in Ontario have been the same, qualitatively, as for the country as a whole, but they have been more severe.

Another interesting point concerns the relative growth of college and university enrolments. Prior to 1966 enrolment grew considerably faster at the universities than at the colleges for both Canada and Ontario. Subsequently, in the two years 1967 and 1968 enrolment suddenly grew much faster at the colleges than at the universities (average rates of 27 per cent vs. 8 per cent for Canada, and 34 per cent vs. 16 per cent for Ontario). Since that period, for the country as a whole, college enrolment has grown more steadily and at a higher average rate than university enrolment. In Ontario, from 1971 to 1976 college enrolment increased more slowly than university enrolment and actually suffered two years of nega-

Figure 25
Full-time enrolment in Ontario community colleges, annual growth rates vs. time,
1961–82

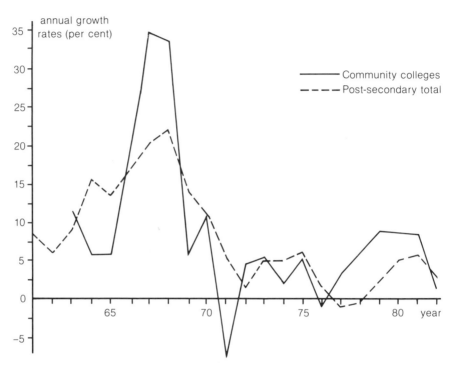

tive growth. Since 1977, however, Ontario has reverted to the national pattern,
with higher enrolment growth for colleges than for universities.

Overall, without too much violence to the facts, we can think of the 1960s as a
decade of rapid post-secondary enrolment growth and of the period since as one
of slow growth. The contrast in average annual growth rates is well marked: 11.3
per cent vs. 3.2 per cent for Canada as a whole, and 13.7 per cent vs. 3.2 per cent
for Ontario alone. To some extent the slow-down reflects the slower growth of the
post-secondary age population since 1970: an average annual growth rate of 2.1
per cent in Canada and 2.2 per cent in Ontario vs. rates of 4.4 per cent in Canada
and 5.1 per cent in Ontario in the 1960s. However, if participation rates had
increased as rapidly since 1970 as they did in the 1960s, the average enrolment
growth rates would have been 9.0 per cent and 10.8 per cent for Canada and
Ontario, respectively. Clearly there must have been a considerable deceleration of
participation rates.

TABLE 14

Percentage composition of full-time, undergraduate enrolment at universities, Canada and Ontario, selected years, 1960–79

School year beginning in	Arts	Science	Business	Education	Engineering	Law	Medicine	Other
CANADA								
1960	39.8	9.1	5.9	9.8	13.6	2.3	3.9	15.6
65	43.7	13.1	5.5	11.3	8.7	2.2	2.4	13.1
70	38.8	15.9	6.0	11.4	8.4	2.7	2.1	14.7
75	34.0	15.8	8.7	10.0	7.9	2.9	2.5	18.2
79	30.2	15.9	11.7	7.7	9.6	3.1	2.6	19.2
ONTARIO								
1960	41.7	7.5	5.1	2.0	14.7	3.1	5.8	20.1
65	48.4	13.1	4.2	1.7	11.4	3.1	3.5	14.6
70	48.5	15.8	3.4	3.6	9.2	2.6	1.9	15.0
75	42.4	16.3	4.7	5.1	8.4	2.9	1.8	18.4
79	36.1	16.8	9.1	2.8	10.3	3.0	1.9	20.0

NOTE: In 1960, 1970, 1975, and 1979 some enrolment in an arts and science category (not disaggregated) was reported. Such enrolment is divided between 'arts' and 'science' here in the same proportions as reported in 'arts' and (separately) 'science.' That this is an appropriate procedure is confirmed by comparison with the 1961–9 figures, where complete disaggregation occurred in the primary data.

SOURCE: Computed from Statistics Canada, *Fall Enrolment in Universities and Colleges*, various issues

There has indeed been a remarkable slow-down in the rise of participation rates. From 1960 to 1970 the overall post-secondary participation rate more than doubled in Ontario, rising from 9 to 19 per cent, and somewhat less than doubled for Canada, increasing from 10 to 18 per cent. Over the twelve years since 1970 there has been an additional increase of only 2.5 percentage points for both Canada and Ontario.

Finally, important changes have taken place in the composition of enrolment within the post-secondary sector. It is difficult to obtain a long time series for composition of college enrolment, but the data for universities are readily available and are shown in Table 14.

One of the most striking things highlighted by Table 14 is the behaviour of arts enrolment. In the early 1960s, arts faculties were the fastest growing part of the university system. From 1960 to 1965, for example, the arts share of full-time undergraduate enrolment rose from 40 to 44 per cent for Canada as a whole, and from 42 to 48 per cent for Ontario alone. (While 1965 was in fact the peak year for Ontario, the arts share rose to 45 per cent in 1966 for the country as a whole before starting to decline.) In the late 1960s, however, arts started to lose ground and since that time has done so steadily. The decline in the importance of arts enrolment has been dramatic. At the national level the 1979 figure – 30 per cent – represented a loss of one-third the peak 1966 enrolment share. In Ontario alone the decline was somewhat less dramatic, but by 1979 the arts share had fallen to 36 per cent, a drop of one-quarter from the 1965 peak of 48 per cent.

In science, as in arts, enrolment increased in relative importance in the early 1960s. Unlike arts, science continued to rise in importance, so that by 1970 it had approximately doubled its enrolment share, to 16 per cent, at both the national and the Ontario levels. Since 1970, however, the science share has been stable. We must look elsewhere to find the gainers that have taken up the ground lost by arts over this period.

In order of importance, the faculties whose enrolment share has increased most in the 1970s are business (a doubling at the national level, to 12 per cent, and a tripling in Ontario, to 9 per cent), the 'other' category (comprising faculties such as agriculture, architecture, fine arts, home economics, journalism, music, nursing, physical education) with increases from 15 per cent for both Canada and Ontario to 19 per cent for Canada and 20 per cent for Ontario, and engineering, whose share rose from 8 per cent for Canada and 9 per cent for Ontario to 10 per cent in both cases.

Earlier in this section we saw that there has been a sizeable shift of enrolment share from the universities towards the colleges since about 1975, both in the country as a whole and in Ontario alone. We pointed out that this reflects precisely the kind of re-allocation of educational resources that according to several recent documents in the labour market policy literature ought to occur in the future. Here again we find that dramatic changes of precisely the type we are told ought to happen in the 1980s already took place in the 1970s. There has been an enormous re-allocation of university-level resources away from arts towards business, engineering, and a wide variety of other vocational forms of study. Scrutiny of the recent studies advocating re-allocation towards more vocational programs reveals little appreciation that such an adjustment has already taken place.

IV RECENT TRENDS IN POST-SECONDARY EDUCATION – EXPLANATIONS

In this section we analyse the causes of the enrolment and expenditure trends identified in the previous section. We show that the observed changes in post-secondary participation rates and enrolment structure can to a great extent be explained with the help of the human capital and informational models of education. A complete analysis of enrolment is not possible, however, without paying attention to factors like cohort size effects in earnings and the state of the market for highly qualified manpower – which step outside the simple framework of these models. Finally, the vicissitudes of expenditures, we argue, can be traced to a substantial degree to changes in the form of federal subsidies to post-secondary education.

IV.1 Basic features of enrolment demand and supply

In Chapter 2 we considered models in which education technology takes a particularly simple form. In both the human capital and signalling models presented the only input into schooling is the student's time. In this subsection we shall first see to what extent the nature of enrolment demand over the last two decades can be explained in models with this very simple technology. Then we shall introduce 'other inputs,' thereby bringing in considerations of supply as well as demand.

In Chapter 2 we found that the following condition determined optimal years of schooling in the human capital model:

$$R\Delta H^s / r = RH \qquad (3)$$

The term on the right-hand side of (3) is the product of the rental rate on human capital, R, and the current stock of human capital, H. In the simple schooling technology we assumed in the human capital model, forgone earnings are the only cost of schooling. The right-hand side of (3) is therefore the marginal cost of raising H by one unit. The left-hand term gives the perpetual increase in earnings resulting from another unit of H, $R\Delta H^s$, discounted to the present by dividing by the interest rate, r. The left-hand term thus gives the marginal benefit of human capital investment. Condition (3) says that one will go to school up until the point where the marginal benefit from doing so falls to the marginal cost.

The R of human capital theory is a wage rate. We see from (3) that a change in wages will not affect the schooling decision. A general rise in wage rates leaves the equality in (3) undisturbed. Thus the general rise in wages experienced in the post-war period would not produce the observed upsurge in post-secondary participation if the only input into schooling were student's time.

It is also easy to discuss the effect of the increase in financial assistance to students that took place in the 1960s (the Canada Student Loan Plan, for example, was introduced in 1964) in the simple human capital framework. A loan plan reduces the interest rate confronting many students. This increases the discounted returns from additional H, and leaves the current costs unchanged. An increase in length of time spent in school is a straightforward prediction. Similarly, a bursary system must raise desired length of schooling. It does so by removing some of the costs on the right-hand side of (3).

Although the increase in financial assistance on the part of governments in the 1960s was very sizeable, it does not seem likely that it was responsible for the bulk of the increase in enrolment. In order to explain the increase in participation rates in the 1960s we have to turn to somewhat different models from those considered in Chapter 2. First, we ask what difference it will make if we allow the use of 'other inputs' as well as student's time. That is, we allow for 'direct costs' of schooling as well as forgone earnings.

The informational model of Chapter 3 was set up with a more interesting education technology than that used in Chapter 2. 'Other inputs,' K, as well as student's time, s, are used to produce information of quality θ. We can use the informational model to investigate what happens under this more general technology. The results obtained are not specific to the informational approach. They would be derived in many other models of education with a similar technology.

Over the post-war period as a whole there has clearly been a considerable decline in the direct costs of schooling relative to the forgone earnings costs.[10] This means that there was a fall in P_K relative to $\mathcal{E}$, reducing the costs of schooling relative to expected returns (since the former depend partly on P_K). Hence the schooling output desired by the representative individual must have risen in order to make marginal cost once more equal to expected marginal returns. At the same time, however, a drop in $P_K/\mathcal{E}$ has a substitution effect. A more 'other inputs intensive' technology of information production should be used. This substitution effect may outweigh the scale effect, with the result that although schooling output increases, time spent in school actually declines.

While we might not be able to predict the effect of a drop in P_K and rise in $\mathcal{E}$ in a free market setting, it is somewhat easier in a world of predominantly public education. It is probably true that the public sector is relatively slow to respond to students' desire for rising K/s. If this is the case, the substitution effect is weakened, and the scale effect may be expected to predominate. We therefore argue that the decline in $P_K/\mathcal{E}$ over the post-war period probably has much to do with the increased length of education observed and with the rise in post-secondary participation rates.

10 While evidence on forgone earnings is necessarily poor, that a considerable relative decline in direct costs has occurred is clear from the time path of tuition fees. Surveys showed that arts and science students' median fees in the 1956–57 academic year were $298 and average fees in 1961–62 were $383. (Statistics Canada, *University Student Expenditure and Income in Canada*, Publication Nos 81-509 and 81-520.) By comparison, the average fee charged for arts students in Ontario by the six largest universities was $833 in 1980–81. (This overstates the average for all arts students in Canada, since Ontario universities had relatively high fees.) In constant 1956–57 dollars, fees increased from $298 in 1956–57 to $354 in 1961–62 but dropped to $259 by 1980–81.

If the decline in the direct costs of schooling relative to indirect had been steady over the last two decades, there should have been a constant trend towards increasing post-secondary participation rates. In fact these participation rates increased rapidly up to 1971 but have only crept up slowly since. While certain special features of demand and supply conditions (discussed below) help to explain this discontinuity, it appears that the explanation may lie partly in the fact that the decline of direct costs relative to indirect has not been steady over the last two decades.

Welch (1979) has argued that cohort size had a strong negative effect on relative earnings in the United States over the period 1967–75.[11] If members of different age groups are imperfect substitutes in production, an especially large cohort is fated to have relatively low earnings throughout its lifetime (although the effect is found to be most pronounced when the cohort is young). Cohorts born in both Canada and the United States between 1945 and 1965 were extraordinarily large. (The peak number of births occurred in Canada in 1959 and in the United States in 1957. The number of births in Canada in 1959 was about 32 per cent greater than in both 1949 and 1969.) We might therefore expect that the baby boom generation would be strongly affected by the cohort size impact on earnings.

In the light of the cohort size effect on earnings, one might conjecture that the participation rate trends of the last two decades could be explained as follows. Up until about 1967 post-secondary graduates belonged to the small pre-1945 cohorts. They therefore experienced steadily rising forgone earnings, direct costs of schooling fell rapidly as a fraction of the total, and desired length of schooling steadily increased. After 1967, however, graduates belonged to the increasingly large baby boom cohorts. Forgone earnings (and expected future earnings) stopped rising so quickly and may even have fallen. The downward progress of the ratio of indirect to total costs slowed, and the trend towards higher desired educational attainment was therefore interrupted. Finally, as we moved into the late 1970s and early 1980s, students entering the post-secondary system began to belong to steadily smaller cohorts. (The peak 1959 cohort would have left high school in 1977–78.) Indirect costs fell relative to total once more and desired

---

11 We are not aware of an age-related time series on earnings that provides direct evidence for Canada on these trends. However, the considerable relative worsening of unemployment rates for the young is consistent with declining relative earnings. More direct evidence is provided by the time series on graduates' starting salaries given by the Pay Research Bureau data. These data appear in our Table 16 (Chapter 6), which shows that after 1970 for honours arts, pass arts and science, and business graduates real starting salaries declined up until 1979 or 1980.

educational attainment again began to increase, giving a fillip to post-secondary participation rates.

While the above argument is clearly speculative, the causation suggested appears to fit the facts rather well. Detailed empirical work on the effects of cohort size on the demand for education is certainly warranted.[12]

IV.2 Supply conditions

To some extent the extraordinary increase in post-secondary participation in the 1960s and subsequent stagnation, as well as the enrolment shifts that have been observed, appear to be explained by certain simple supply factors.

During the 1960s there was a considerable increase in the number of universities, an explosion of non-university post-secondary institutions (principally community colleges), and a broadening of programs offered at the typical institution. One result was a much more even geographic distribution of post-secondary institutions and programs. This extension of the post-secondary system, a supply side factor, would be expected to increase participation rates, because it would dramatically decrease the true direct costs of post-secondary participation for many students. Indeed, in his recent detailed study of the college attendance behaviour of U.S. males, Bishop (1977) finds that direct costs of college attendance (e.g., tuition, travel costs, and room and board) have a significant large negative effect on the probability of college attendance. On this basis he suggests that 'an important part of the upward trend in enrollment rates during the fifties and sixties can be attributed to the establishment of ... colleges in states and metropolitan areas where they had not previously existed, the expansion of student-aid programs, and the liberalization of admissions policies resulting from the creation of community colleges. By 1970 the impact of these policy shifts may have largely run their course' (302).

The federal government has played an important role over the years in subsidizing post-secondary expenditures. The magnitude and form of subsidy have gone through dramatic changes. It appears that these changes may have influenced both the overall scale of supply of post-secondary places, and the composition of that supply in ways that account not only for some of the observed enrolment trends, but for important expenditure trends as well.

During the last two decades there have been three successive regimes as far as federal support to post-secondary education is concerned.[13] From 1951 to 1967

12 Martin Dooley of McMaster University is currently engaged in research that examines the cohort size effect on earnings of Canadian men over the period since 1972, using Statistics Canada's Survey of Consumer Finance (SCF) data.

13 The following discussion is based on Leslie's careful treatment of the subject. See Leslie (1980), 146–59.

the federal government made direct grants to the universities, offering a flat, per-student subsidy. Each province was allocated an aggregate subsidy based on its population. This total was then allocated among the universities in a province in proportion to their enrolment. The scale of the grants was such that, on average, universities received from 14 to 23 per cent of their revenue from direct federal grants in the period 1954–64 (Leslie, 1980, 147).

One would expect a scheme such as that used by the federal government up to 1967 to have complex and interesting effects. In provinces with only one university, there would have been no stimulus to enrolment, since the total subsidy for the single university would be fixed by provincial population and would not be related to the number of students. In provinces with several universities, like Ontario, an individual institution would have faced a generous federal subsidy to enrolment at the margin. But note that this subsidy was of a very special kind. Because it was a flat subsidy per student, enrolment in the cheapest programs received the highest proportional rate of subsidy. To some extent this high rate of subsidy may explain the shift toward arts and science enrolment in the early 1960s (especially strong in Ontario, the province with the largest number of universities). Remarkably, this shift terminated in 1967, only one year before the flat subsidy came to an end and was replaced by a uniform proportional subsidy on all expenditures.

In 1968 the federal government moved to an extremely generous, open-ended scheme, undertaking to finance one-half the operating costs of all post-secondary institutions in the country. This scheme remained in place until 1977. What effects would we expect from such a scheme?

Since the 50 per cent rate of subsidy adopted after 1968 represented an increase in the scale of subsidy, we would expect even more impetus towards expansion of post-secondary enrolment in the period 1968–77 than before. We would also expect a shift in enrolment growth away from the cheapest programs, like arts and science at the universities, towards the more expensive. Finally, since all forms of post-secondary education were subsidized in the same generous manner, we would expect faster growth than previously for the community colleges.

The changes we would have predicted to result from the 1968–77 arrangements for the most part have been witnessed. As discussed earlier, after 1967 there was a dramatic shift in university enrolment away from arts, towards the more vocational and more expensive programs. Also, from 1968 to 1977 college enrolment rose steadily from 33 to 39 per cent of the (full-time) post-secondary total for Canada as a whole. However, as we have already seen, overall enrolment growth decelerated over the period.

As shown above, one reason that post-secondary enrolment growth should have decelerated in the 1970s, despite the federal government's move to a more universal subsidy at a higher rate, was the influence of the large number of people in the baby boom cohorts on the forgone earnings and expected lifetime earnings of those cohorts. In part the reason for the slow-down may lie in certain additional enrolment demand factors. However, the reason for the apparent contradiction may lie partly on the supply side. The new federal subsidy did not apply to enrolment, as the previous scheme had done. It was a subsidy to expenditure. One implication has already been discussed: a shift in enrolment supply towards the more expensive programs. Such a shift must involve some tendency for *total* enrolment supply to grow more slowly. But in addition, the universities were free to spend their subsidies on research, rather than on lower tuition fees or higher-quality instruction, which presumably would have provided more stimulus to enrolment.

In 1977 federal financing for post-secondary education moved into its current phase. Under the title 'Established Programs Financing' (EPF) the federal government now offers a grant to the provinces (partly in the form of tax points and partly in cash payments) to finance health and education expenditures. In fact the provinces are free to treat these transfers as lump sum. There is therefore no incentive effect on post-secondary enrolment or expenditure. Switching from a 50 per cent subsidy on all post-secondary operating expenditure to no subsidy (at the margin) ought to decrease provincial expenditure on post-secondary education but would have no substitution effect between different programs at the universities or between the universities and colleges.

To some extent, enrolment and expenditure trends in the late 1970s and early 1980s are consistent with the supply side forces created by the change in federal subsidy regime. For example, whereas between 1970 and 1975 real per capita spending at the post-secondary level rose 4.4 per cent (deflating by the CPI) for the country as a whole, between 1975 and 1980 there was no change. (See Table 12.) The predicted lack of any substitution effects also seems to be borne out. The trends towards a lower arts enrolment share and an enrolment shift from the universities to the colleges, established under the 1968–77 regime, continued into the post–1977 period, as we have seen earlier in this chapter. While these trends are consistent with federal supply-side influences, expenditure trends in Ontario are rather puzzling.

It is true that over the EPF period real per capita spending at Ontario colleges and universities has been declining. For the colleges this situation represents a reversal of the increased per capita spending over the early 1970s. (Again, see Table 12.) At the universities, however, per capita spending has been falling throughout the 1970s. In fact the rate of decline over 1970–75 (14.6 per cent) was considerably greater than that over 1975–80 (6.4 per cent). Why should spending have flagged so much more during a period of 50 per cent subsidy than in one of zero (marginal) subsidy? This question is especially puzzling in view of (1) the opposite behaviour recorded in the other nine provinces, and (2) the continuity of administration in Ontario. Leslie (1980, 90) offers the following explanation. Ontario expanded its universities much more rapidly than the other provinces in the 1960s. (See our Figures 22 and 24.) The sharp enrolment deceleration of the early 1970s therefore came as more of a shock to Ontario than to other provincial governments. Ontario feared that it had already 'over-expanded' and therefore pursued a policy of retrenchment.

IV.3 Demand conditions
In the preceding subsection we examined special conditions affecting the supply of places in post-secondary institutions. In this subsection we examine factors affecting enrolment demand.

In analysing the determinants of enrolment demand it is important to recognize that there are changes in the tightness of the market for post-secondary graduates that vary independently of overall labour market conditions. In other words, substitutability between university- and college-educated manpower – highly qualified manpower or 'HQM' – and other types of labour is imperfect. Special conditions of excess demand and supply can therefore exist in the market for HQM. We would expect them to have a direct impact on the demand for post-secondary enrolment. If there is excess demand for HQM, starting salaries for graduates will be high and enrolment will tend to increase. If there is excess supply, we would expect the opposite to occur.

Imperfect substitutability between HQM and other labour cannot be captured in the simple human capital model presented in Chapter 2, where all labour is homogeneous. However, it *is* a feature of the informational model. Workers with higher education output θ, other things being equal, have less uncertain characteristics and are not perfect substitutes for workers with lower θ. We shall argue below that there has long been a trend towards increasing specialization and division of labour, and that this process has led to an increase in the relative demand for workers with more information, that is, with better-known characteristics. This means that secularly increasing specialization has acted as a constant force to increase the relative demand for HQM.

Some of the most important changes in enrolment demand over the last two decades may be explained largely by developments in the market for HQM. For example, the relative demand for HQM has tended to increase because of (1) sectoral shifts away from agriculture and manufacturing towards services, (2) the rising importance of public sector employment, and (3) technological change that has favoured HQM (an example of which is increasing specialization, with the impact hypothesized above). It is believed by many that the relative increase in the demand for HQM, rather than the decline in direct costs of schooling relative to indirect discussed in Subsection V.1, is the major reason for the secular trend towards increased length of schooling and rising post-secondary participation rates.[14]

Some also believe that conditions in the market for HQM can help explain the enrolment slow-down of the 1970s. Freeman (1975) has argued that until 1967, in the United States, the increase in relative demand for 'college graduates' (includes university graduates) was stronger than the increase in supply. After that date supply began to outstrip demand. The result, he suggests, was a decline in earnings differentials for the more educated, which in turn was the cause of the enrolment slow-down. While there is no parallel Canadian study, one might make the same case for Canada, where we also had an extremely rapid increase in the number of post-secondary graduates in the late 1960s, and both a decrease in graduates' starting salaries relative to general earnings and a sharp enrolment slow-down, in the early 1970s.[15]

If the secular increase in the relative demand for HQM had continued, one would have expected the enrolment slow-down of the early 1970s to have been fairly short-lived, assuming that enrolment demand is largely driven by the market for HQM. That is, if the demand curve for HQM was steadily marching out, a drop in earnings differentials according to education would have been temporary. The decline in the number of graduates induced by this drop would have restored earnings differentials, and enrolment could once more rise quite rapidly (but not as rapidly as it did prior to the collapse of differentials) without affecting the earnings differential.

In fact, post-secondary enrolment demand did not return to a steady upward march after an early 1970s hesitation. Its trend through the 1970s was one of sluggish growth. The only way this pattern could be explained in the framework that concentrates on the relative demand for and supply of HQM, it would seem, is by a break in the steady growth of the demand for HQM. Just such a break was clearly caused by the decline in public sector demand for HQM.

Whereas between 1960 and 1970 total public sector employment in Canada grew by 52 per cent, rising from 13.6 to 15.5 per cent of total employment, from 1970 to 1980 the growth rate was only 25 per cent, and public sector jobs declined

---

14 Freeman (1975) expresses the dominant view that the increased relative demand for HQM is most important. Bishop (1977) dissents. See also the discussion in Stager (1981, 114–19).
15 See Table 16 (Chapter 6) for evidence on starting salaries.

to 14.5 per cent of total employment.[16] The impact of the slow-down was especially severe on university enrolment, because the decline was caused in large part by weakening demand for teachers. (Taking teachers out of the totals, public sector employment grew 45 per cent in the 1960s and 32 per cent in the 1970s.) Clark and Zsigmond (1981) found that 42 per cent of those graduating from university in 1976 in Canada who were in employment two years later had jobs in the education sector. It is not hard to understand that the virtual drying-up of openings for teachers at the elementary and secondary levels would have a severe impact on university enrolment, especially in faculties such as arts. If the demand for teachers had grown as fast in the 1970s as in the 1960s, rough calculations indicate that total post-secondary enrolment would have increased by something like 57 per cent over the decade, rather than 35 per cent, and the post-secondary participation rate would have risen to about 23 per cent in 1980, from 18.3 per cent in 1970, rather than to the observed 19.5 per cent.[17]

Finally, in this subsection, we should like to explore two ways in which our informational model can help explain changes in enrolment demand over the last two decades. One, the analysis of the impact of secularly increasing specialization and division of labour, has already been touched on. The other concerns the impact on the demand for post-secondary education of recent changes in elementary and secondary education.

16 Data on total public sector employment are not available. Statistics Canada does have separate publications on federal, provincial, and local government employment. (Publication Nos 72-004, 72-006, and 72-009. See No. 72-505 for local government prior to 1967.) They provide fairly complete totals. Not only civil servants but employees of all crown corporations, agencies, etc. are included in the federal and provincial figures. Omissions include the entire labour force of the BC provincial government (figures have been reported to Statistics Canada only in recent years) and employment in municipal enterprises (transit, power, school boards, hospitals, etc.). We have compensated for the school board omission by including the totals for full-time elementary and secondary school teachers found in Statistics Canada, *Education in Canada*, Publication No. 81-229.

17 If the number of teachers had grown at the same rate over the 1970s as in the 1960s – 78% – by 1980 there would have been about 560000 full-time teachers instead of the actual 327000. If the extra 233000 had been produced at a steady rate, there would have been an additional 23300 post-secondary graduates per year. In mid-decade there were about 140000 earning first degrees or diplomas each year. (See Statistics Canada, Publication No. 81-229.) Thus in order to fill the additional requirement for teachers, an increase of about 16 per cent in the number of graduates (and therefore in enrolment) would have been required. If enrolment had been 16 per cent higher in 1980, enrolment growth over the 1970s would have been 57 per cent, and the post-secondary participation rate in 1980 would have been 22–26 per cent.

The effects of increased division of labour are easy to analyse in the informational model, once we realize how they show up in the technologies of α and β production. At first it is a little difficult to see how increased specialization can be accommodated in the model, since we have assumed just two types of people and two 'production processes.' The key is to think of them as typical tasks drawn from a world in which there are many. We may ask how these representative tasks would differ between a world of low division and one of high division of labour.

There are two types of skill in our model – general and specialized – represented by α_0 and β_0, on the one hand, and α_1 and β_1 on the other. Everyone has the same endowment of the general skill, but people have different specialized skills. Another way of thinking of this could be that there are many abilities equally distributed over the population, except that each person has an especially large endowment of one ability. With low division of labour each job would require the use of a large number of abilities. Everyone would be fairly proficient at every job, but slightly more proficient at those requiring his / her special ability. With high division of labour, everyone would still be able to do all jobs, but since each job required only a small number of abilities, those whose special endowment corresponded with the job would be far more proficient than others at that job.

Although a basically uniform distribution of abilities with 'special' endowments of single abilities can be only an approximation, it appears to capture something essential about the real world. It is well known that many abilities (e.g., mathematical, musical), have an extremely unequal distribution. We therefore argue that it is appropriate to think of an increase in the component of output that can be produced only by 'special' skills, α_1 and β_1, relative to the component produced by 'general' skills, α_0 and β_0, as reflecting increased specialization or division of labour.

In Chapter 3 it was explained that, except under extreme assumptions, an increase in α_1 and β_1, relative to α_0 and β_0, leads to a general desire for a rise in the schooling output, θ; that is, workers want to become better informed about their true abilities before entering the labour market. We would expect this to lead to a desire for increased length of schooling, unless students are being offered increasingly other-inputs-intensive education, making greater θ possible with less inputs of time. Thus, secularly increasing specialization and division of labour should lead to a continual trend towards higher educational attainment, likely to be expressed in increased length of schooling. In other words, according to the informational model, increasing specialization is responsible for continually increasing relative demand for highly qualified manpower, or HQM.

The second insight offered by the informational model concerns developments at the elementary and secondary levels. Because education at this level is not primarily vocational, those concerned with the impact of education and training on labour markets tend to forget that important changes have been taking place in the public schools, and that these changes can have consequences at the post-secondary level.

We saw earlier that real per capita spending at the elementary and secondary level has been increasing both absolutely, and relative to post-secondary spending, throughout the 1960s and 1970s. In fact, real spending per elementary or secondary student is now about twice as high relative to spending per university student as it was in 1960 (deflating by the CPI). In addition, there has been a well noted trend towards a broader and more flexible curriculum, as well as towards innovative teaching techniques. We think this trend likely implies (1) that more schooling output can now be produced with smaller inputs of student time, whether the output is human capital or information; and (2) that more information is being accumulated by the typical elementary or secondary student, because a wider range of subjects may be investigated.

The implication for post-secondary education of greater outputs at the elementary and secondary level is clear. If people get more output before leaving the schools, other things being constant, there will be less need to add further output at the post-secondary level. In other words, each improvement in the quality of elementary and secondary education should reduce the demand for post-secondary education.[18] This development may help explain the levelling-off of participation rates in post-secondary education in the 1970s. It may also help explain the reduced arts enrolment share, if a primary purpose of arts education is information acquisition.

Since there is a climate of opinion that the last two decades have seen 'declining standards' in the schools, the above argument may seem novel, and perhaps questionable. The idea that the quality of education in the schools has generally been declining appears to be founded on the observations that students (1) have less compulsory subjects and, in particular, need spend less time at 'core' subjects like English and mathematics; and (2) do poorly, overall, in tests of English ability, mathematics, general knowledge, etc. While disappointment with the basic academic abilities of high school graduates is hardly new, some deterioration is not inconsistent with our argument. More information investment, and

18 This prediction is quite unambiguous. Better elementary and secondary education may be thought of as increasing the 'endowments' of human capital and information possessed by high school graduates. Higher endowments mean higher costs of post-secondary education (i.e., greater forgone earnings). Other things being constant, there higher costs must reduce (1) the number who choose to pursue post-secondary education, and (2) the desired length of post-secondary studies for those who do go on.

perhaps more human capital accumulation, today likely requires greater emphasis on subjects outside the traditional core areas.[19]

V FUTURE TRENDS IN POST-SECONDARY ENROLMENTS

If our discussion of enrolment trends over the last two decades has any value, it ought to allow us to say something about what will happen in the future. The post-secondary sector in Canada now seems to be at a difficult pass. Demographics dictate that there will be a 20 per cent decline in the number of young people in the eighteen to twenty-four year age group over the next ten or twelve years. (See Leslie, 1980, 34. After 1994 the number in this group will increase once more, but will still be 10 per cent below its current level in the year 2000.) Hence, an increase in the national post-secondary participation rate from its current level of about 21 to 25 per cent will be necessary over the next decade, just to keep post-secondary enrolments from declining. Fortunately, from the point of view of post-secondary institutions, there is some hope that such an increase may occur.

Over the last decade there has been a steady increase in part-time post-secondary enrolment. The part-time category now (1981–82) forms about 14 per cent of the 'full-time equivalent' undergraduate enrolment at Ontario universities, for example. While some might expect this trend to continue in the future, one astute observer at least believes that further large increases in part-time enrolment are unlikely (Leslie, 1980, 44).

A promising development for Ontario universities is the planned staging-in of a new secondary school regime over the remainder of the 1980s. This will make it possible for large numbers of students to enter university after only four instead of the current five years of high school. There will be two favourable effects on university enrolment. (Deleterious effects on college enrolment could, of course, be realized.) First, if the new system is phased in, say, over ten years, eleven cohorts of high school graduates will enter university over that ten-year period. Thus, over the decade the number of university entrants would be increased by 10 per cent. Secondly, since it will now be 'cheaper' to go on to university, the proportion of young people who take that route will likely increase. In addition, it

19 We should perhaps recall that emphasis on accurate grammar, spelling, and basic mathematics originated in a time when there was heavy reliance on hand calculation, manual filing and data manipulation, and written communication. While many may find the change hard to accept, these skills are no doubt *generally* less important today, given the use of computers and calculators for data processing, and telephones, xerox machines, etc. in communication. This is not to say that such skills are no longer important for managerial, technical, and professional workers. They may simply be less important for the typical, mid-level white-collar worker.

should be noted that since in our view high school education consists largely of information investment, university entrants in Ontario will in the future likely have a smaller endowment of information (unless there are further large gains in 'productivity' in the schools). This situation may strengthen the relative enrolment demand in the university faculties where information investment bulks largest, that is, principally arts and science.

More fundamentally, over the next decade there will be a continued reversal of the cohort size effect of the early and mid-1970s that we have discussed in this section. For the next decade post-secondary graduates will belong to steadily smaller cohorts. Both their forgone and expected future earnings should rise relative to direct costs of schooling (barring a dramatic increase in tuition fees), leading to increased average desired education output and probably higher post-secondary participation rates.

An additional reason that post-secondary enrolment prospects may not be as bleak as they seem lies in the state of the market for highly qualified manpower (HQM). The trend should be strong towards increased relative demand for HQM, which we associate, among other factors, with the secular rise in person-specific information occasioned by the trend towards greater specialization and division of labour. Its retardation by weak public sector demand is now over. (This is not to say that public sector demand is again strong. However, the weakening of public sector demand led to a downward shift in the growth path of HQM; once that downward shift was over, the stock of HQM could again grow fairly quickly.)

Finally, there may be implications for the *composition* of future post-secondary enrolment of what is widely believed to be the recent acceleration in technological change (chips, robotics, etc.). It has often been argued that with rapid technical progress it is dangerous to pursue 'too narrow' an education. It is considered more advisable to obtain a more 'general' education to ensure flexibility in response to future technical change. This argument may point to an effect of technical progress on the relative attractiveness of investing in human capital (skills) vs. person-specific information. If technical change regularly makes skills obsolete, should not more rapid change make lower initial skill acquisition appropriate? And if frequent career changes will be necessary – a fate often predicted for today's young people – will it not be especially important to know one's inherent skills and abilities? After all, whereas without technical change the information investment is used only once to help decide what skills to acquire, with rapid technical change and frequent 're-tooling,' person-specific information will be used as such an input repeatedly over the lifetime. While these predictions have not been rigorously derived, it appears that if we are in fact witnessing an acceleration of technical change, we can expect in the future to see less relative demand for narrowly vocational studies and more for programs which are especially suitable for investment in person-specific information – perhaps, for example, the arts and sciences at the post-secondary level.

VI CONCLUSION

This chapter has described the current structure of and recent changes in education in Canada, and has looked for explanations, both in terms of the simple economic theories of education examined in earlier chapters, and more general frameworks. We found, first, that in Ontario today about two-thirds of young people obtain a high school diploma, and of these one-half go on to complete post-secondary studies. Of the half who go on, about a third go to community college and the rest to university. Of the one-third of all young people who do not obtain a high school diploma, a sizeable fraction attend a trade or vocational school. The overall fraction who never obtain any qualification is thus probably around 20–25 per cent; of these individuals, many may be expected to take part in manpower training at some point in their working lives.

We have pointed out that in a world where both human capital accumulation ('skill acquisition') and information investment occur, it makes sense for the latter to come first. People should explore their abilities before they invest in narrow skills. It is clear that the perhaps 10 per cent of young people who terminate formal schooling in trade or vocational school and the approximately 13 per cent who complete community college for the most part have gone from information investment to a fairly intensive program of skill acquisition before leaving formal schooling. On the other hand, of the overall one-third whose last qualification is a high school diploma and the approximately 20 per cent who finish after a BA there is likely only a minority who pursue intensive skill acquisition before entering the labour force. The public seems suspicious of these dominant forms of schooling. The lack of skill acquisition makes them appear poor preparation for the job market. We have argued that such concern is misplaced. A large proportion of aggregate skill acquisition takes place on the job. Those who do not enter a period of intensive skill acquisition while still at school may typically go on to such training on the job. This process may be entirely natural and desirable.

Turning to changes that have occurred over the last two decades, we have examined not only enrolments but patterns of expenditure as well. Overall the 1960s can be characterized as a period of rapid post-secondary enrolment growth, and the 1970s as one of slower growth. Important details are that since about 1966, for Canada as a whole, college enrolment has grown much more quickly than university enrolment, so that whereas during the mid 1960s about 75 per cent of post-secondary students were in universities, this figure has now dropped to about 60 per cent. In Ontario, on the other hand, while during the late 1960s and late 1970s there was more rapid growth of college than university enrolment, the period 1971–76 was one of very slow college growth. The net result is that the current share of universities in total post-secondary enrolment is very similar to what it was in the mid-1960s: slightly less than 70 per cent.

The rapid rise of post-secondary enrolment in the 1960s was partly due to the increase of the post-secondary age (eighteen to twenty-four) population. However, the most important factor was the approximate doubling of the post-secondary participation rate from the 9–10 per cent range to 18–20 per cent. Similarly, the enrolment slow-down of the 1970s was for the most part due to a levelling-off of participation rates; after 1970 for both Canada as a whole, and Ontario alone they had increased by only another 2.5 percentage points by 1982.

A further important element in the enrolment picture is that after 1967 the proportion of university enrolment accounted for by arts faculties began a decline, which has continued to the present. While in 1966 the arts' share of enrolment was 45 per cent in Canada and 48 per cent in Ontario, by 1979 the figures had dropped to 30 per cent and 36 per cent, respectively. The major winners in terms of enrolment shift were commerce and business administration – up from 6 per cent to 12 per cent for Canada and from 4 per cent to 9 per cent for Ontario over the 1966–80 period. Science, engineering, and a number of the smaller faculties were the other beneficiaries.

A significant point to emerge from the mere description of enrolment trends is that to a surprising extent the kinds of changes in post-secondary education that several recent documents in the labour market policy literature argue should occur in the 1980s have already happened! As the figures just reviewed indicate, during the 1970s there was a very large shift of enrolment from the universities to the community colleges (if we look only at the late 1970s this pattern applies to Ontario as well) and away from arts towards more vocational programs at the universities. While further movement in these directions may be warranted, the scale of the changes that have already occurred suggests that new forms of intervention may not be necessary to secure further movement, if it is indeed desirable, in the future.

On the expenditure side we have seen that real operating expenditures at universities have been steadily declining relative to those at the college, or elementary-secondary levels. In Ontario this trend is especially marked. Over the period 1970 to 1980 we estimate that while real operating expenditures per student at the elementary-secondary level rose 9 per cent, they stayed approximately constant at the colleges and dropped by 20 per cent at the universities. Although the universities may have been able to prevent significant damage, it is clear that the quality of university education must have been declining relative to that at other levels, in particular the elementary-secondary.

Turning to explanations of recent trends, we have argued that most economic theories of education would suggest a fundamental tendency towards a desire for more education output, as a result of the secular decline in the indirect costs of schooling (tuition, books, equipment, travel costs, etc.) relative to the direct costs (forgone earnings). However, this underlying tendency does not have to be expressed in ever-rising post-secondary participation rates. To some extent it can be satisfied by increased education output at the elementary-secondary level or indeed by increased on-the-job training. Finally, temporary demand and supply conditions may result in stagnation or decline of participation rates.

The participation rate slow-down of the 1970s, we have argued, may owe much to the age-cohort-size effect on earnings. After about 1967 post-secondary graduates belonged to the increasingly large post-war baby boom cohorts. There is evidence from the United States that extraordinarily large age cohorts suffer reduced relative earnings opportunities throughout their lifetimes. This may have been an important force behind the falling real starting salaries for graduates in the 1970s. In addition, the relatively poorer earnings prospects of the baby boom cohorts may have caused a slowing of the secular decline in direct costs of education relative to forgone earnings. This slowing would tend to reduce the rate of growth in desired educational attainment and thus in post-secondary participation rates.

Other special supply and demand conditions arising over the last two decades have also likely had strong impacts on enrolments. On the enrolment supply side the geographical extension of the post-secondary system in the 1960s may have been responsible for a large part of the increase in participation rates at that time. In addition, changes in the structure of federal support for post-secondary education appear to have had important supply-side effects. Prior to 1967 the federal government provided a flat subsidy per university student. This form of subsidy ought to have encouraged enrolment growth at the universities primarily in the cheapest programs, an influence apparently reflected in the increasing enrolment share of arts and science in the early 1960s. From 1967 to 1977, a 50 per cent subsidy to all post-secondary operating costs was in force. This factor helps explain the shift towards community colleges (in all provinces except Ontario), and away from arts enrolment at the universities. Finally, the effective disappearance of any marginal federal subsidy to university expenditure after 1977 may have something to do with the levelling-off of real per capita expenditures at both the college and university levels outside Ontario in the late 1970s.

On the enrolment demand side further insights are available, if the imperfect substitutability of university and college-trained workers, or highly qualified manpower (HQM), for other kinds of labour is taken into account. (Such imperfect substitutability is a crucial feature of the informational model of education, one that distinguishes it from the human capital model.) There has been a secular trend towards increased relative demand for HQM, as a result of sectoral shifts in production, increased public sector employment, and technological change – an example of which is increased specialization and division of labour, predicted to increase the demand for education in the informational approach. This development helps to explain the secular trend towards more lengthy schooling. But conditions in the market for HQM may also help to explain the enrolment slow-down in the 1970s, especially in the universities and in faculties such as arts in particular. There has been a considerable slow-down of public sector employment growth, largely owing to the decreased need for elementary and secondary school teachers.

A further, more speculative reason for weaker demand for post-secondary education in the 1970s lies in changes in elementary and secondary education. There has been a steady increase in real per capita spending, as well as in the flexibility and breadth of curriculum. We have argued that this expansion probably means that the typical high school graduate has a greater endowment of person-specific information than in the past. He/she therefore has less need to continue education at the post-secondary level and is less likely to pursue a great deal of information investment – for example, in faculties of arts and science – if the choice to continue formal schooling is made.

Finally, we have commented on the likely future course of post-secondary enrolment. Although over the next decade the population of post-secondary age in Canada will drop by about 20 per cent, there are grounds for believing that the participation rate may rise enough largely to offset this decline: the phasing out of grade thirteen will increase the flow of high school graduates eligible to go on to university, the cohort size effect is now working in favour of lengthier schooling, and the relative demand for highly qualified manpower (HQM) is recovering from the slow-down in public sector employment in the mid-1970s. We have also pointed out that there may be a trend towards less enrolment demand for narrowly vocational studies and towards more general arts and science programs, as a result of the apparently increased pace of technological change.

6
Education and training in Canada:
current issues

I INTRODUCTION

In the conditions of high unemployment and structural adjustments in the industrial labour force of the early 1980s, labour market, education, and training policy has been charged with new interest. It is repeatedly suggested that our large public expenditures on education and training are misdirected to a significant degree. It is not misleading to say that a consensus has emerged in the labour market policy literature that too much is being spent on largely non-vocational studies at universities and too little on technological education at the colleges and universities and on training for skilled trades. There are suggestions that the federal government should take steps to encourage a re-allocation of resources from the former to the latter.

The main purpose of this chapter is to examine the recent labour market policy literature. We use the insights gained from our examination of alternative economic theories of education, guidelines for policy, and recent trends in education in Canada in evaluating this literature. Section II critically sets out the positions that have been taken in the current debate. In Section III we provide our response.

II THE CURRENT DEBATE

II.1 *Introduction*
The current discussion of education and training priorities in Canada has been somewhat one-sided. Within the last three years studies have been issued by Employment and Immigration Canada, Statistics Canada, the Economic Council of Canada, the Ontario Manpower Commission, and a parliamentary task force, all of which argue for a re-allocation of resources towards higher skill training in manpower programs and/or more technological or job-oriented

studies in the post-secondary sector, as well as away from post-secondary education towards other forms of training. This point of view reflects a deep-seated concern that we are failing to prepare young people adequately for participation in labour markets, and that we are thereby doing ourselves considerable economic harm.

The obvious losers from the suggested reallocation, the universities, have responded vigorously to the studies cited. However, this response, which will be briefly sketched below, appears to have fallen largely on deaf ears. No doubt the universities are viewed as having too much self-interest at stake to be objective.

In the remainder of this section we shall summarize critically the studies in favour of re-allocation, as well as the universities' response in opposition. Greatest attention will be paid to the report of the Federal Task Force on Labour Market Development (Employment and Immigration Canada, 1981) – known as the 'Dodge report,' after David Dodge, its executive co-ordinator. This study is the most comprehensive of those calling for re-allocation of resources, and it has also been by far the most influential.

II.2 *The 'Dodge report'*

The current trend towards vocationalism stands in marked contrast to the buoyant enthusiasm for all forms of education and training that marked the 1960s and was expressed, for example, in the *First Annual Review* of the Economic Council of Canada in 1964. Gradually in the late 1960s and early 1970s this enthusiasm began to wane, for at least two reasons. First, it soon became clear that the preliminary academic – Basic Training for Skill Development (BSTD) – and low-level skill training offered under the Canada Manpower Training Program (which started in 1966) had little impact on the employability of trainees. The second reason was the disillusionment with university education that followed the alarming increase in expenditure on universities in the late 1960s and the slide in graduates' starting salaries and employment prospects in the early 1970s.

By the time the federal government appointed its task force on labour market developments in the 1980s the disillusionment with much formal education and training was complete. In 1977 the federal government had already ceased to give any encouragement at the margin to provincial spending on education (under Established Programs Financing – EPF). It had also accepted the recommendations of a 1977 joint evaluation of manpower training by the Department of Employment and Immigration and the Treasury Board secretariat. This report 'called for a strong re-emphasis on the development of skills required by the economy as the objective of all federal training.' In line with this recommendation, during the period after 1977 there was a running-down of the lower levels of

BTSD and agreement in principle with the provinces that manpower training funds should in future be allocated more according to labour market demand conditions. (See Employment and Immigration Canada, 1981, 171.)

The Dodge report provided a detailed argument in favour of the kind of reallocation of education and training resources that the federal government and many others had by the end of the 1970s apparently come to feel was necessary. Its starting point was an ambitious manpower forecasting exercise for the 1980s. (See Employment and Immigration Canada, 1981, chap. 4.) Alternative manpower projections were offered, but those favoured were based on the following assumptions governing the projected relative growth of different industries (see Employment and Immigration Canada, 1981, 47–50):

1. Demographics would produce slow growth in the health and education sectors and in aggregate personal consumption.
2. Heavy investment in the energy sector, and growth in exports (due to an improved competitive position and an increase in world trade starting in 1982) would induce faster growth in manufacturing than in recent years.
3. Continued restraint by government would keep the public sector expanding slowly.

Already we can see that the projected basis for manufacturing growth was wide of the mark: by 1982 the mega-projects had collapsed, and the trade picture had become poor. This discrepancy illustrates one reason why manpower forecasts are often falsified ex post: events have a way of diverging from even the most reasonable of predictions.[1]

The danger that events could play havoc with its projections was recognized by the task force (see, e.g., Employment and Immigration Canada, 1981, 47). It therefore presented two forecasts based on alternative high- (A) and low- (B) growth scenarios. It was believed that these forcasts covered 'a reasonable range of plausible outcomes.' But in addition, a scenario (C) based on the medium-term projection of the Department of Finance (1980) was also examined. This scenario assumed much slower growth of the manufacturing sector than either alternatives A or B. After the fact, it would therefore seem to have an edge in realism, although not a large one, since none of the projections anticipated the depth of the recession that began in 1981.

The manpower projections are of the usual 'fixed-coefficients' variety. Thus, once industrial growth rates are projected, the demand for labour by occupation

---

1 See Selleck (1982b, 39–52) for documentation of how previous manpower forecasting exercises in Canada for specific kinds of highly qualified manpower (e.g., engineers) have proved ex post to have been seriously erroneous. See also Foot (1980) for a discussion of possible sources of error in manpower forecasting.

TABLE 15

Alternative manpower projections, 1980–85, Federal Task Force on Labour Market Development

	Demand	Supply*	Imbalance†	Imbalance as per cent of demand
I. High-skill trades projection**	(Annual averages, '000s)			
A	53.3 ⎫		−30.0 ⎧	−56.3
B	48.6 ⎬	23.3	−25.3 ⎨	−52.1
C	54.9 ⎭		−31.6 ⎩	−57.6
II. Highly qualified manpower†† projection**				
A	56.7 ⎫		+ 6.2 ⎧	+10.9
B	51.0 ⎬	62.9	+11.9 ⎨	+23.3
C	59.2 ⎭		+ 3.7 ⎩	+ 6.3

* Assumes zero immigration
† Supply–demand
** A = High growth scenario.
  B = Low growth scenario.
  C = Scenario based on Department of Finance medium-term projections (October 1980).
†† University degree-holders
SOURCE: Employment and Immigration Canada (1981, Tables 4-14 and 4-15, 66 and 67)

drops out immediately, since no change in intra-industry occupational structure is allowed. Projected demands are compared with anticipated supply only in the cases of highly qualified manpower (HQM) (here including only university graduates) and the higher-skill trades. Assuming zero immigration, the projected aggregate demands, supplies, and 'imbalances' (excess supply) are summarized in Table 15. The period covered includes only 1980–85, reflecting the task force's concern about the magnitude of possible errors.[2] Confining the analysis to this period helps, for example, by limiting projections of university graduates and journeymen largely to those already enrolled in university or as apprentices at the time of the forecast.

---

2 The task force took a commendably conservative approach in not attempting to extend its forecasts of imbalance either over a wider range of occupations, or further into the future. Freeman (1980b) concludes that the major difficulty with fixed-coefficients, 'manpower require-ments' models is not on the demand side, where his work indicates they do quite well, but on the supply side, where methods are less well-established. Concentrating on a subset of all possible occupations and looking forward only a few years ought to reduce error on the supply side.

As Table 15 shows, very sizeable excess demand in the higher-skill trades (measuring from 52 to 58 per cent of total demand), and moderately large excess supply of university graduates (from 6 to 23 per cent) are projected. Note the greater sensitivity of the university graduate imbalance than the higher-skill trade imbalance to alternative scenarios. Since events have given the lie to scenarios A and B, C, with its lower growth in manufacturing employment (approximately half that in A or B – see Employment and Immigration Canada, 1981, 51), seems most 'realistic.' We may perhaps interpret it as saying that if Canada was to have experienced a normal level of unemployment over 1980–85, but the energy and world trade situations had been about what we have experienced, there would have been only a small excess supply of university graduates. As it is, with the highest rates of unemployment since the 1930s, at the end of the day 1980–85 will no doubt have seen considerable excess supply of university graduates, as of most other kinds of labour.

If the task force had been highly confident in its A and B projections, it could have constructed an argument for reallocation of education and training resources without appeal to other kinds of evidence. Of course, to say that such manpower projections could be 'correct' is not to say that the excess demands and supplies they forecast would necessarily materialize. We would expect the tendency towards imbalance to lead to relative wage changes that would choke off excess demand and absorb excess supply. Those changes in relative wages would, however, imply changes in the social benefits of (and rates of return to) different forms of training. Something like this argument appears implicit in one strong conclusion that the task force drew from its forecasts: that increased federal support for training in the higher-skill trades is warranted. Provided that the immigration source has really dried up,[3] it is difficult to fault the implicit logic. Initiatives such as Employment and Immigration Canada's Critical Trades Skill Training (CTST) program, set up in 1978 to help the private sector develop a training capacity in a select group of high-skill industrial trades, may be appropriate under the circumstances.

Not surprisingly, the task force did not feel it could argue for a reduction in support for university education simply on the basis of its manpower forecasts. Although not stated explicitly, the reasoning was probably as follows. First, the

---

3 As the task force points out (Employment and Immigration Canada, 1981, 187), 'Canadian wages and working conditions are relatively less attractive now than in the past, in comparison with those prevailing in western European countries which have traditionally supplied this country with higher level skills.' The result has been a dramatic reduction in immigration of highly skilled workers. Whereas in 1974 there were 7855 immigrant entrants to the higher-skill manufacturing trade, providing 66 per cent of all entrants, by 1979 the number had declined to 3775 – just 38 per cent of all entrants (Employment and Immigration Canada, 1981, 162).

forecasts are subject to many possible errors, so that the small *projected* excess supply of university graduates might well turn into a *realized* excess demand. It could not be confidently predicted, therefore, that the social rate of return to university education would decline. Also, even if it was felt that this rate of return was certain to decline, it could have been at a high level at the start of the period, so that continued strong support would be warranted.

Partly in order to get a better idea if a reduction in aggregate federal support for the universities would be in order and partly to examine problems *within* the universities and colleges, the task force examined four kinds of evidence on the performance of the post-secondary sector.

First, the task force pointed out, it would be desirable to have current social cost-benefit evidence (and associated rate of return estimates) for post-secondary education, with detail for individual programs and faculties. Unfortunately, as we have seen in our Chapter 4, and as the task force recognizes, no estimates are available for Canada since 1972. Nevertheless, the task force finds some indication in more recent studies for the United States and the United Kingdom that the decline in the social rate of return that Mehmet found for Canada between 1969 and 1972 has probably continued: 'The Task Force has found evidence from analysis of Canadian and foreign cost / benefit studies that the overall size of the post-secondary sector is too large and has concluded from this that it should be contracted somewhat ...' (Employment and Immigration, Canada, 1981, 154). It also draws on the careful summary by Stager (1981) of both pre-1972 evidence for Canada and foreign evidence on rates of return across disciplines to argue that reallocation of resources from 'general arts and science and social work to engineering, business, economics, and technology' would be desirable.

We find it disturbing that recommendations should be made on the scale of expenditure on post-secondary education and on re-allocations across programs on the basis of studies that are all at least a decade out of date and evidence from other countries. The task force, itself, suggests that 'it is difficult to draw conclusions from this analysis.' In our opinion it is impossible.

There is clearly a great need for a comprehensive and detailed scholarly examination of social costs and benefits of different forms of post-secondary education and training in Canada for the period since 1972. Any plans to alter the overall scale of federal support for post-secondary education should be held in abeyance until such research has been carried out.

A second piece of evidence examined by the task force was the 1978 survey by Statistics Canada of the employment experience of 1976 post-secondary graduates two years after leaving school. (See Clark and Zsigmond, 1981.) The task force confined itself to the observation that the results showed that 'certain fields of study are associated with high (labour force) participation rates, low rates of both unemployment and underemployment, and higher salaries. For university graduates these include business and commerce, education, engineering, architecture, dentistry and pharmacy ... For college graduates they include data processing, medical and dental services, and various technologies' (Employment and Immigration Canada, 1981, 154–5). Others have devoted more attention to the variation in rates of 'underemployment.' Being underemployed is defined as having a job where either (1) one's formal qualifications are not required by the employer, or (2) one's qualifications are 'required' but are unnecessary in the worker's view. The underemployment rate was found to be 38 per cent for university graduates, but only 25 per cent for college graduates. The rate was particularly high for university graduates in the humanities (50 per cent) and social sciences (47 per cent).

Third, the task force looked at a time series on starting salaries for university graduates by faculty for the period 1965–77.[4] Mean starting salaries are presented as a ratio of average industrial earnings. It is found that in all disciplines this ratio declined considerably after 1969, from an approximate 20 per cent decline for engineering and honours science to about a 30 per cent drop for honours arts. Curiously, little is made of this evidence. It is suggested that the general decline probably represents a return to the normalcy of the 1950s and early 1960s, rather than a 'surplus' of graduates in the 1970s. Also, changes in relative starting salaries across disciplines are not highlighted.

In fact the starting salary data provide much better evidence for the task force's re-allocation argument than, for example, the rate of return 'evidence' on which it lays greater stress. These data indicate a stable ratio of starting salaries to average industrial earnings for engineering and honours science after 1972 but a continued decline for honours arts, pass arts and science, and commerce. Thus it may be that while the rate of return to engineering and science studies held constant through the 1970s, the rate to arts and commerce declined. (Note that this finding is not inconsistent with constancy of the average rate of return to university, since significant enrolment shifts were taking place over the period, e.g., away from arts.)

In Table 16 we provide a more detailed and updated version of the starting salary data presented by the task force. Here we give the actual starting salaries in

---

4 This comes from the federal government's Pay Research Bureau, which annually surveys starting salaries for university and college graduates taken on by about 75–100 large Canadian corporations. One should be aware that the series may sometimes be misleading. For example, half the honours science graduates hired by these large corporations in a single year might be in high-demand areas like computer science, and geophysics, while the proportion of all honours science graduates in these areas might be much smaller.

constant 1970 dollars, rather than a ratio to the average industrial wage, and we provide figures for honours computer science, as well as for business and technology graduates at the college level, for 1976–81. These data show that since 1970 there has been a considerable increase in the starting salaries of engineering and honours science graduates relative to honours arts, pass arts and science, and business graduates, whose relative salaries have stayed roughly constant. The increase from 1970 to 1981 is about 25 per cent for both engineering and honours science. Since 1976 the table shows there has also been about a 10 per cent increase in honours computer science starting salaries relative to arts, and a small increase in starting salaries of business and technology college graduates relative to arts graduates from universities.

The task force might have argued that the changes in relative starting salaries indicate the enrolment shifts that took place in the 1970s, although in the correct direction, were not always large enough. The approximate doubling of the commerce enrolment share in Canada as a whole has apparently been sufficient to prevent commerce starting salaries from rising relative to arts. This represents a success on the part of the universities. It indicates that in some respects, at least, there is sufficient flexibility in response to changes in enrolment demand. On the other hand, the steady increase in relative engineering and honours science starting salaries might be interpreted as indicating that the smaller increases in enrolment shares for these disciplines (see Table 14) represented an inadequate supply response.

Finally, the task force took a brief look at trends in the composition of full-time university undergraduate enrolment over the period 1960–77. Unfortunately, it did not do a very careful job, and managed to create a highly misleading impression. A table was presented (Table 9-2, 156) which purported to show that the proportion in 'arts, science, and education' rose from 64.1 per cent in 1960 to 67.0 per cent in 1977. (In other respects the table was unexceptionable, indicating the considerable increase in business enrolment, and the small shift to engineering over the period 1970–77.) The impression these numbers give is of a university system out of control – needlessly increasing the share of its resources devoted to non-vocational arts and education programs over a period when the relative demand for such graduates was disastrously declining.[5]

In fact the impression of an increase in relative resources devoted to arts-type programs conveyed by the task force is entirely the result of inappropriate aggregation. First, a number of unspecified faculties are included in the 'arts, science, and education' category. If they are omitted, the data behind our Table 14

---

5 This impression was fostered by the reference to the arts, science and education category in the text as 'arts, education, and related disciplines.'

TABLE 16

Mean monthly starting salaries of university and college graduates, Canada selected years, 1965–81

Selected years	University						College	
	Engineering	Hons sci.	Hons Comp. sci.	Hons arts	Pass arts or sci.*	Pass + hons business†	Business	Technology
	Constant 1970 dollars							
1965	586	561	–	526	497	537	–	–
70	672	650	–	645	588	616	–	–
75	690	640	–	561	538	580	–	–
76	698	649	640	579	544	598	523	593
77	705	659	649	563	546	589	533	586
78	699	661	639	572	523	–	512	590
79	696	669	656	545	513	563	505	622
80	719	669	650	568	510	551	516	598
81	829	780	755	622	566	622	585	673
	Relative amounts (Hons arts = 100)							
1965	111.2	106.7	–	100.0	94.5	102.1	–	–
70	104.2	100.8	–	100.0	91.2	95.5	–	–
75	122.9	114.0	–	100.0	95.9	103.3	–	–
76	120.5	112.1	110.6	100.0	94.0	103.3	90.3	102.5
77	125.2	117.2	115.4	100.0	97.1	104.6	94.7	104.1
78	122.2	115.5	111.6	100.0	91.4	–	89.5	103.1
79	127.7	122.8	120.4	100.0	94.2	103.3	92.6	114.1
80	126.6	117.8	114.5	100.0	89.7	97.0	90.7	105.3
81	133.3	125.3	121.4	100.0	91.0	100.0	94.1	108.2

* Includes only pass arts for 1978–81

† Includes only honours business for 1979–81

SOURCES: Pay Research Bureau, Public Service Staff Relations Board, *Survey of Actual and Anticipated Recruiting Salaries for University and College Graduates.* Taken from various issues for 1978–81, and from Zsigmond et al. (1978, 185)

show that the enrolment share of arts, science, and education actually *fell* from 58.7 per cent in 1960 to 57.3 per cent in 1977. Second, lumping together arts and education with science is also very misleading. The science enrolment share jumped from 9.1 per cent in 1960 to 15.5 per cent in 1977, while arts and education on their own dropped from 49.6 per cent to 41.8 per cent. Arts by itself dropped from 39.8 per cent to 32.0 per cent.

What the task force appears to have concluded from its perusal of these four forms of evidence is the following:

1. The rate of return 'evidence' indicated the desirability of reducing somewhat the total resources devoted to post-secondary education.

2. The rate of return evidence and Statistics Canada's 1978 survey reinforced the notion that there are certain high-demand disciplines at the post-secondary level that should be encouraged. The task force's list includes: 'engineering (especially those fields related to primary industry development, the continuous process industries, heavy construction electronics, and biotechnology),' some areas of pure science, and some business courses at the graduate level in the universities; and technological training in the colleges.

3. The composition 'evidence' suggests that the universities have severe difficulties in responding to changes in enrolment demand.

As we have pointed out, in actuality there is *no* rate of return 'evidence,' and when the enrolment composition data are analysed correctly, we find that the universities have in fact managed dramatic enrolment shifts over the 1970s in response to changing demand conditions. Dismissing the high rates of unemployment and underemployment found for arts graduates in the 1978 Statistics Canada survey as unsurprising for a period of transition in which demand for these graduates was falling (with a resulting decline in enrolment), we may dispense with the second conclusion as well.

Despite our view that the federal task force provided little proof that intervention is required to induce enrolment responsiveness in the post-secondary sector, we do find the conclusion is to an extent valid. In Subsection III.3 we present our reasoning. It is based on a more careful examination of starting salary and enrolment composition trends than that carried out by the task force.

The task force made a number of recommendations about how the form of federal financing of post-secondary education should be altered to encourage enrolment responsiveness (see Employment and Immigration Canada, 1981, 158-9):

1. Some portion of federal expenditures should be tied to the 'base support given the institutions by the provinces.' This 'would be important in maintaining the academic base in disciplines currently not in high demand.'

2. Tuition fees should be allowed to rise substantially and should be more closely related to the marginal cost of providing instruction by discipline. (Such

changes are clearly outside the powers of the federal government. Reduction in federal support, however, would probably necessitate increased reliance on fees.) This would lead to greater responsiveness to enrolment demand.
3. Federal expenditures on student aid should be increased to ensure that access was not reduced by the higher fees. Aid should be tied to the type of program entered, partly to encourage students to enter high-demand areas and partly to offset the high fees required in areas with high costs.
4. Institutions should be encouraged to tap other private sector sources of funding. The federal government should offer to match corporate contributions to establish new programs, etc. It should also provide grants to cover the administrative costs of co-op programs.
5. The federal government should provide thrust funding to assist in the establishment of new programs in areas of high labour market demand.

Note that the manner in which a portion of federal expenditures should be tied to the provinces' 'base support' was not specified. If the federal government merely gave each province a fixed amount to be distributed among the institutions in proportion to operating grants, it would not in fact be departing from the current lump sum grant approach. (A fixed total, to be spent on directed ends, has only an 'income effect'; that is, it merely swells provincial coffers, unless less would actually be spent on the specified ends in the absence of the federal grant than the amount of that grant.) On the other hand, if the federal government promised to pay, say, 20 per cent of the operating costs of all post-secondary institutions it would be encouraging overall post-secondary enrolment growth, contrary to the aims of the task force.

II.3 *Literature related to the Dodge report*
Much of the message of the Dodge report, with some variation, has been reiterated by studies produced by the Parliamentary Task Force on Employment Opportunities for the 80's (the 'Allmand Committee'), the Ontario Manpower Commission (OMC), the Economic Council of Canada, and Statistics Canada. These studies will be discussed in less detail than the Dodge report, since they have perhaps been less influential.

The Allmand committee eschewed the use of formal analysis. It used its resources instead to conduct a cross-country tour with numerous hearings at which employers, trade unions, municipal governments, educational institutions, and others made their views known. The result was a set of recommendations (the 'Allmand report') similar to those of the Dodge report, without the detailed supporting evidence. Again, a re-allocation of resources towards higher-skill training, and away from low-level skill training and university education is advocated. Governments, it is argued, should alter their funding of universities and colleges to stimulate a shift within these institutions towards the type of training required by 'the industrial and business needs of the country and to occupations where there are skill shortages.' It should be noted, however, that the committee pointed out that many experts had advised them of the great uncertainty attached to forecasts of future occupational imbalances. (See, e.g., Parliamentary Task Force, 1981, 37, 44, 116, 120.)

Like the Dodge report, the OMC *Labour Market Outlook for Ontario, 1981–86* (Siddiqui et al., 1981) was based on a detailed labour market forecast. A major result is the prediction that while on average 22250 university graduates will enter the Ontario labour market annually in the period studied, on average there will be only 7567 job openings each year requiring a university degree, even in a 'high-growth' scenario. Since the overall supply of university and college graduates is predicted to match approximately the demand, the conclusion drawn is that Ontario is wastefully providing university education to a large number of people who could receive sufficient job qualification by attending college.

The excess supply of university graduates predicted for Ontario is, on the face of it, far more severe than predicted by the federal task force for the country as a whole over almost precisely the same period. While the OMC projects an excess supply of 194 per cent, the federal task force predicted an excess of from 6 to 23 per cent (depending on the scenario). It is not clear whether this discrepancy actually reflects a greater likely excess for Ontario, since it is apparently largely the result of a difference in procedure. The OMC carefully classified all occupations according to whether a university degree was required or whether the job could be done by either a college or a university graduate. In contrast, the task force used the current intra-industry utilization of university graduates as its guide to the demand for such graduates.

It appears that the OMC approach may cause unnecessary alarm. It is not likely that the productivity of the average university and college graduate trained in a particular occupation (e.g., nursing, business) is exactly the same. Employers may prefer university graduates for legitimate reasons, although they may be willing to accept a good college graduate as a substitute for an average university graduate. It is not clear that it is a bad idea for students to train at university for these occupations, although it is not strictly 'necessary.'

A second comment is that the feeling that college education is less costly than university education – which must underlie the suggestion that we ought to fill a vacancy with a college graduate if a university degree is not really necessary – is not well founded. It is true that, as shown in Table 12, operating expenditure per full-time student at the universities is about 40 per cent higher than at the colleges. However, the true cost of undergraduate instruction is not necessarily higher. Part of the 40 per cent higher cost reflects support for faculty members' non-sponsored research, and part is due to expensive graduate programs.

An important point about the OMC report is that it advocates much more strongly than the Dodge report a shift in resources from the universities toward the colleges. The Dodge report emphasizes the need for a reallocation within the post-secondary sector towards more technological training and training in areas of high labour market demand. To the extent that there is greater emphasis on technological training at the college level, it therefore would support some shift of resources from the universities to the colleges, but it did not see the wholesale need for this shift argued by the OMC.

Another document that placed considerable emphasis on the need to reallocate resources from the universities to the colleges was Clark and Zsigmond's (1981) report on the 1978 Statistics Canada survey of graduates. The purpose of this report was primarily to provide guidance for high school leavers, their parents, and teachers, about the relative desirability of various post-secondary alternatives. A wealth of useful detail is presented. Some pieces of information would clearly be helpful for some prospective college or university students – for example, one-half of all physics graduates said they wished they had studied another subject. However, in our opinion, the results of the survey were presented in a somewhat misleading way, and erroneous policy inferences were drawn.[6]

It is repeatedly stated by Clark and Zsigmond that post-secondary students want job-related studies and are happiest when they have obtained such training. In fact, the published tabulations from the survey provide little indication that this is the case (unless it is true that university is equally as job-related as college). It is true that rates of unemployment and 'underemployment' for university graduates, especially those in the humanities and social sciences, were found to be higher than those for college graduates. However, the conclusion that university students must have been less happy with their studies than college graduates does not follow. In fact, about the same proportion of BAs and college graduates stated they regretted their field of study (25.5 per cent vs. 25.8 per cent). Also about the same proportion of BAs and college graduates in employment were dissatisfied with the jobs they had obtained (12.7 per cent vs. 12.5 per cent). More strikingly, Clark and Zsigmond (153) go out of their way to tell us that most college graduates wish they had gone to university!

It is undoubtedly the case that college study is, on average, more job-related and vocational. It is also clear that there is a stronger link between training and

---

6 An interesting minor example of a rather questionable conclusion is the inference that because a larger proportion of university than college graduates said they would like to return for additional study at some point in the future, it must be the case that university students are not adequately trained the first time around. (See Clark and Zsigmond, 1981, 157.) Surely the willingness to return for even more university education should be taken as evidence that the preliminary experience was favourable.

job obtained. However, on the basis of the data published by Clark and Zsigmond it is *not* clear that graduates themselves regarded such education as the most desirable. In our opinion, the attempt to support vocationalism by an appeal to the views and experience of post-secondary graduates is not very successful.

More recently, much of what was said in the literature already discussed has been re-emphasized by Betcherman's (1982) Economic Council of Canada study, which is based on a national survey of firms' skill shortages and responses via training, recruitment, etc. It finds that of the 1354 establishments surveyed, half experienced some difficulty in filling skill requirements in the 1977–79 period. The type of skill shortages experienced are what one would expect from the Dodge report: 'The most critical shortages ... involved certain high-level, blue-collar skills within the product fabricating and repair and the machining categories. Significant hiring difficulties were also cited for some jobs involving professional and technical personnel. More prominent here were shortages involving the sciences and engineering group. For the most part, these hard-to-find skills were reported by respondents in all regions of the country' (65). While not really a policy document, this study does conclude that 'an obvious priority for government involvement concerns the development of skills for technical and trades occupations' (70).

Finally, the Economic Council (1982) has recently issued a policy document on labour market policy, *In Short Supply – Jobs and Skills in the 1980's.* This report draws on the Betcherman survey and new manpower forecasts to confirm the Dodge report's prediction of continuing manpower shortages for some kinds of skilled workers. The document devotes considerable attention to the problem of unemployment. Increased federal support for manpower training, especially in co-operation with industry, and in longer-term higher-skills programs is recommended. In addition, there is considerable emphasis on the perceived need for greater government involvement in disseminating labour market information. It is recommended that 'an independent research institute charged specifically with developing and co-ordinating a human-resource information network ...' should be established.[7]

---

7 We have argued, in Section II of Chapter 4, that government assistance to the dissemination of labour market information may be justified by arguments similar to those used to justify subsidies to education on efficiency grounds. Perhaps most importantly, the gains to individuals acquiring such information accrue to society at large, as well as to the individual, in the form of reduced unemployment insurance pay-outs, increased tax revenue, etc. Note, however, that there is no argument that the extra information should be provided directly by government. Better results might be achieved by subsidizing private employment agencies, want ads, etc.

II.4 *The universities' response*

A persistent theme of much recent literature on education and training in Canada has been a questioning of the role of the universities. The universities have not been loath to defend themselves, but their rejoinders to successive attacks have received little attention. The Dodge and Allmand reports and Clark and Zsigmond's (1981) *Job Market Reality for Post-Secondary Graduates*, for example, have been the subject of detailed rebuttals by the AUCC or the Council of Ontario Universities.

To some extent the universities have defended themselves on the grounds that university education is more than job preparation. However, they have also vigorously disputed the charge that they are falling down on the labour market preparation count. The AUCC rejoinder to the Dodge report (AUCC, 1981), for example, argues as follows:

1. University graduates have a broader education than that obtained in vocational training. They are therefore more flexible and capable of dealing successfully with the marked changes that will occur in technology and organization over their working lives.[8]
2. Manpower forecasting is too unreliable to be used as the basis for government intervention in university affairs to secure labour market objectives.
3. Stager, on whose work the task force based its summary of cost-benefit evidence, suggested that 'there may already have been an excessively strong reaction ...' (in post-secondary financing) 'to the unexpected "dip" in university enrollments in the early 1970's' (Stager, 1981, 124).
4. The Clark and Zsigmond (1981) evidence on the labour market experience of arts graduates is misleading, because those entering the labour market with an arts BA are a rather special group. To some extent they form a residual group who were not 'creamed off' into professional or graduate school.
5. Comparisons of starting salaries for university graduates with average industrial earnings over the period 1965–77 are misleading. (No very convincing argument for this position is given.) The average earnings of all university graduates relative to those of high school graduates showed little change over the period 1959–78.
6. The belief that the universities have been highly unresponsive to changes in enrolment demand is unfounded. In Ontario, for example; 'despite financial difficulties and static overall enrolment, university output in commerce and administration ... from 1977 to 1981 increased by 60.7%, in engineering by 35.1%, and in computer science by 34.6%' (AUCC, 1981, 73).

---

8 This point has been made frequently. See, for example, Weisbrod (1964, 23).

These points dispute the validity of the 'evidence' used in the Dodge report (and elsewhere – e.g., Clark and Zsigmond, 1981) to criticize the universities' performance in preparing their graduates for the labour market. In some respects the rebuttal is similar to that we have offered above, but note the new issues raised in points 1 and 4. The suggestion that university graduates have more 'breadth' is of particular interest here, since it seems to accord well with the emphasis we have placed on the importance of person-specific information accumulation in programs like the humanities and social sciences (and to a lesser extent the sciences) at the universities. Breadth is acquired by studying a wide range of subjects. The lasting effect of such sampling is probably more the knowledge of one's talent for and / or interest in a broad range of subjects, than a basket of diverse skills. The argument in point 4 that arts BAs have lower average 'ability' than, say, all university entrants, does not fit into the framework of any simple economic model of education, but it has undeniable force.

Finally, it is interesting to note that the universities have disputed the claimed need for interventionist federal policy to promote enrolment responsiveness on the grounds that intervention might well be misguided, as well as on the grounds that there is sufficient responsiveness without it. The argument is that we know forecasted surpluses or shortages of particular kinds of graduates are unreliable. In the universities' view the federal government has no crystal ball that will allow it to determine which university programs to encourage by, say, temporary increases in student aid, in order to achieve the goal of avoiding labour market imbalance.

II.5 *Recent policy developments*
The recent literature espousing the need for re-allocation of education and training resources has complemented shifts in policy occurring at both the Ontario and the federal levels.

At the federal level a major realignment of the goals and operating procedures of Employment and Immigration Canada's manpower training programs was announced in January 1982. Under the National Training Program the whole training system is to be based in future on a manpower forecasting system (the Canadian Occupational Projection System – COPS) to be developed in co-operation with the private sector. Training resources will be shifted continuously away from occupations of skill surplus towards those of shortage. In addition, a substantial increase in financial aid to industries providing training in designated jobs is projected.

In Ontario there has been considerable discussion of secondary education, involving criticism of grade thirteen, the quality of job preparation received by the majority of high school students who do not go on to grade thirteen, and falling standards. The government's Secondary Education Review Project (SERP) recommended that grade thirteen should be abolished, standards should be raised, and greater efforts should be made to give non-university entrants good job preparation.

The response of the Ontario government to SERP has been to accept, in large part, the phasing out of grade thirteen.[9] In future there will be only one Ontario high school diploma, requiring thirty credits (a credit involves 110–120 hours of work) for all students. Of the thirty credits sixteen will be required instead of the current nine. Those students wishing to go on to university will have to obtain six university-entrance credits, corresponding to the type of work now done in grade thirteen. While many (perhaps most) university entrants will complete their diplomas in four years, a fifth year will still be possible for those who do not obtain their full thirty credits in the first four years.

As discussed in the previous chapter, one important implication of the gradual phasing-out of grade thirteen in Ontario will be a fillip to university enrolment, just when it is most required. (As discussed in the last chapter, the number of Canadians in the age group eighteen to twenty-four will decline about 20 per cent over the next decade.) Whether the announced changes will result in improved job preparation for non-university entrants, however, is not clear.

A further important series of developments followed the indication by the federal government in the fall of 1980 that it wished to renegotiate Established Programs Financing (EPF). Post-secondary education was explicitly identified as the prime target. Subsequently the federal government unilaterally removed the revenue guarantee, one of the three components in the fiscal transfers under EPF, thereby reducing its commitments to the provinces. At the same time, while urging negotiations, it indicated that it was prepared to move unilaterally if it could not secure agreement with the provinces. The desired type of change in fiscal arrangements has not been set out explicitly, but it would apparently allow the federal government to promote its manpower planning aims, along the lines advocated by the Dodge report. This policy was made clear in the November 1981 budget paper dealing with federal-provincial fiscal arrangements:

Federal support for human resources development should ... be reassessed. The issue is no longer simply growth and program expansion, but the focus and direction required to restore and maintain the vitality of Canada's economy. Concerted and sustained efforts are required to avoid university and college graduates finding themselves unemployed because of an over-supply of their particular skills, while industrial expansion is hampered by shortages of other skills. (Dept. of Finance, 1981, 38)

9 'Tougher High School System on Way,' *London Free Press*, 30 November 1982, 1

It is also clear that there is a desire by the federal government simply to reduce the EPF drain on the exchequer. This appears to be the reason for the announcement in March 1982 that the 'six and five' limits on expenditures would apply to EPF payments.

Finally, the recent reduction in projected EPF payments implied by their inclusion in the 'six and five' program has been accompanied by a sizeable increase in federal student aid. For the first time, part-time students will be given access to the Canada Student Loan Plan (CSLP), and the financing limits will be raised from $1800 per academic year to $3200. It is anticipated that the increased cost of CSLP will be of about the same magnitude as the decreased EPF payments.

The partial switch from block grants under EPF to increased student aid is particularly interesting, because it fits in with the policy change recommended in the Dodge report. It will be interesting to see whether the reduced federal block grants lead to an increase in tuition fees and greater enrolment responsiveness, as the Dodge report predicted.

III OUR REACTION TO THE CURRENT DEBATE

III.1 *On vocationalism*
The previous section has documented the current high tide of vocationalism in Canada. Increased emphasis on job preparation is being advocated at each level of the education and training systems, and implementation of increased vocationalism is well underway. In addition, re-allocation of resources towards institutions and programs with a heavier vocational content has been not only widely recommended but already substantially undertaken.

Current circumstances may well make increased vocational study appropriate. After all, enrolment demand has swung in that direction, lending credibility to the opinions of policy makers and experts. However, we find alarming the perception that if education is to give people better job prospects and therefore reduce unemployment and poverty and increase prosperity, the *only* way this goal can be accomplished is through greater skill acquisition. It is apparently not recognized that activities other than the narrowly vocational can contribute to earnings and employability.

Policy makers clearly do not appreciate that much of the activity in our schools, colleges, and universities is more accurately thought of as investment in person-specific information rather than in skills or human capital. Further, it is not understood that building up information on inherent abilities has the same kind of job market pay-off as investing in skills. Investment in information raises earnings, employability, and output by raising the quality of job-worker matches. In increasing the vocational content of education, planners may unknowingly reduce the information accumulation element. While this may increase earnings and employability if the marginal product of skill acquisition is higher than that of information investment, it will harm job market prospects if the reverse is true.

While there may have been a net pay-off of switching from information investment to skill acquisition in the late 1970s and early 1980s, it is not necessarily the case that it will be a good idea to keep on switching in the future, or even to maintain the mix that has now been reached. As argued in the previous chapter, the currently perceived acceleration in technological change may bode ill for vocational studies. When technical progress quickens many believe the pay-off to skills (whose rate of obsolescence goes up) falls relative to the profitability of more general education. The latter is believed to ensure flexibility in response to technical change. We believe that this general education may be thought of largely as investment in person-specific information. By trying out alternative studies the individual explores his inherent abilities and prepares himself for repeated decisions on changes in career. That is, the more information one has on one's inherent capacities, the better choices one will make in deciding what new skills to learn when technological progress makes the old ones obsolete.

If the rate of technological progress is truly accelerating, it seems likely that a trend in enrolment demand away from narrow vocational studies towards more general education may soon emerge. While the kind of education system we argue in favour of – one that simulates a free competitive market – would result in rapid adjustments, there is considerable danger in our view that under current arrangements, with their large element of central planning, this will not occur. The present trudge towards greater vocationalism, perhaps justified by the needs of the late and early 1980s, may continue under its own momentum into a period when much reduced vocationalism is in order.

III.2 *The need for re-allocation of resources away from post-secondary sector*
If the total public resources to be spent on education and training in Canada were fixed, it seems clear that a re-allocation of resources away from the post-secondary sector towards apprenticeship programs and on-the-job training (OJT) would be desirable. The latter are subsidized at a much lower rate. By a straightforward economic efficiency argument, as discussed in Chapter 4, it would likely pay to subsidize formal education at a lower rate and informal education at a higher one.

If total resources devoted to education and training are not fixed, it is not clear that any decrease in expenditures on post-secondary education is warranted. In brief, we need to know the social rate of return to this form of education. If it is close to the high levels that were repeatedly estimated in the 1960s, then no diminution in expenditures appears desirable. The fact that the rate of return to, say, apprenticeship training is higher, or has recently increased, would not suggest that resources should be taken away from socially profitable investment in post-secondary education. Additional resources should certainly be devoted to apprenticeship training, but there would be no rationale in this scenario for a simultaneous decrease in post-secondary spending.

We are greatly in need of a comprehensive and detailed scholarly examination of the social costs and benefits of post-secondary education, and other forms of training. As we have already pointed out, there is no Canadian study that has attempted to estimate rates of return to post-secondary education for the period since 1972. As our Chapter 5 has shown, there have been dramatic changes in enrolment composition and funding since that time. Little confidence can be placed in the differential structure of rates of return to different forms of education estimated for the earlier period.

As a final note, it is clear that any argument for shifting resources away from the post-secondary sector for Canada as a whole must apply in considerably attenuated form to Ontario. In Ontario, as we saw in detail in the last chapter, there has been a prolonged running-down of post-secondary expenditure, particularly at the university level, since the early 1970s. Serious study indeed would be required before it could be responsibly suggested that there should be a further shift of support away from the post-secondary sector.

III.3 Re-allocation within the post-secondary sector

The argument that there should be re-allocation of resources within the post-secondary sector in response to changes in enrolment demand brought on by labour market developments is ironclad. The further argument that the current system of higher education is incapable of producing such re-allocation, however, does not follow. As we have discussed in Chapter 4, universities and colleges in Canada exist in a highly competitive framework. Their individual fortunes depend to a large degree on their success in attracting students, and, as the record of the past ten years indicates, they do respond rapidly and effectively to at least some changes in enrolment demand.

Although empirical evidence is not available, there is some reason to expect that the current post-secondary system may be insufficiently responsive to changes in enrolment demand, particularly when these changes involve an increase in the demand for more costly programs. As we shall see, however, this lack of responsiveness is a result of the funding regimes imposed by provincial governments, rather than of any inherent sluggishness on the part of universities and colleges.

It is not hard to find explanations for the lack of responsiveness of the post-secondary system to increase in enrolment demand for more costly programs. When there is an increase in demand for a particular kind of labour, there will be two effects in the market for education. On the one hand, the enrolment demand curve will shift upwards. On the other, the marginal cost of increasing enrolment will tend to rise, since it will involve hiring, for example, more engineers to teach engineering, just when engineers' wages are rapidly rising. In an unregulated education industry one would expect the outward shift of the demand curve to dominate, with a resulting strong increase in enrolment (and increase in tuition fees). But we do not have an unregulated education industry.

In fact, our educational institutions have almost no control over the price they charge for instructional services. They receive enrolment-related operating grants from their provincial governments, with implicit prices for the provision of training in the different faculties and at different levels. Typically, these prices are not changed in response to fluctuations in the cost of providing different forms of training. The other part of the total price received is made up by tuition fees. The institutions do not control them either, and fees typically differ less across programs than costs of instruction do.

What happens in our system when there is an increase in demand for a particular type of graduate is that the price received by a university or college for producing that type of graduate stays fixed, while the true equilibrium price rises. The result, as in any case where regulation enforces a subequilibrium price, is excess demand. In addition, there will be no induced increase in enrolment, unless there was initially some excess capacity or the quality of instruction is reduced (e.g., by increasing class size).

It is easy to see that lack of enrolment responsiveness should be most severe where the marginal cost of expanding enrolment tends to be increased by strong demand in the labour market that graduates are entering. This will be a problem in any professional faculty and in specialized disciplines like the sciences. The success of the universities and colleges in expanding commerce education over the last ten or twelve years is probably a reflection of the fact that enrolment and employment of instructors could be increased rapidly without much effect on marginal cost. Compared with engineers or computer scientists, commerce and business instructors represent a much less specialized and more readily augmentable resource.

Lack of enrolment responsiveness may have become a more serious problem in Ontario in recent years, owing to the nature of the formula funding arrangements introduced in 1978–79.[10] Prior to 1978 the universities' grants were related to a moving average of their weighted enrolments. Under such a system full payment from the provincial government for, say, enrolling an extra engineer is

10 The following discussion is based on Leslie (1980, 292–4).

not received immediately, but *will* be received after the number of years governing the moving average have passed by (e.g., with a three-year moving average, full payment has taken place after three years). Under the current scheme, however, only one-half of an operating grant is based on a (three-year) moving average of weighted enrolment. The other half is determined by the university's weighted enrolment in the base period, 1974–75–1976–77. Thus enrolling an extra engineer results in only half-payment from the province. (Another way of looking at this situation is that the university will continue to earn a payment, indefinitely, for the 'extra engineer' of 1974–75–1976–77.) A return to the simple moving average approach would clearly bring an immediate gain in enrolment responsiveness.[11]

In thinking about the consequences of halving the weight on current enrolment in the operating grant formula, it may be useful to think of the system as having initially been in competitive equilibrium, with enrolments such that all producers were at the minimum points on their U-shaped average cost curves. Thus to begin with, let us assume, price (tuition fee plus formula grant) equalled both marginal and average cost. Reducing the formula grant by one-half would greatly reduce the (constant) price. Thus enrolment in every program desired by each institution would fall (in order to keep price equal to marginal cost). This would not be immediately or fully realized, no doubt, owing to the bad public relations results and the high capital intensity of educational institutions. Most of the adjustment might therefore come in the form of a reduction in quality. (Some of the adjustment would come in this form even if the universities could throw caution to the winds and behave in a simple, profit-maximizing fashion.) In any case, holding quality constant, there would be no financial incentive to expand programs to accommodate increases in enrolment demand in any area.

To an extent, the predictions of the previous paragraph have been borne out by university behaviour in Ontario in the last few years. A number of universities have placed limits on enrolment, and methods of revising the criteria for the minimum acceptable high school graduate are now being actively discussed. The switch to lower quality also appears evident in the rapid relative expansion of enrolment at some of the institutions specializing in handling large numbers of

11 It has been suggested to us that the current formula is being exploited by some universities, which have accommodated large numbers of undergraduates at the expense of program quality in order to appropriate a larger portion of the global subsidy. It is feared that a return to a formula based 100 per cent on moving average weighted enrolment would exacerbate this problem. We believe the opposite is the case. The strong position of the 'lower quality' institutions appears to us to be the result of the halving in the weight placed on current enrolment in 1978, as set out in the following analysis in the text. Restoring the 100 per cent weight on moving average current enrolment would improve the profitability of higher quality programs and that of the institutions offering them.

undergraduates. The disinclination to expand enrolment appears to be borne out by the continuing excess demand for places in, for example, computer science.

Whether or not the operating grant formula is altered, most of the lack of enrolment responsiveness could be removed by giving the institutions full control over tuition fees, as advocated for the universities, for example, by Peter Leslie (1980, 350) in his recent compendious review of university education in Canada for the AUCC. Whatever the operating grant formula, if the universities and colleges could set their own fees, we can safely predict an elimination of excess enrolment demands. (This does not mean, of course, that the resulting pattern of enrolments and fees would be as desirable as it would if the operating grant formula were reformed.)

One reason that provincial governments may acquiesce in funding arrangements that do not encourage enrolment responsiveness is that the benefits of subsidizing post-secondary education are not entirely captured by the province where the education takes place.[12] To take an example, in 1976, 46 per cent of all graduating engineers in Canada graduated in Ontario, but only 12 per cent graduated in Alberta and BC. A high proportion of the Ontario graduates would probably have found employment in the West. What incentive was there, one may ask, for the Ontario government to provide additional funds for engineering education at this time?

It has been suggested by Leslie (1980, 400) that the federal government should respond to the regional imbalance in output and employment of graduates by compensating net exporting provinces and imposing a special tax on net importers. Such equalization was implicit in the pre-1977, pre-EPF funding regimes, with their flat, per student subsidies or matching grants. Under the previous systems the marginal reward for adding students or spending more money on them could be viewed in part as payment for the benefits to other provinces of the education provided by a given province. Stager (1981, 151) has pointed out that the federal government can increase provinces' willingness to be net exporters by channelling more of its support for post-secondary education through (liberalized) student assistance. Presumably provinces would react by raising fees, and thereby end up with increased marginal inducement to take on students, regardless of destination after graduation. This is another way of (indirectly) relating federal support to post-secondary output, in order to provide payment for the external benefits to the rest of the country of the education provided by any province.

A final point that needs to be addressed is the question of whether some change in the relative support for university and community college education is needed.

---

12 See Leslie (1980, 400–1) and Stager (1981, 151–2).

This is very much an Ontario issue. As we saw in Chapter 5, whereas for the country as a whole college enrolment grew much faster than university enrolment over the 1970s, it did not do so in Ontario. (The period of more rapid college growth in Ontario began only in 1976.) The result is that whereas nationally 40.5 per cent of all post-secondary students are in colleges, the proportion was only 32.0 per cent for Ontario in 1980–81. Both the Ontario Manpower Commission and officials of the Ontario Ministry of Education strongly feel that college enrolment should be greatly expanded in Ontario.[13] The OMC bases its view on projected massive excess supply of university graduates, which will have to be accommodated by giving the university graduates jobs that could have been filled by college graduates. Officials in the Ministry of Education, as well as many others, have further been influenced by the very large apparent excess demand for college attendance.[14]

If both colleges and universities had full control of tuition fees, and if enrolment demand was really stronger at the colleges, we would see an enrolment shift in that direction. This change would be accompanied by a bidding-up of college relative to university fees. The tendency for a fee differential to arise would act as a signal to the provincial government that it ought to increase its support for colleges and reduce that for universities.

In the current situation, where colleges have no control of fees and universities have very little, we could easily have a prolonged situation in which college growth was being unadvisably restricted. However, given present information it is not clear that we are in such a period. It is simply very difficult in a situation where the market mechanism is not being used to gain an accurate view about the strength of relative demand for different post-secondary programs.

IV. CONCLUSION

This chapter has examined the current debate surrounding education and training policy in Canada – a debate involving a confrontation between a number of

13 The feelings of officials in the Ministry of Education were outlined in 'Ontario School Overhaul Focusses on Jobs,' *The Globe and Mail*, 6 January 1982, 1.
14 In 1980–81 the number of college applicants (93 161) exceeded new registrants (42 546) by 119 per cent (data provided by the Special Projects Office of the Ontario Ministry of Colleges and Universities). Interestingly, the number of applicants to Ontario universities exceeds registrants by a similar proportion. Also in 1980–81 there were 61 685 applicants and 33 619 new registrants for apparent excess demand of 84 per cent. Whether these apparent excess demands reflect a true problem is unclear. What is clear, however, is that there is no basis in these kinds of figures for the claim that there is great excess demand at the colleges and a rough balance at the universities.

agencies concerned with labour market policy (including Employment and Immigration Canada) on the one hand, and the representatives of higher education on the other. It has centred on the twin issues of whether a re-allocation of resources away from the post-secondary sector towards more vocational training would be desirable, and whether governments should work towards reallocation of resources and greater enrolment demand responsiveness within the post-secondary sector.

We have examined in detail the arguments provided by the principal proponent of re-allocation, the Federal Task Force on Labour Market Development, whose highly influential report (the Dodge report) was issued in the fall of 1981. This document does not make a strong case for a re-allocation of resources away from the post-secondary sector. There is no evidence available on the social costs and benefits of post-secondary education in Canada for the period after 1972. We therefore simply do not know if public spending on post-secondary education currently represents a good investment. There is clearly a need for a comprehensive and detailed cost-benefit study that would allow us to examine the social rate of return to different forms of post-secondary study. Studies such as Statistics Canada's survey of graduates or the various manpower forecasting exercises that have been undertaken, while in certain respects very interesting, cannot come to grips with the fundamental question of whether post-secondary spending at the current level is justified in terms of a strict accounting of social costs and benefits.

While we do not regard the case for reduced public support for post-secondary education as having been proved, it is undoubtedly true that if the funds that can be spent on education and training in Canada are fixed, increased support for apprenticeship and other forms of on-the-job training (and therefore reduced post-secondary spending) would produce significant gains. This is clear from the simple efficiency argument that since we subsidize formal education at a very high rate and training in industry at a much lower rate the social rate of return to investment in the latter is likely higher. Recently, the drying-up of immigration as a source of skilled workers has meant that the social return to training for the higher-skill trades has likely increased in Canada.

The argument for federal intervention to secure re-allocation of resources within the post-secondary sector has not been made as well as it could have been, but we have argued that it may hold some weight. There are reasons to believe that our post-secondary systems may be insufficiently responsive to changes in enrolment demand. One is that provincial governments engage in heavy regulation of the 'prices' that universities and colleges receive for their instructional services. These prices are extraordinarily inflexible. The result is that whenever there is an increase in demand for graduates in an area where instructional inputs (principally teachers) are a specialized resource, we can expect the supply response on the part of universities and colleges to be less strong than is desirable. Another reason for lack of enrolment responsiveness is the current system of formula funding for Ontario's universities. This puts equal weight on moving average weighted enrolment and base year figures, thereby greatly reducing funding sensitivity to enrolment changes. A final difficulty is that of regional imbalance: the interprovincial structure of post-secondary output differs greatly from the structure of hiring of new graduates. This discrepancy may help explain, for example, the reluctance of Ontario, which produces a large surplus of graduates, to spend on the universities in the late 1970s and early 1980s.

Finally, a point that we have stressed is that the current emphasis on 'techno-logical' and higher skill trade training represents a vocationalism which largely ignores the role of investment in person-specific information in education. There is a trade-off between skill training and investment in information. It is a mistake to believe that every increase in the skill content of education must lead to greater employability and higher earnings. Such increases may come at the expense of information investment and therefore reduce the quality of job-worker matching. An optimal mix of investment in skill and information, rather than exclusive reliance on one form of education, must be sought.

7
Policy conclusions

I INTRODUCTION

In this book our principal goal has been to explore the insights that can be gained by using simple economic models to interpret what takes place in our education and training systems. We have argued that the human capital model and our new approach, which models investment in information about skills and abilities, provide complementary interpretations of observed education and training. In general, the relative importance of human capital accumulation increases as the student passes through his schooling career. However, in some cases the bulk of a student's energies may be devoted largely to information investment right up to the time of leaving formal schooling. Such students are destined to pursue most of their human capital accumulation on the job.

We have put the human capital and informational models to two uses. First, we have asked how they can help explain the important post-secondary enrolment trends over the last two decades. Second, we have used these models as an input in establishing guidelines for public policy towards education and training. Here we will summarize the results of these two exercises. We conclude the chapter by setting out specific policy initiatives recommended for the federal and Ontario governments.

II ANALYSIS OF RECENT ENROLMENT TRENDS

The analysis of post-secondary enrolment trends in Chapter 5 takes on considerable importance because of the 20 per cent decline in the population of post-secondary age (eighteen to twenty-four) that will take place over the next decade. (It will rise again to its current level in the first years of the next century.) This development lends particular interest to the likely future behaviour of post-secondary participation rates.

We have argued that there are two reasons for an underlying secular tendency towards increased educational attainment. First, the direct costs of education (tuition, books, equipment, etc.) have been continually declining relative to forgone earnings. Second, the steady increase in specialization and division of labour is predicted by the informational model to lead to increased relative demand for more educated labour. While the continuation of the relative decline in direct costs of post-secondary education is contingent on government policy, we expect that both these forces will continue to operate over the remaining years of the century.

In fact, there is an argument that the likely rate of decline of direct costs of education relative to forgone (and expected lifetime) earnings will accelerate over the 1980s, giving a boost to post-secondary participation rates exactly when needed. There is some evidence that larger age cohorts experience lower earnings relative to smaller cohorts throughout their lifetimes. Over the period from about 1967 to 1978 the students entering post-secondary education in Ontario belonged to steadily larger age cohorts. Since about 1978, however, this trend has been reversed, and entering students have belonged to increasingly smaller cohorts. As of about 1982 the last of the baby boom generation reached college or university entrance age. Over the next decade the relevant cohort sizes will fall dramatically, likely leading to rapidly rising forgone (and expected lifetime) earnings.

An important point that emerges when there are inputs of goods as well as time in the education production function is that more education can be produced with less time spent in school if goods inputs are increased sufficiently. As we saw in Chapter 5, over the last two decades there has been a substantial increase in real spending per student at the elementary and secondary levels, combined with a broader and more flexible curriculum. As a result, the typical high school graduate today has accumulated more information than his counterpart of ten or twenty years ago. He / she therefore has much less need to invest in information at the post-secondary level. Although other factors are in play, we have suggested this as a contributory explanation of the participation rate slow-down of the 1970s, as well as of the enrolment shift away from arts towards more vocational studies.

If improvements in elementary and secondary education continue to be made, we would expect more dampening of the underlying tendency for participation rates to rise. On the other hand, if further progress at the elementary and secondary level is halted, post secondary participation rates will have a greater tendency to increase.

Another consideration of some importance is that the drying-up of public sector jobs for graduates (especially teaching) in the 1970s should have had a one-time impact on the trend in participation rates. Over the 1970s, we have argued, this lack helped cause an interruption in the secular trend towards greater participation. This cause for interruption no longer exists.

If governments wish to offset the effects of the decline in the post-secondary age population by stimulating participation rates, our analysis would suggest that they should increase spending at the post-secondary level relative to the elementary and secondary levels. We must point out, however, that such a strategy is not necessarily desirable. If rates of subsidy for different levels of education and for students of different types have been set correctly (i.e., more or less equally, except where differential externalities dictate otherwise), why should governments not allow post-secondary enrolments to decline, if they start to do so?

It is sometimes argued that the sensitivity of enrolment to changing demand should be dampened to maintain stability in the post-secondary sector. The response to temporary decline in the demand for engineers, for example, should not be to lay off engineering professors, because over the long run costs are minimized by having a stable work force. It is not clear that this argument has a great deal of force when the anticipated enrolment trough may last for fifteen or twenty years – as would be the case in Canada if participation rates were constant through the remainder of this century.

While special action to prevent enrolment decline may not be warranted, changes in policy that are justified by other considerations may have the side-effect of offsetting such decline to some extent. Giving post-secondary institutions more control over tuition fees, for example, would allow them much more scope to respond to the changing structure of enrolment demand. This is particularly true in Ontario, where the province has been providing falling real support for the universities for many years, without allowing tuition fee increases sufficient to offset the loss of revenue.

III BASIC POLICY GUIDELINES

In our Chapter 4 we set out an economic rationale for government intervention in education and training and spelled out the policy guidelines that are implied. An alternative rationale for intervention with far-reaching policy implications has recently been propounded by the federal government and others.

We argued that there are two fundamental economic criteria that might justify public intervention in education. One is to achieve greater economic efficiency, and the other is to pursue redistribution. Intervention on efficiency grounds is warranted, first, if there are thought to be significant positive externalities of education; their presence indicates a need for general subsidies to education and training. The other potential efficiency basis for intervention is that private insurance markets for earnings are incomplete, which results in students' experiencing difficulties in borrowing to finance education. The state can deal with this problem by making loans available to students in amounts sufficient to ensure that no one need terminate schooling artificially early, owing to a lack of borrowing opportunities. Such loans ensure that the external benefits of education will in fact be received.

It is important to note that the externalities argument for subsidies applies to on-the-job training (OJT), as well as to formal education. (One externality, for example, results from reduced probability and duration of unemployment, since society in general shares the costs of unemployment through the unemployment insurance system.)

In the past most OJT has proceeded with very little explicit subsidy, in contrast to formal schooling, thus implying that there would be an efficiency gain if any given fixed total to be spent in support of education were more evenly divided between formal education and OJT.

We should also repeat that there is no case for government intervention to resolve labour market 'imbalances' per se. Surpluses and shortages would be dealt with as quickly as is efficient in competitive markets without government interference. Unlike other imbalances, those in labour markets may take years to disappear, owing to the time required to train new workers. This delay is inescapable and is not a justification for government intervention. Arbitrarily speeding up adjustment may be inefficient.

Although there is no general case for governments to correct labour market imbalances, if one level of government pursues policies that exacerbate imbalances, it may be desirable for another level to take offsetting action. In Canada, we have argued, policies that enjoy wide public support but slow down the adjustment processes that correct imbalances are, owing to the constitutional division of powers, implemented by the provinces. Tuition fee policies and the form of provincial funding effectively fix prices in the post-secondary sector, with easily understood consequences for institutions' responsiveness to altered demand for graduates of different types; apprenticeship regulations discourage employers from providing some forms of training; and minimum wage laws discourage on-the-job training generally. If policies to remove or offset these distortions can be devised, action whose by-product is the amelioration of imbalances may be warranted.

Intervention may be justified on equity as well as efficiency grounds. The equity rationale is not to provide universal access to education – the comprehensive student loan plan warranted on efficiency grounds alone will give us that

– but to use education as a redistributive tool. Equity-motivated intervention is warranted if forms of support for education that are genuinely redistributive can be devised, and donors (i.e., taxpayers) strongly prefer in-kind education transfers to cash transfers. (It should be noted that the insistence on in-kind transfers bears a cost – the difference between the cost of placing an extra dollar in a donee's hands via the in-kind transfer and the cost of achieving the same transfer in cash.)

Subsidizing post-secondary education, even by means-tested grants, clearly does not achieve redistribution towards the lowest expected lifetime earners. Two ways to achieve the goal are (1) to improve elementary and secondary education (something which has in fact been done, if we are to believe the evidence on per capita spending over the last two decades); and (2) to subsidize OJT for the youngest workers.

The argument for subsidizing OJT as a redistributive tool reinforces the argument for subsidy on efficiency grounds. The only difficulty is that sometimes OJT is not easily monitored. This does not mean, however, that its support is unfeasible. Empirical evidence suggests that a significant part of workers' effort is generally devoted to training in the initial years of employment.[1] A close approximation to OJT subsidy can therefore be achieved by providing wage subsidies for young labour force entrants. To add more of a redistributive element, we have suggested that the rate of subsidy should be inversely related to age. Thus, the worker who enters the labour force at age eighteen could benefit from substantial wage subsidies for his first few years of work, while a university graduate would receive much less benefit (if any).

Finally, we have pointed out that direct state provision of education and training, as opposed to the mere subsidization of a competitive education industry, involves certain costs. There is no natural mechanism to ensure the correct mix and amount of different kinds of education – for example of investment in skills on the one hand and in person-specific information on the other. We have therefore argued that much greater use of the market mechanism should be made – via a voucher system or tax credit for independent school fees in the elementary and secondary schools, and by giving post-secondary institutions freedom to compete more effectively.

IV SPECIFIC POLICY RECOMMENDATIONS

As our final contribution we should like to outline the specific federal and Ontario government policy initiatives in education and training that our study suggests.

1 See, for example, Mincer (1974).

IV.1 *Federal policy*

Our study suggests that federal initiatives are needed in both manpower training and post-secondary funding.

We argued in Chapter 4 that on both efficiency and equity grounds it would be desirable to have general subsidies to on-the-job training in the initial years of working life. As outlined in the previous section, an appropriate mechanism would be a system of wage subsidies for young workers inversely related to age. To emphasize the redistributive element, we suggest a flat-rate scheme. Subsidies of something like $1.50 an hour for all workers aged fifteen to eighteen, $1.00 for those nineteen to twenty, and $0.50 for those twenty-one and twenty-two might be appropriate.

Rough calculations indicate that gross subsidies under the system of OJT subsidy suggested in the previous paragraph would total about $2 billion annually.[2] That is, such a program would inevitably be very expensive. (The federal manpower training budget as of 1982 was about $1 billion, and total post-secondary expenditure about $8 billion.) In the current atmosphere of government restraint, additional expenditure on this scale seems unlikely to be undertaken. In line with our claim in previous chapters that if the global subsidy to education and training from all levels of government cannot be increased, a re-allocation of expenditure from formal education towards OJT is warranted, we would recommend that the funds required to finance our suggested wage subsidies for young workers be obtained by reducing expenditure on formal education. Unfortunately, the federal government does not have the policy tools necessary to effect that re-allocation unilaterally, as discussed below. Federal-provincial co-operation, which may be difficult to obtain, is required.

We have declined to comment in detail on the design of federal manpower training policy. As is often pointed out, there has been a proliferation of manpower programs as well as no dearth of critical assessments. We have no expertise that would allow us to add a great deal to this discussion. However, we can make some general comments.

Manpower training arises mainly to mitigate the difficulties faced by the 'structurally' unemployed. They can be either young workers whose education has not rendered them sufficiently attractive potential employees or older workers who must retrain as a result of technological or other changes. The problems of those in the first category would be considerably eased by our

---

2 This calculation is based on the currently observed composition of the labour force aged fifteen to twenty-two. Ignoring the effect of the proposed subsidies on labour force participation rates is not too misleading, because, as often pointed out in this study, the population of young people will decline rapidly over the next ten years.

proposal for general wage subsidies for young workers. Such subsidies are predicted to improve both the employment opportunities and degree of training received by young workers. Nevertheless, some young members of the labour force will continue to have severe problems in finding work. In addition, our wage subsidies would not help unemployed older workers. For these reasons public support for retraining would continue to be required.

Recently, Employment and Immigration Canada adopted a new 'National Training Program' under which manpower training in the future will primarily take place in skills in high labour market demand (as evaluated by the Canadian Occupational Projection System – COPS). While this initiative may represent an improvement on previous arrangements, it would be inconsistent with the general approach to government's role in education and training that we are espousing in this study not to point out the possibility of further improvement.

We see no essential reason why the strategy of exploiting the market mechanism to get the right mix and amount of different forms of training could not be applied to manpower training as well as to more formal education. Why should manpower trainees not be allowed the same kind of freedom of choice as, say, post-secondary students? They could, for example, be given vouchers that could be redeemed at any accredited institution for manpower training – including private schools and ordinary firms, as well as provincial technical colleges. Employment and Immigration Canada would no doubt wish to continue its manpower forecasting in order to provide trainees with information designed to help them make appropriate choices. In our view, however, we have much stronger assurance of good choices, and of manpower training resources' being well allocated, if the trainees are free to act as they believe is best in the light of information both from sources like COPS and from their own private sources.

Finally, there is the question of the form of federal funding of post-secondary education. Until 1977 federal support was provided by means of matching grants. Alarm over rapidly increasing provincial expenditures, not only in post-secondary education but also in health, led to 'Established Programs Financing' (EPF) – in force since 1977. EPF provides block grants (partly in the form of tax points and partly in cash) based on the size of federal support for health and education in 1975–76, escalated through time according to the growth rate of GNP. These grants are invariant with respect to actual provincial expenditures on health and education. For a variety of reasons different agencies of the federal government view EPF as a matter of concern: some because the expenditures are seen as placing too much strain on the federal deficit; others (like Employment and Immigration) because the transfers have no incentive effects on provincial spending priorities.

Evidently Employment and Immigration Canada would like to see the education component of EPF replaced by some method of finance that would encourage provinces to expand post-secondary education in some areas and contract it in others. Specifically, expansion in 'high technology' occupations or those in high demand would be encouraged, and elsewhere the aim would be contraction. The Federal Task Force on Labour Market Development has proposed three principal tools for achieving such an objective:

1. a reduction in basic federal support for post-secondary education, which would force an increase in tuition fees; the greater the reliance on fees, the greater enrolment responsiveness;
2. increased spending on student aid by the federal government, with differential rates of aid across programs, depending on differences in fees and strength of demand for graduates;
3. federal grants matching private sector contributions to establish new programs in growth areas and federal support for co-operative education.

While discretionary support for different types of post-secondary training motivated by anticipated shortages of particular types of graduates has some dangers, given the difficulties in manpower forecasting, we have argued that the way provincial governments finance post-secondary institutions creates some rigidity, which the federal government might legitimately want to offset. For that reason initiatives like those suggested by the federal task force might seem attractive if it were believed that they were likely to provide scope for enrolment responsiveness.

Let us focus our attention on the two central planks of the new funding mechanism proposed by the federal task force (the third seems relatively unobjectionable). On the first point, while a reduction in basic federal support might be a good idea, it would not be likely to lead to much greater reliance on tuition fees. Since the EPF transfers are lump sum, their reduction would have an impact on *all* forms of provincial spending and therefore probably a fairly small impact on post-secondary spending. This small impact could be for the best, however, since provinces would probably prevent tuition fees from rising sufficiently to offset reduced operating grants to the colleges and universities. In short, the likely result of reductions in federal transfers to support education would be a small increase in fees, insufficient to prevent a decline in college and university revenue per student, leading (ultimately) to reduced quality of post-secondary education.

The second lever the federal task force would use to encourage enrolment responsiveness – increasing student aid – appears more promising than reducing federal transfers to the provinces. Provinces would likely increase tuition fees in response to increased federal student aid, since increased fees would be made palatable to the public by the increased aid, and higher fees could be used to take the strain off provincial budgets by somewhat reducing operating grants. The recent substantial increase in borrowing limits under the CSLP is to be applauded.

Is there anything else the federal government could do to encourage enrolment responsiveness? If part of current lump sum grants under EPF could be tied instead to an appropriately weighted index of post-secondary enrolment, federal dollars would encourage enrolment demand responsiveness rather than merely swelling provincial coffers. (Federal funds could also be made partly contingent on the provinces' increasing tuition fee revenue.) Detailed federal-provincial consultation would of course be required to implement such a change. However, it seems to us that the federal government is in a sufficiently strong bargaining position to secure a new regime wherein post-secondary funding was related to enrolment.

While we agree with the federal task force that increased student aid can be used to encourage increases in tuition fees and therefore greater enrolment responsiveness, we do not believe it is wise to provide differential aid based on the type of program the student is enrolled in. There are serious dangers associated with intervention to secure short-term labour market goals. Where universities and colleges are operating in reasonably competitive conditions and shifts in enrolment demand do not affect the more expensive programs (i.e., those most difficult to expand under provincial funding systems), the mere prediction of a surplus or shortage does not justify federal alarm or intervention. And even where provincial funding arrangements make expansion in the area of predicted shortage difficult, it is not clear that federal intervention is always warranted. In order to decide on the sort of marginal incentives to provide, federal planners would have to forecast demand conditions three to five years down the road on a regular and detailed basis. Experience with previous manpower forecasting shows that the danger of anticipated booms and busts' failing to materialize is real.

Finally, as raised earlier in this subsection in our discussion of subsidies to OJT, there should be a second goal of federal initiatives in post-secondary funding, in addition to the objective of securing greater enrolment responsiveness. We recommended that the federal government should attempt to promote a re-allocation of the total subsidy to education and training provided by all levels of government away from formal education towards OJT. Merely reducing federal support for post-secondary education is not a satisfactory method of effecting this re-allocation, we would argue, because of the likely provincial response: inadequate increases in tuition fees and further post-secondary underfunding. The poor results of simply cutting federal support imply a need, in our view, for some hard bargaining directed at obtaining a re-allocation of resources without undesirable side-effects. The federal government could, for example, reduce its support for post-secondary education but at the same time threaten not to introduce the wage subsidy for young workers in a province unless tuition fees were raised sufficiently to bring post-secondary revenues up to some target level.

IV.2 *Recommended policy for the Ontario government*

There is a great deal of current concern about the quality of education in Ontario (as elsewhere in Canada) – at all levels of the system. Since the schools, colleges, and universities are all under varying degrees of provincial control, this dissatis- faction raises the question of provincial policy initiatives.

We have argued at length, in Chapter 4, that the only reliable way to ensure technical efficiency in education and the correct mix and amount of different forms of education – human capital formation, investment in person-specific information, etc. – is to use the market mechanism. It is far too difficult to *plan* an education system so that by state direction of resources the goals of efficiency in production and correct composition of output can be achieved. An indication of the difficulty is given by the fact that while the province has bowed to the apparent general desire for 'higher standards' in the secondary schools with a reform that will considerably reduce flexibility of course selection, some argue that it is becoming increasingly important to preserve curricular choice because of the apparently accelerating pace of technical change. We may therefore have a diametrical opposition of views among thoughtful and knowledgeable observers who share a concern for educational quality. In our view this illustrates why an attempt to run an education system on the basis of central planning must fail. The planners have no crystal ball that allows them to discern the optimal methods and curriculum.

There is a strong need in Ontario for much more parent and student choice among institutions at the elementary and secondary level. Currently there is an element of choice between the public and separate systems and between schools within each system. However, this does not appear to ensure sufficient choice to simulate a competitive outcome. We would like to see introduced something like British Columbia's Independent Schools Support Act of 1977. As outlined in Chapter 4, this legislation provides a sizeable per student subsidy to accredited independent schools, thereby considerably increasing the element of choice for parents and students.

It should be noted that a significant by-product of allowing choice between public and independent schools would be provision of an objective test of the quality of the public system. At present there are mixed opinions about which way the public schools ought to move – towards more vocational emphasis, greater stress on 'basics,' or towards greater flexibility. The changes that are genuinely warranted would be easier to see if we could observe how the programs freely chosen at independent schools by those who opted out differed from the public school menu.

At the post-secondary level less radical change is required, because many of the elements of competition are already in place – there are numerous alternative institutions, faculties, and programs, all in direct competition for students, and the institutions have considerable control over the kind of studies they offer students. The principal barriers to competition are controls on price (regulation of tuition fees) and on programs (provincial authorization is required before a wide range of new types of program may be introduced).

Previously in this book (especially in Chapter 4) we have discussed methods of increasing freedom of choice and competition in the post-secondary systems. We propose not to repeat the rationale for these methods at this stage but to outline how they can be applied in the particular case of Ontario. We recommend the implementation of the following three changes in provincial policy towards colleges and universities:

1. The institutions should have full control over tuition fees. This is a vital prerequisite for the operation of the market mechanism. Prices must be flexible in order to play their allocative role and in order to transmit information on required changes in allocation through the system.
2. The institutions should be given full control over which programs are offered. It is no good having flexible prices signalling required changes if the institutions do not have full freedom to innovate and to try to capture student demand.
3. At the university level, the formula for determining operating grants should be reformed. Its one-half basis in 1974–77 enrolments should be terminated. A return to 100 per cent reliance on a moving average of current enrolments should be restored. If the moving average of current enrolment is weighted only 50 per cent, provincial operating grants lose a great deal of their power to induce appropriate response of universities to student demand, as outlined in the previous chapter.

It will be objected by some that the above package would expose colleges and universities too greatly to the rigours of the marketplace. There is a fear of 'destabilization,' which may appear eminently justified in view of the sudden enrolment shocks of the last two decades. There is also an anxiety that the liberal arts may be cut back so much that the essential character of the universities is threatened.

While the measures we advocate would undoubtedly increase the exposure of post-secondary institutions to market forces, we do not envisage these negative results. Use of the price mechanism could actually reduce the amplitude of enrolment swings and would cushion the institutions from the effects of changes in the structure of enrolment demand. When demand for a program increases, at present the institutions are urged from many quarters to expand – with no increase in the financial reward and frequently with rapidly rising input costs. With flexible tuition fees, however, an increase in price can be used both to choke off the excess demand and to raise the revenue required to expand, without reducing quality. Conversely, when demand falls, a decline in price can be used to encourage students to enter a program temporarily out of fashion.

Protection from 'destabilization' can be increased by lengthening the span of the moving average of current enrolment used in the operating grant formula. Even under, say, a five-year moving average there is *eventual* full reward for answering student demand. And with a long moving average, institutional revenues would move quite gradually – slowly enough for the excess costs of undesirably quick adjustments to be avoided.[3]

Also, it is far from clear that the long-term viability of the liberal arts is threatened by encouraging institutional responsiveness to enrolment demand. The need for this type of program has too strong a basis to be permanently or seriously eroded. While the number of students who wish to *specialize* in the liberal arts may be permanently smaller in the future than it was, say, in the 1960s (when we must recall so many graduates were destined for teaching), there should be strong demand for some liberal arts study by those who end up specializing elsewhere. This demand is based on the following: a strong consumption component (presumably buoyant in our ever more highly educated society); an important skills element (writing and analytical skills, knowledge of political processes and government, etc.); and, finally, the likely considerable importance of the liberal arts in person-specific information investment.

IV.3 *Conclusion*

In conclusion, in order to ensure that our education and training systems in future provide the correct mix and amount of alternative elements – human capital or skills accumulation, investment in person-specific information, and other forms

---

3 It has been suggested that there remains a problem of supporting capacity in programs that go out of fashion but that we can reliably expect will come back into demand. Here, an analogy may help. In a recession a manufacturer will not lay off as many skilled workers as it would if it were expected that the downturn in business was permanent. Temporary losses on the wage account are accepted as an investment whose pay-off comes in the form of an appropriate labour force when demand picks up. This occurs without government intervention (actually despite it, since unemployment insurance likely induces more lay-offs in this situation than would otherwise occur). In the universities' case we can rely on a like mechanism. Unpopular faculties and programs will not be cut to the bone by profit-maximizing universities, as long as it is anticipated that demand will pick up in the future.

of education – we believe that the federal and provincial governments should work to organize these systems as far as possible along competitive free market lines. Studies such as the present one can provide some insight about what goes on in the education and training systems, but even with the most careful scrutiny it is not possible to acquire the comprehensive and detailed knowledge that would be necessary to achieve efficiency in education via central planning.

In the absence of a move towards more competitive conditions what lessons does this study have for policy makers? The major moral is perhaps that they should recognize that skill acquisition is not the only element of education that is justified from a job market point of view. A great deal of the current activity in our education and training systems is more accurately characterized as investment in information rather than in vocational skills. The current trend towards increased vocational training ignores the fact that greater emphasis on skills may mean a diminution in this other basic element of education. We may turn out graduates who are on average more skilled, but who also have less information about their inherent capacities and therefore end up on average with poorer job-worker matches.

While it may be an appropriate strategy now to increase skill acquisition at the cost of reducing the average quality of job-worker matches, it is clear that this will not always be the case. If planners are at least aware that there is another element in education, aside from skill acquisition, that is important for the job market success of graduates, they may react more quickly when the signs that a switch back from vocationalism is necessary begin to be seen. The ability to react quickly may be especially important in the near future if, as many expect, the rapid, perhaps increasing current pace of technological change leads students to conclude that they are better off investing to a greater extent in person-specific information and to a lesser extent in narrow skills that may rapidly become obsolete.

Appendix

In this appendix we provide formal demonstrations of the propositions advanced in Chapter 3. Since it is intended to be a rigorous complement to the chapter, rather than a substitute for it, we assume the reader to be familiar with the model, its notation, and the intuition behind the results.

The analysis in Chapter 3 is fully rigorous up to and including the development of the expression for expected income. We therefore start at that point.

A.1 EXPECTED INCOME

Let $\mathcal{E}(\theta, \pi)$ denote the expected income corresponding to $(\theta, \pi) \in \{[1/2, 1] \times [0, 1]\}$. $\mathcal{E}(\cdot)$ has the properties

$$\mathcal{E}(\theta, \pi) = \begin{cases} \alpha_0 + \alpha_1 \pi & \text{for } \theta\epsilon[1/2, \pi], \quad \text{and } \pi\epsilon[1/2, 1] \\ \bar{O} + \alpha_1[\dfrac{\theta + \pi}{2} - 1/2] + \beta_1[\dfrac{\theta + (1 - \pi)}{2} - 1/2] & \theta\epsilon[\max(\pi, 1 - \pi), 1] \\ \beta_0 + \beta_1(1 - \pi) & \text{for } \theta\epsilon[1/2, 1 - \pi], \text{ and } \pi\epsilon[0, 1/2]. \end{cases}$$

Using subscripts to denote partial differentiation, for $\theta\epsilon[\max(\pi, 1 - \pi), 1]$ we have

$$\mathcal{E}_\theta = (\alpha_1 + \beta_1)/2, \tag{A1}$$
$$\mathcal{E}_\pi = (\alpha_1 - \beta_1)/2, \tag{A2}$$

and

$$\mathcal{E}_{\theta\theta} = \mathcal{E}_{\pi\pi} = \mathcal{E}_{\theta\pi} = 0, \tag{A3}$$

A.2 COST OF INFORMATION ACCUMULATION

The cost of information accumulation depends on θ, π, and P_K. This relationship is developed by minimizing the input cost of obtaining a given level of θ. Of course, the technological relationship between θ, s, and K must be specified first.

A.2.a *Information quality technology*

Let $\Omega = \{[0, 1] \times [0, \infty]\}$. θ is produced according to

$$\theta = h(s, K), \tag{A4}$$

where for all $(s, K) \epsilon \Omega$, $h(\cdot)$ is twice continuously differentiable in both arguments and strictly concave. In addition it is assumed that: $\forall (s, K) \epsilon \Omega$,

$$h(0, K) = h(s, 0) = 0, \tag{A5}$$
$$K \neq 0 \rightarrow h_s(s, K) > 0, \tag{A6}$$
$$s \neq 0 \rightarrow h_K(s, K) > 0, \tag{A7}$$

and

$$\lim_{\substack{s \to 1 \\ K \to \infty}} h(s, K) = \bar{\theta} < 1. \tag{A8}$$

(A5)–(A8) are conventional. For simplicity it is also assumed that neither s nor K is ever inferior: $\forall (s, K) \epsilon \Omega$, both

$$h_s h_{KK} - h_K h_{sK} < 0, \tag{A9}$$

and

$$h_s h_{sK} - h_K h_{ss} > 0. \tag{A10}$$

A.2.b *Cost minimization*

The cost minimization problem assumes that the expression for $\mathcal{E}(\theta, \pi)$, when $\theta \epsilon[\max(\pi, 1 - \pi), 1]$ is the relevant one for all θ. This assumption is harmless, because, as explained in the text, the only interior θ that are potentially optimal are those for which this expression is indeed appropriate. The cost minimization problem is

$$\min_{s, K \epsilon \Omega} s\mathcal{E} + P_K K$$

$$\text{s.t. } \theta = h(s, K).$$

The Lagrange function is

$$\mathcal{L}(s, K, \lambda) = s\mathcal{E} + P_K K + \lambda[\theta - h(s, K)],$$

where λ is a non-negative undetermined multiplier. The first-order necessary conditions are

$$\mathcal{L}_s = \mathcal{E} - \lambda h_s = 0, \tag{A11}$$

$$\mathscr{L}_K = P_K - \lambda h_K = 0, \tag{A12}$$

and

$$\mathscr{L}_\lambda = \theta - h(\cdot) = 0, \tag{A13}$$

where all functions are evaluated at the optimal values of s, K, and λ. The second-order necessary conditions, which are also sufficient here, are

$$h_{ss}h_{KK} - h_{sK}^2 > 0 \tag{A14}$$

and

$$-h_K^2 h_{ss} + 2h_s h_K h_{sK} - h_s^2 h_{KK} > 0, \tag{A15}$$

where s, K, and λ again take on their optimal values.

Assuming (A14) and (A15) to be satisfied, (A11)–(A13) yield continuously differentiable functions $\bar{s}(\theta, \pi, P_K)$, $\bar{K}(\theta, \pi, P_K)$, and $\lambda(\theta, \pi, P_K)$. The first two functions are interpreted as output-compensated factor demand functions. The properties of these functions are required for the derivation of the properties of the cost function and the comparative statics analysis on θ.

A.2.c *Properties of $\bar{s}(\cdot)$, $\bar{K}(\cdot)$, and $\lambda(\cdot)$*

Total differentiation of the system (A11)–(A13), with minor manipulation, yields

$$\begin{bmatrix} \lambda h_{ss} & \lambda h_{sK} & h_s \\ \lambda h_{Ks} & \lambda h_{KK} & h_K \\ h_s & h_K & 0 \end{bmatrix} \begin{bmatrix} ds \\ dK \\ d\lambda \end{bmatrix} = \begin{bmatrix} \mathcal{E}_\theta & \mathcal{E}_\pi & 0 \\ 0 & 0 & 1 \\ 1 & 0 & 0 \end{bmatrix} \begin{bmatrix} d\theta \\ d\pi \\ dP_K \end{bmatrix} \tag{A16}$$

(A15) implies that the 3×3 matrix on the left-hand side of (A16) has a positive determinant, which we shall call D.

Consider $d\theta > 0$ and $d\pi = dP_K = 0$. Solving (A16) yields

$$\bar{s}_\theta = 1/D\{-h_K^2 \mathcal{E}_\theta + \lambda(h_K h_{sK} - h_s h_{KK})\} \gtrless 0, \tag{A17}$$

$$\bar{K}_\theta = 1/D\{h_s h_K \mathcal{E}_\theta + \lambda(h_s h_{Ks} - h_K h_{ss})\} > 0, \tag{A18}$$

and

$$\lambda_\theta = 1/D\{\lambda \mathcal{E}_\theta(h_K h_{Ks} - h_s h_{KK}) + \lambda^2(h_{ss}h_{KK} - h_{sK}^2)\} > 0. \tag{A19}$$

As discussed in the text, that the restrictions imposed so far are not sufficient to sign $\bar{s}_\theta$ is somewhat inconvenient. However, it is not hard to show that $\bar{s}_\theta > 0$ is clearly the leading case and delineate the circumstances under which it will fail. The nature of the additional restrictions imposed by assuming $\bar{s}_\theta > 0$ is therefore clarified.

To that end consider the following: Let $\eta_W{}^Z$ be the general notation for the elasticity of Z with respect to W: $(dZ/Z) \div (dW/W)$. By inspection, (A17) yields

$$\bar{s}_\theta > 0 \leftrightarrow \lambda(h_K h_{sK} - h_s h_{KK}) > h_K{}^2 \mathcal{E}_\theta. \tag{A20}$$

Using (11) and the fact that

$$- \partial(h_K/h_s)/\partial K = (h_K h_{sK} - h_s h_{KK})/h_s{}^2$$

(which is positive under (A9)), minor manipulation gives an alternative representation of (A20):

$$\bar{s}_\theta > 0 \leftrightarrow -\eta_K{}^{h_K/h_s} > \eta_K{}^\theta \eta_\theta{}^\varepsilon. \tag{A21}$$

Concavity of $h( )$ implies $\eta_K{}^\theta < 1$. From (A1) it can be shown that $\eta_\varepsilon{}^\theta < 1$. So

$$-\eta_K{}^{h_K/h_s} > 1 \rightarrow \bar{s}_\theta > 0. \tag{A22}$$

Evidence on $-\eta_K{}^{h_K/h_s}$ is a little hard to come by, but $-\eta_K{}^{h_K/h_s} = 1/\sigma$ for the CES technology, where σ is the elasticity of substitution. Thus $\bar{s}_\theta > 0$ is clearly the leading case and may be expected to hold, provided s and K are not too highly substitutable (recalling that (A22) is merely a sufficient condition).

The effects of changes in π and P_K are more straightforward. Proceeding as above,

$$\bar{s}_\pi = (1/D) -h_K{}^2 \mathcal{E}_\pi < 0, \tag{A23}$$

$$\bar{K}_\pi = (1/D) h_s h_K \mathcal{E}_\pi > 0, \tag{A24}$$

$$\lambda_\pi = (1/D)\lambda \mathcal{E}_\pi (h_K h_{sK} - h_s h_{KK}) > 0, \tag{A25}$$

$$\bar{s}_{P_K} = 1/D h_s h_K > 0, \tag{A26}$$

$$\bar{K}_{P_K} = (1/D) -h_s{}^2 < 0, \tag{A27}$$

and

$$\lambda_{P_K} = (1/D)\lambda(h_s h_{sK} - h_K h_{ss}) > 0. \tag{A28}$$

A.2.d *The cost function and its properties*
The cost function for information quality is the value of the cost minimizing bundle of factors:

$$C(\theta, \pi, P_K) = \bar{s}(\theta, \pi, P_K)\mathcal{E}(\theta, \pi) + P_K \bar{K}(\theta, \pi, P_K). \tag{A29}$$

Marginal cost (C_θ) is positive and increasing when $\bar{s}_\theta > 0$. For $\bar{s}_\theta < 0$, it is possible to construct cases wherein $C_{\theta\theta} < 0$ holds. These examples correspond to large values of $\eta_\theta{}^\varepsilon$ and thus suggest that declining marginal cost is not relevant in our case. However, these examples are merely suggestive. Accordingly, this is one point at which the assumption $s_\theta > 0$ may be a real restriction.

Differentiation of (A29) yields

$$C_\theta = \bar{s}\mathcal{E}_\theta + \mathcal{E}\bar{s}_\theta + P_K\bar{K}_\theta. \tag{A30}$$

(A11)–(A13), (A17), and (A18) yield

$$C_\theta = \lambda + \bar{s}\mathcal{E}_\theta > 0. \tag{A31}$$

Differentiation of (A30) yields (again using (A11)–(A13), (A17), and (A18))

$$C_{\theta\theta} = \lambda_\theta + \bar{s}_\theta \mathcal{E}_\theta > 0, \tag{A32}$$

from (A19), (A1), and $\bar{s}_\theta > 0$.

Proceeding in a similar fashion yields

$$C_\pi = \bar{s}\mathcal{E}_\pi > 0 \tag{A33}$$

from (A2);

$$C_{\pi\pi} = \bar{s}_\pi \mathcal{E}_\pi < 0 \tag{A34}$$

from (A23) and (A2); and

$$C_{\theta\pi} = \bar{s}_\theta \mathcal{E}_\pi > 0 \tag{A35}$$

from (A2) and $\bar{s}_\theta > 0$. (A35) is a standard result from the theory of the firm. When a factor price rises, costs rise; but marginal costs rise or fall depending upon whether the factor is normal or inferior.

Moreover,

$$C_{P_K} = \bar{K} > 0; \tag{A36}$$

$$C_{P_K P_K} = \bar{K}_{P_K} < 0 \tag{A37}$$

from (A27); and

$$C_{\theta P_K} = \bar{K}_\theta > 0 \tag{A38}$$

from (A18).

A.3 OPTIMAL INVESTMENT

The discussion of optimal investment presented in the text is fully rigorous. Assuming $\theta > 1/2$ is optimal, the first-order necessary condition for a maximum is

$$\mathcal{E}_\theta = C_\theta. \tag{A39}$$

The second-order necessary condition (also sufficient here) is $C_{\theta\theta} > 0$. Let $\theta*$ denote the solution to (A39). As discussed in the text, $\theta* > \max(\pi, 1 - \pi)$ is obvious. Whether $\theta*$ or $\theta = 1/2$ is optimal depends on whether

$$\mathcal{E}(\theta*, \pi) - C(\theta*, \pi, P_K) > \mathcal{E}(1/2, \pi). \tag{A40}$$

$\theta = 1/2$ is optimal when (A40) fails.

The only point that needs discussion in addition to that provided in the text is as follows: there exist values of π, denoted π_L and π_U, such that $\theta = \theta*$ is optimal if and only if $\pi \in [\pi_L, \pi_U]$, where $\pi_L \in [0, 1/2)$ and $\pi_U \in (1/2, 1]$. Further, $\pi_U < 1 - \pi_L$.

To see the first point, define $V(\pi)$ to be the net expected life income when $\theta = 1/2$, less that when $\theta = \theta*$:

$$V(\pi) = \mathcal{E}(1/2, \pi) - [\mathcal{E}(\theta*, \pi) - C(\theta*, \pi, P_K)]. \tag{A41}$$

First consider $\pi \in (1/2, 1]$. $V(1/2) < 0$ and $V(1) > 0$ are obvious. Since $V(\cdot)$ is continuous in π, a unique π_U exists if and only if $dV / d\pi > 0$. Evaluating the derivative,

$$dV / d\pi = \alpha_1 - [(\mathcal{E}_\theta - C_\theta)d\theta / d\pi + \mathcal{E}_\pi - C_\pi]$$

$$= \alpha_1 - (\mathcal{E}_\pi - C_\pi) \qquad \text{because } \theta* \text{ satisfies (A39)}$$

$$= \alpha_1 - [(\alpha_1 - \beta_1)/2] + C_\pi \qquad \text{from (A2)}$$

$$= [(\alpha_1 + \beta_1)/2] + C_\pi > 0 \qquad \text{from (A33)}.$$

The proof for $\pi < 1/2$ is analogous.

The second point is that $\pi_U < 1 - \pi_L$. To see this, define $\tilde{\pi} \equiv 1 - \pi_L$. Consider raising π from π_L to $\tilde{\pi}$. Then ask whether $\theta > 1/2$ is preferred to $\theta = 1/2$ if $\pi = \tilde{\pi}$. If not, then $\tilde{\pi} = 1 - \pi_L > \pi_U$.

When π is raised from π_L to $\tilde{\pi}$, $\mathcal{E}(1/2, \pi)$ rises from $\beta_0 + \beta_1(1 - \pi_L)$ to $\alpha_0 + \alpha_1\tilde{\pi}$.

Now,

$$\alpha_0 + \alpha_1\tilde{\pi} = \bar{0} + \alpha_1(\pi - 1/2)$$

and

$$\beta_0 + \beta_1(1 - \pi_L) = \bar{0} + \beta_1[(1 - \pi_L) - 1/2]$$

$$= \bar{0} + \beta_1(\tilde{\pi} - 1/2).$$

Clearly then,

$$(\alpha_0 + \alpha_1\tilde{\pi}) - [\beta_0 + \beta_1(1 - \pi_L)] = (\alpha_1 - \beta_1)(\tilde{\pi} - 1/2).$$

thus $\mathcal{E}(1/2, \pi)$ rises by $(\alpha_1 - \beta_1)(\tilde{\pi} - 1/2)$.

The net expected life income for $\theta > 1/2$ changes from $\mathcal{E}(\theta_L, \pi_L) - C(\theta_L, \pi_L, P_K)$ to $\mathcal{E}(\tilde{\theta}, \tilde{\pi}) - C(\tilde{\theta}, \tilde{\pi}, P_K)$, where θ_L and $\tilde{\theta}$ are the levels of θ associated with π_L and $\tilde{\pi}$, respectively. Note that $\tilde{\theta} > 1/2$ may be assumed. For if $\tilde{\theta} = 1/2$, $\pi_U \leqslant \tilde{\pi}$ is immediate.

Now consider $\mathcal{E}(\tilde{\theta}, \tilde{\pi}) - \mathcal{E}(\theta_L, \pi_L)$. Since $\mathcal{E}_{\pi\pi} = \mathcal{E}_{\theta\pi} = 0$,

$$\mathcal{E}(\tilde{\theta}, \tilde{\pi}) - \mathcal{E}(\theta_L, \pi_L) = \mathcal{E}_\pi(\tilde{\pi} - \pi_L) + \mathcal{E}_\theta(\tilde{\theta} - \theta_L)$$

$$= [(\alpha_1 - \beta_1)/2](\tilde{\pi} - \pi_L) + [(\alpha_1 + \beta_1)/2](\tilde{\theta} - \theta_L)$$

$$= (\alpha_1 - \beta_1)(\tilde{\pi} - 1/2) + [(\alpha_1 + \beta_1)/2](\tilde{\theta} - \theta_L).$$

Further, when π_L is raised to $\tilde{\pi}$, costs change from $C(\theta_L, \pi_L, P_K)$ to $C(\tilde{\theta}, \tilde{\pi}, P_K)$. Thus if $\theta = 1/2$ and $\theta = \theta_L$ are valued equally for $\pi = \pi_L$, $\theta = 1/2$ is preferred to $\tilde{\theta} > 1/2$ for $\pi = \tilde{\pi}$ if and only if *net* returns for $\theta > 1/2$ rise by less than expected income for $\theta = 1/2$:

$$[(\alpha_1 - \beta_1)(\tilde{\pi} - 1/2) + \{(\alpha_1 + \beta_1)/2\}(\tilde{\theta} - \theta_L)] - [C(\tilde{\theta}, \tilde{\pi}, P_K) - C(\theta_L, \pi_L, P_K)]$$
$$< (\alpha_1 - \beta_1)(\tilde{\pi} - 1/2).$$

This simplifies to: $\theta = 1/2$ is preferred if $\pi = \tilde{\pi}$ if and only if

$$(\alpha_1 + \beta_1)/2 > [C(\tilde{\theta}, \tilde{\pi}, P_K) - C(\theta_L, \pi_L, P_K)]/(\tilde{\theta} - \theta_L)$$

Now

$$C(\tilde{\theta}, \tilde{\pi}, P_K) = C(\theta_L, \pi_L, P_K) + \int_{\pi_L}^{\tilde{\pi}} (dC/d\pi)d\pi$$

$$= C(\theta_L, \pi_L, P_K) + \int_{\pi_L}^{\tilde{\pi}} (C_\pi + C_\theta d\theta/d\pi)d\pi.$$

Now for any π, provided $C_{\theta\theta} > 0$, $C_\theta = \mathcal{E}_\theta$, where $\mathcal{E}_\theta$ does not depend on π. Also $C_\pi > 0$. Therefore

$$C(\tilde{\theta}, \tilde{\pi}, P_K) > C(\theta_L, \pi_L, P_K) + \mathcal{E}_\theta \int_{\pi_L}^{\tilde{\pi}} (d\theta/d\pi)d\pi$$

$$= C(\theta_L, \pi_L, P_K) + [(\alpha_1 + \beta_1)/2](\tilde{\theta} - \theta_L).$$

Equivalently, since $\tilde{\theta} - \theta_L < 0$ holds (see below), $d\theta/d\pi < 0$),

$$[C(\tilde{\theta}, \tilde{\pi}, P_K) - C(\theta_L, \pi_L, P_K)]/(\tilde{\theta} - \theta_L) < (\alpha_1 + \beta_1)/2.$$

The proof for $\tilde{\theta} > \theta_L$ is similar.

A.4 COMPARATIVE STATICS

In this section $\pi \in [\pi_L, \pi_U]$ is assumed. We therefore examine the impact of parameter changes on the interior solution $\theta = \theta^*$. In the final section the impact of parameter changes on π_L and π_U is considered.

A.4a *Changes in π*
Using the implicit function theorem, total differentiation of (A39) yields

$$d\theta / d\pi = -C_{\theta\pi} / C_{\theta\theta} < 0 \tag{A42}$$

by the second-order conditions and (A35). From subsection A.2.b, the impact of a change in π on s is

$$ds / d\pi = \bar{s}_\pi + \bar{s}_\theta d\theta / d\pi < 0,$$

from (A23), (A42) and the assumption $s_\theta > 0$. Similarly

$$dK / d\pi = \bar{K}_\pi + \bar{K}_\theta d\theta / d\pi \gtrless 0$$

from (A18), (A24), and (A42).

The change in net expected life income is

$$d\mathcal{E} / d\pi = \mathcal{E}_\pi + (\mathcal{E}_\theta - C_\theta) d\theta / d\pi - C_\pi$$
$$= (1 - s)\mathcal{E}_\pi > 0$$

from (A2), (A33), and (A39).

The impact of an increase in π on total investment expenditures is

$$dC / d\pi = C_\pi + C_\theta d\theta / d\pi \gtrless 0 \tag{A43}$$

from (A32), (A33), and (A42). (A43) can be coaxed into

$$dC / d\pi = s\mathcal{E}_\pi (1 - \eta_\theta{}^s / \eta_\theta{}^{C\theta}), \tag{A44}$$

where $\eta_\theta{}^s$ and $\eta_\theta{}^{C\theta}$ denote the elasticities of s and C_θ with respect to θ, *holding π fixed*. When π rises, the cost function shifts up for a given θ. But one effect of raising π is a decline in θ, which in turn leads to some fall in expenditures. The new level of expenditures will actually be lower than the original amount if either (1) marginal cost is relatively unresponsive to θ, in which case the reduction in θ will be large; or (2) the utilization of s is very sensitive to scale, in which case a small reduction in θ yields a large decline in the use of the factor whose price has risen.

A.4.b *Changes in P_K*
Proceeding as in the previous subsection:

$$d\theta / dP_K = -C_{\theta P_K} / C_{\theta\theta} < 0, \tag{A45}$$

by the second-order conditions and (A38).
Next,

$$dK / dP_K = \bar{K}_{P_K} + \bar{K}_\theta d\theta / dP_K < 0,$$

by (A18), (A27), and (A45). Also,

$$ds / dP_K = \bar{s}_{P_K} + \bar{s}_\theta d\theta / dP_K \gtrless 0$$

from the assumption $\bar{s}_\theta > 0$, (A26), and (A45). Further,

$$d\mathcal{E} / dP_K = (\mathcal{E}_\theta - C_\theta)d\theta / dP_K - C_{P_K}$$
$$= -K < 0$$

from (A39) and (A36). Finally, manipulation yields

$$dC / dP_K = K(1 - \eta_\theta^K / \eta_\theta^C \theta) \gtrless 0,$$

which may be interpreted in a fashion similar to (A44).

A.4.c *Changes in the offer functions*

The two changes considered in the text are an upward shift in the offer functions, holding the *marginal* value of correct allocation fixed, and an increment to the marginal value of correct allocation, holding the no information offer ($\bar{O}$) fixed.

The upward shift in the offer function can be parameterized as $d\bar{O} > 0$, and $d\alpha_1 = d\beta_1 = 0$. This changes the optimal factor mix and shifts the cost function. Specifically,

$$s_{\bar{O}} = (1 / D) - h_K^2 < 0, \tag{A46}$$

$$K_{\bar{O}} = (1 / D)h_s h_K > 0, \tag{A47}$$

$$C_{\bar{O}} = \bar{s} > 0, \tag{A48}$$

and

$$C_{\theta\bar{O}} = \bar{s}_\theta > 0. \tag{A49}$$

Given (A46)–(A49), we may proceed as in the previous two subsections.

$$d\theta / d\bar{O} = -C_{\theta\bar{O}} / C_{\theta\theta} < 0 \tag{A50}$$

by the second-order conditions and (A48). Next,

$$ds / d\bar{O} = \bar{s}_{\bar{O}} + \bar{s}_\theta d\theta / d\bar{O} < 0,$$

by (A46), the assumption $\bar{s}_\theta > 0$, and (A50). Also,

$$dK / d\bar{O} = K_{\bar{O}} + K_\theta d\theta / d\bar{O} \gtrless 0,$$

by (A18), (A47), and (A50). Furthermore,

$$d\mathcal{E} / d\bar{O} = \mathcal{E}_{\bar{\sigma}} - C_{\bar{\sigma}} + (\mathcal{E}_\theta - C_\theta)d\theta / d\bar{O} = 1 - s > 0$$

from (A39), (A48), and the observation that $\mathcal{E}_{\bar{\sigma}} = 1$ (Section A.1). Finally,

$$dC / d\bar{O}_\theta = s(1 - \eta_\theta^{\ s} / \eta_\theta^{\ C\theta}),$$

again similar to (A44).

Increasing the marginal value of information is a little more complicated. Formally, set $d\bar{O} = 0$, and $d\alpha_1 = d\beta_1 \equiv d\xi$. This implies $d\alpha_0 = d\beta_0 = (d\xi) / 2$. It follows that

$$\mathcal{E}_\xi = \theta - 1/2 > 0, \tag{A51}$$

$$\mathcal{E}_{\theta\xi} = 1, \tag{A52}$$

$$s_\xi = (1 / D) \cdot - (\theta - 1/2)h_K^2 < 0, \tag{A53}$$

$$K_\xi = (1 / D)(\theta - 1/2)h_s h_K > 0 \tag{A54}$$

$$C_\xi = s(\theta - 1/2) > 0, \tag{A55}$$

and

$$C_{\theta\xi} = s[1 + \{(\theta - 1/2) / \theta\}\eta_\theta^{\ s}] > 0. \tag{A56}$$

Proceeding as above yields

$$d\theta / d\xi = (\mathcal{E}_{\theta\xi} - C_{\theta\xi}) / C_{\theta\theta} = (1 / C_{\theta\theta})[1 - s(1 + \{(\theta - 1/2) / \theta\}\eta_\theta^{\ s}]. \tag{A57}$$

If $\eta_\theta^{\ s}$ is sufficiently large, the effect of an increase in ξ on the *level* of the price of time could be large enough to cause θ to fall. However, we shall assume $d\theta / d\xi > 0$. Realistically $s \leq 1/3$ must surely hold. Also $0 \leq (\theta - 1/2) / \theta \leq 1/2$. In this case $\eta_\theta^{\ s} > 4$ is a necessary condition for $d\theta/d\xi < 0$. Thus $d\theta/d\xi > 0$ would appear to be the leading case. Given that, we obtain

$$ds / d\xi = s_\xi + s_\theta d\theta / d\xi \gtreqless 0$$

from the assumption $s_\theta > 0$, (A53), and the assumption $d\theta / d\xi > 0$. Next,

$$dK / d\xi = K_\xi + K_\theta d\theta / d\xi > 0$$

from (A18), (A54), and the assumption $d\theta / d\xi > 0$. Moreover,

$$d\mathcal{E} / d\xi = \mathcal{E}_\xi - C_\xi + (\mathcal{E}_\theta - C_\theta)d\theta / d\xi = (1 - s)(\theta - 1/2) > 0$$

from (A39), (A52), and (A55). Finally,

$$dC / d\xi = C_\xi + C_\theta d\theta / d\xi > 0$$

from (A30), (A55), and (A57).

A.4.d *Effects of parameter changes on π_L and π_U*

The algebra involved in obtaining the impact of parameter changes on π_L and π_U is straightforward but quite tedious. However, the results are very simple. Consequently we merely describe the results.

The effects of parameter changes on π_L are symmetric to those for π_U. It therefore suffices to focus on π_U.

An increase in P_K reduces π_U. This is obvious because the net expected life income received if the worker does not invest is independent of P_K, while expected life wealth for $\theta > 1/2$ declines with P_K. Thus an increase in P_K reduces investment both through causing a decline in the number of workers for whom it pays to invest at all, as well as via reducing the level of investment for those who are not at the extensive margin π_U.

Similarly, an increase in $\bar{O}$ ($d\bar{O} > 0$, $d\alpha_1 = d\beta_1 = 0$) raises both the expected life income associated with no investment and the gross income associated with $\theta > 1/2$, by the same amount. But costs also rise with $\bar{O}$. Therefore π_U falls as $\bar{O}$ rises, generating the same kinds of reduction in investment as an increase in P_K does.

An increase in the marginal value of information ($dO = 0$, $d\alpha_1 = d\beta_1 = -2d\alpha_0 = -2d\beta_0 \equiv d\xi$) has an ambiguous impact on π_U. The impact of $d\xi > 0$ is to raise the expected life income in the absence of investment by less than it increases the expected life income for $\theta > 1/2$. Thus the fact that $d\xi > 0$ also raises costs does not necessarily render $\theta = 1/2$ preferable to $\theta > 1/2$ for the marginal worker. Thus an increase in the marginal value of information is expected to raise investment principally by increasing the scale of investment for those already investing.

Bibliography

Arrow, K. (1973) 'Higher education as a filter,' *Journal of Public Economics* 2, 193–216

Association of Universities and Colleges of Canada (AUCC) (1981) 'AUCC response to the Task Force report on *Labour Market Development in the 1980's*' in Council of Ontario Universities (1982)

Axelrod, P. (1982) *Scholars and Dollars; Politics, Economics, and the Universities of Ontario 1945–1980* (Toronto: University of Toronto Press)

Azariadis, C. (1979) 'Implicit contracts and related topics: a survey' Centre for Applied Research in Economics and the Social Sciences, Working Paper No. 79–17, November

Becker, G.S. (1975) *Human Capital* Second Edition (First Edition, 1964) (New York: National Bureau of Economic Research)

Betcherman, G. (1982) *Meeting Skill Requirements, Report of the Human Resources Survey* (Ottawa: Economic Council of Canada)

Bishop, J. (1977) 'The effect of public policies on the demand for higher education' *Journal of Human Resources* 12, 285–307

Boadway, R. (1980) *Intergovernmental Transfers in Canada* (Toronto: Canadian Tax Foundation)

Buttrick J.A. (1977) *Educational Problems in Ontario and Some Policy Options* Occasional Paper No. 4 (Toronto: Ontario Economic Council)

Carnoy, M., and D. Marenbach (1975) 'The return to schooling in the United States, 1939–69.' *Journal of Human Resources* 10, 312–31

Clark, W. and Z. Zsigmond (1981) *Job Market Reality for Post-Secondary Graduates* Publication No. 81–572 (Ottawa: Statistics Canada)

Commission on Post-Secondary Education in Ontario (1972) *The Learning Society* (Toronto: no publisher)

Cook, G., and D. Stager (1969) *Student Financial Assistance Programs* (Toronto: Institute for Policy Analysis, University of Toronto)

Council of Ministers of Education (1981) *Report of the Federal-Provincial Task Force on Student Assistance* (Ottawa: Secretary of State)

Council of Ontario Universities (1979) *An Uncertain Future* (Toronto: the Council)

– (1982) *Federal-Provincial Relations and Support for Universities* (Toronto: the Council)

Crean, J.F. (1973) 'Forgone earnings and the demand for education: some empirical evidence.' *Canadian Journal of Economics* 6, 23–42

– (1975) 'The income redistributive effects of public spending on higher education.' *Journal of Human Resources* 10, 116–21a

Denison, E.F. (1979) *Accounting for Slower Economic Growth, the United States in the 1970's* (Washington, DC: The Brookings Institution)

Department of Finance, Canada (1980) *Economic Review, a perspective on the Decade*, April (Ottawa: Ministry of Supply and Services)

– (1981) *Fiscal Arrangements in the Eighties – Proposals of the Government of Canada* (Ottawa: Department of Finance)

Dominion Bureau of Statistics (see also Statistics Canada) (1959) *University Student Expenditure in Canada, 1956–57.* D.B.S. Publication No. 81–509 (Ottawa: Queen's Printer)

– (1963) *University Student Expenditure and Income in Canada 1961–62, Part II – Canadian Undergraduate Students.* D.B.S. Publication No. 81–520 (Ottawa: Queen's Printer)

Economic Council of Canada (1970) *Seventh Annual Review: Patterns of Growth* (Ottawa: Queen's Printer)

– (1971) *Eighth Annual Review, Design for Decision-Making, An Application to Human Resources Policies* (Ottawa: Information Canada)

– (1982) *In Short Supply: Jobs and Skills in the 1980's* (Ottawa: Ministry of Supply and Services)

Employment and Immigration Canada (1981) *Labour Market Development in the 1980's* (the 'Dodge report') (Ottawa: Ministry of Supply and Services)

Feldstein, M. (1977) 'Does the United States save too little?' *American Economic Review* 67, 116–21

Foot, D. (1980) *Labour Market Analysis with Canadian Macroeconometric Models: A Review* (Toronto: Centre for Industrial Relations, University of Toronto)

Freeman, R.B. (1971) *The Market for College-Trained Manpower, A Study in the Economics of Career Choice* (Cambridge, MA: Harvard University Press)

– (1975) 'Overinvestment in college training?' *Journal of Human Resources* 10, 287–311

– (1980a) 'The facts about the declining economic value of college.' *Journal of Human Resources* 15, 124–42

– (1980b) 'An empirical analysis of the fixed coefficient "Manpower requirements" model, 1960–1970.' *Journal of Human Resources* 15, 176–99

Friedman, M. (1955) 'The role of government in public education.' In Solow, R., ed., *Economics and the Public Interest* (New Brunswick, NJ: Rutgers University Press)

– (1982) *Capitalism and Freedom* (first published 1962) (Chicago: University of Chicago Press)

Friedman, M. and S. Kuznets (1945) *Income From Individual Professional Practice* (New York: National Bureau of Economic Research)

Galbraith, J.K. (1967) *The New Industrial State* (New York: Signet)

Gunderson, M. (1974a) 'The case for government supported training programs.' *Industrial Relations Industrielles* 29, 709–23

– (1974b) 'Training in Canada: progress and problems.' *International Journal of Social Economics* 4, 1–24

Hare, P. and D. Ulph (1979) 'On education and distribution.' *Journal of Political Economy* 87, S193–212

Hashimoto, M. (1982) 'Minimum wage effects on training on the job.' *American Economic Review* 72, 1070–87

Judy, R.W. (1970) 'The income-redistributive effects of aid to higher education.' in L.H. Officer and L.B. Smith, eds, *Canadian Economic Problems and Policies* (Toronto: McGraw-Hill)

Leslie, P. (1980) *Canadian Universities 1980 and Beyond: Enrolment, Structural Change and Finance* (Ottawa: Association of Universities and Colleges of Canada)

Levhari, D. and Y. Weiss (1974) 'The effect of risk on the investment in human capital.' *American Economic Review* 64, 950–63

MacDonald, G.M. (1980) 'Person-specific information in the labor market.' *Journal of Political Economy* 88, 578–97

– (1981) 'The impact of schooling on wages.' *Econometrica* 49, 1349–59

Maeroff, G. (1983) *School and College: Partnerships in Education* (Princeton, NJ: Carnegie Foundation)

Manley-Casimir, M.E., ed. (1982) *Family Choice in Schooling: Issues and Dilemmas* (Lexington, MA: Lexington Books, D.C. Heath)

McMahon, W.W. and A.P. Wagner (1981) 'Expected returns to investment in higher education.' *Journal of Human Resources* 16, 274–85

Mehmet, O. (1977) 'Economic returns to undergraduate fields of study in Canadian universities: 1961–1972.' *Industrial Relations / Relations Industrielles* 32, 321–37

– (1978) *Who Benefits from the Ontario University System?* Occasional Paper
   No. 7 (Toronto: Ontario Economic Council)
Meltz, N.M. and D.A.A. Stager (1979) 'Trends in the occupational structure of
   earnings in Canada: 1931–71.' *Canadian Journal of Economics* 12, 312–15
Mincer, J. (1962) 'On-the-job training: costs, returns, and some implications.'
   Journal of Political Economy 70 (October Supplement), 50–79
– (1974) *Schooling, Experience and Earnings* (New York: Columbia–National
   Bureau of Economic Research)
Nadiri, M.T. and M.A. Schankerman (1981) 'Technical change, returns to scale,
   and the productivity slowdown.' *American Economic Review* 71, Papers and
   Proceedings, 314–19
Nerlove, M. (1972) 'On tuition and the costs of higher education: prolegomena
   to a conceptual framework.' *Journal of Political Economy* 80, S178–218
– (1975) 'Some problems in the use of income-contingent loans for the finance
   of higher education.' *Journal of Political Economy* 83, 157–83
Noordeh, A. 'The redistributive effects of investment in post-secondary edu-
   cation: a life cycle analysis.' PHD thesis, Carleton University (forthcoming)
Ontario Council on University Affairs (OCUA) (1982) *Eighth Annual Report*,
   Toronto
Parliamentary Task Force on Employment Opportunities for the 80's (1981)
   Work for Tomorrow (the Allmand report) (Ottawa: Speaker of the House of
   Commons)
Provincial Committee on Aims and Objectives of Education in the Schools of
   Ontario (1968) *Living and Learning* (Toronto: Department of Education)
Riley, J. (1976) 'Information, screening and human capital.' *American Economic
   Review* 66, 254–60
– (1979a) 'Testing the educational screening hypothesis.' *Journal of Political
   Economy* 87, S227–52
– (1979b) 'Informational equilibrium.' *Econometrica* 47, 331–59
Rosen, S. (1973) 'Income generating functions and capital accumulation.' Dis-
   cussion Paper No. 306, Harvard Institute for Economic Research
– (1977) 'Human capital: relations between education and earnings.' In M.
   Intriligator, ed., *Frontiers of Quantitative Economics, Vol. IIIB* (Amsterdam:
   North-Holland)
Rothschild M. and J. Stiglitz (1976) 'Equilibrium in competitive insurance
   markets: an essay on the economies of imperfect information.' *Quarterly Jour-
   nal of Economics* 90, 629–49
Rumberger, ? (1980) 'The economic decline of college graduates: fact or fallacy?'
   Journal of Human Resources 15, 99–112

Selleck, L. (1982a) 'A critique of job market reality for post-secondary graduates.' *Canadian Journal of Higher Education* 12, 57–67

– (1982b) 'Manpower planning and higher education policy.' Council of Ontario Universities (unpublished)

Siddiqui, F., R. Vafa, C.Y. Hsu, and B. Murti (1981) *Labour Market Outlook for Ontario, 1981–86* (Toronto: Ontario Manpower Commission).

Smith, A. (1900) *An Inquiry into the Nature and Causes of the Wealth of Nations,* Second Edition (first edition, 1776) (Toronto: Routledge)

Spence, A.M. (1973) 'Job market signalling.' *Quarterly Journal of Economics* 87, 353–74

– (1974) 'Competitive and optimal responses to signals: an analysis of efficiency and distribution.' *Journal of Economic Theory* 7, 296–332

Stager, D. (1981) *Federal Involvement in Post-Secondary Education for Highly Qualified Labour.* Technical Study 35 of the Task Force on Labour Market Development in the 1980s (Ottawa: Ministry of Supply and Services)

– 'Economics of higher education: research publications in English in Canada, 1971 to 1981." *Canadian Journal of Higher Education* 12, 17–28

Statistics Canada (see also Dominion Bureau of Statistics) (annual) *Education in Canada.* Statistics Canada Publication No. 81–229 (Ottawa: Ministry of Supply and Services)

– (annual) *Elementary-Secondary School Enrolment.* Statistics Canada Publication No. 81–210 (Ottawa: Ministry of Supply and Services)

– (annual) *Enrolment in Community Colleges* (Statistics Canada Publication No. 81–222)(Ottawa: Ministry of Supply and Services)

– (annual) *Fall Enrolment in Universities and Colleges.* Statistics Canada Publication No. 81–204 (Ottawa: Ministry of Supply and Services)

– (annual) *Financial Statistics of Education.* Statistics Canada Publication No. 81–208 (Ottawa: Ministry of Supply and Services)

– (annual) *Estimates of Population by Sex and Age for Canada and the Provinces.* Statistics Canada Publication No. 91–202 (Ottawa: Ministry of Supply and Services)

Stiglitz, J.E. (1975) 'The theory of "screening," education and the distribution of income.' *American Economic Review* 65, 283–300

Vanderkamp, J. (1981) 'University enrolments in the eighties and nineties.' Unpublished paper, University of Guelph

Weisbrod, B.A. (1962) 'Education and investment in human capital.' *Journal of Political Economy* 70 (October Supplement) 106–23

– (1964) *External Benefits of Public Education, An Economic Analysis* (Princeton, NJ: Princeton University Industrial Relations Section)

Welch, F. (1979) 'Effects of cohort size on earnings: the Baby Boom babies' Financial Bust.' *Journal of Political Economy* 87, S65–98

West, E. (1975) *Student Loans: A Reappraisal* (Toronto: Ontario Economic Council)

– (1982) 'The public monopoly and the seeds of self-destruction.' In Manley-Casimir (1982)

Wilson, J.D. and M. Lazerson (1982) 'Historical and constitutional perspectives on family choice in schooling: the Canadian case.' In Manley-Casimir (1982)

Zsigmond, Z., G. Picot, W. Clark, and M.S. Devereaux (1978) *Out of School – Into the Labour Force*, Statistics Canada Publication No. 81–570 (Ottawa: Ministry of Supply and Services)